Molly

317

377-4857

Molly 312 377 4857

Praise for Mary Jo Foley

"Mary Jo Foley is 'Ms. Microsoft.' She
everything that's going on at 1 Microso

—*Robert Scoble, A-list blogg*
and auth

"When I want to know what's going o
Mary Jo Foley. She knows more about
than most insiders."

—*Ed Bott, awa*
(h

"Mary Jo Foley has the correct scoop
does, usually long before everyone els
releases. I'm ordering copies of Micro
company, and if your career has anyt
suggest you do the same."

—*Scott Braden, author*

Microsoft® 2.0

Microsoft® 2.0

How Microsoft Plans to Stay Relevant in the Post-Gates Era

Mary Jo Foley

John Wiley and Sons

Microsoft® 2.0: How Microsoft Plans to Stay Relevant in the Post-Gates Era

Published by
Wiley Publishing, Inc.
10475 Crosspoint Boulevard
Indianapolis, IN 46256
www.wiley.com

Published by Wiley Publishing, Inc., Indianapolis, Indiana
Published simultaneously in Canada

ISBN: 978-0-470-19138-5

Manufactured in the United States of America
10 9 8 7 6 5 4 3 2 1

For general information on our other products and services or to obtain technical support, please contact our Customer Care Department within the U.S. at (800) 762-2974, outside the U.S. at (317) 572-3993 or fax (317) 572-4002.

Library of Congress Cataloging-in-Publication Data is available from the publisher.

To Bill Gates: Thank you for building a company that continues to be one of the most interesting and intriguing in the world. It's been a heck of a lot more fun writing about software (plus services) than shoes—at least for this reporter.

About the Author

Mary Jo Foley has covered the tech industry for 25 years and has been keeping a close eye on Microsoft strategy, products, and technologies for most of that time. An accomplished journalist, she has worked for various print and online publications including *PC Magazine*, CNET's News.com, ZDNet, *PCWeek/eWEEK*, and *Redmond* magazine. As a commentator on the IT and business communities, Foley has appeared on CNBC, CNN, and Fox News as well as radio programs for the BBC, ABC Radio, and NPR. Her "All About Microsoft" blog (`http://blogs.zdnet.com/microsoft/`) is among the top business blogs and her perspective is valued throughout the tech community.

Credits

Acquisitions Editor
Katie Mohr

Senior Development Editor
Tom Dinse

Production Editor
Debra Banninger

Copy Editor
Cate Caffrey

Editorial Manager
Mary Beth Wakefield

Production Manager
Tim Tate

**Vice President and Executive
Group Publisher**
Richard Swadley

Vice President and Executive Publisher
Joseph B. Wikert

Project Coordinator, Cover
Lynsey Stanford

Compositor
Maureen Forys, Happenstance
Type-O-Rama

Proofreader
Nancy Carrasco

Indexer
Robert Swanson

Contents

Foreword:
The Microsoft 2.0 World
(According to
Mini-Microsoft)

For those truly enmeshed in the Microsoft culture, Who da'Punk—aka "Mini-Microsoft"—needs no introduction. But for those of you who don't know Microsoft's most (in)famous and anonymous internal blogger, here is a quick bio:

Mini-Microsoft kicked off the blog http://minimsft.blogspot.com in June 2004 with the mission of slimming down Microsoft into "a lean, mean, efficient customer-pleasing, profit-making machine!" Mini said the things many Softies wanted to say, but were too scared of losing their jobs to do so. Quickly, the comments on Mini's site became a must-read for anyone interested in the internal pulse at Microsoft.

Over the past four years, Mini has championed everything from bringing back towels for employees to revising Microsoft's stack-ranking system. And, unlike "Fake Steve Jobs" and other "anonymous" bloggers, Mini's real identity is still a secret.

I asked Mini to write the Foreword for this book because we share certain characteristics: We are not Microsoft haters. We both know that the company can and should do better—and will need to if it hopes to remain competitive over the next few years/decades.

Without further ado, here's what Mini has to say about this book, as well as Microsoft's future:

Before you delve into this book, I'm going to give you a word—a single word—to read. And I want to prepare you.

When I give you this word, I want you to take a moment and think back upon the first time this word stuck to your consciousness. What did it mean to you then? And what does it mean to you now? How has this word, and what it represents, affected your life, and how do you see your future entwined with what's behind this word?

Wow, big stuff. But really, take the time to reflect on what it means to you. Ready? OK, here we go!

Microsoft

What are you thinking about when you read the word *Microsoft*? Go ahead, take some time. Look up from this lovely book and reflect on your attachment to "Microsoft." It's okay, ponder. People in the bookstore or the café where you might be reading this will assume you just came across something deeply profound. Trust me, profoundness will kick in shortly after this Foreword.

As I write this, Microsoft has been part of my life for well over 25 years. The very first little consumer microcomputer I used, tooting along at less than 1 MHz, booted into Microsoft Basic (and later, Microsoft Extended Basic). As the years went by, I coveted the compilers Microsoft wrote for the IBM PC. I bought my first Apple Macintosh strictly because of Microsoft Word for the Mac. And in the middle of the early browser wars, I switched to Microsoft Internet Explorer because it was faster (and I think it had avoided implementing the <blink> tag, which was a good thing).

Somewhere along the way, I found myself with a shiny new Microsoft blue badge. That was quite a surprising turn in my life given that I was no Microsoft fan. Shortly after I joined Microsoft, it became clear that Microsoft was the place for me: Everyone was smart, people spoke their minds, leaders focused on doing good things for the customer, and anyone could step up to drive important tasks or initiatives. You were truly limited only by your talent and your passion. It was a wonderful meritocracy.

Life Was Good

Years passed. And then slowly and gradually things changed at Microsoft. And not for the better. First, we totally blew any respect we had in the technical influencer world by declaring that browsing technology was tightly coupled with the core essence of an operating system. See, we have this embarrassingly kludged-together video to show you so! Oh, no, I wondered: Who's in charge here?

Later, the pre-reset Windows Longhorn—codename for what was eventually released as Windows Vista—had a crazy file system called *WinFS* and system features depending on new, slow, unproven technology (the byte-code-interpreted .NET Common Language Runtime). After all the Windows folks working on WindowsXP SP2 re-engaged with Longhorn, their first big question (after a shocked "WTF?") was: Who's in charge here?

Microsoft employees found themselves dealing with a constantly changing performance review system and strange, demoralizing compensation cutbacks. First, the midyear review reward was dropped, and the evaluation turned into a career discussion. The self-evaluation on new Microsoft Company Values appeared with no guidance. The values section morphed around with each iteration, making review-to-review progress impossible, and then disappeared altogether. The distasteful fixed curve used for evaluating employees against each other came under increasing scrutiny. Batches of stock options, once the path to Microsoft Millionaire status—perhaps another legendary item you think of when Microsoft is mentioned—expired worthless and below their strike price. And then one day, pleasant employee benefits like reduced price stock purchasing (ESPP) were made less attractive, and the towel service from our locker rooms was cancelled. Cost cutting through towels? Who's in charge here?

And all along the way, through these years, Microsoft's employee ranks continued to bloat larger and larger. Rampant hiring without any obvious need continued aggressively, until the doubling of people in offices started to be replaced by tripling people in offices. Oh, right, if you hire people, you need to ensure that you have office space for them. One last time: Who's in charge here?

In the midst of all this, I started a public discussion for these issues and other salacious items. Over time, it has had moments of intense Microsoftie participation, railing against Microsoft and its leadership.

Why? Why care so passionately? Non-Microsoftie participants in the discussion point out that all of these problems at Microsoft are nothing compared to some corporations. We Microsofties have it good. Why are you so critical?

Because It Is Microsoft

Because we have an aspiration of what Microsoft can be, and we are disappointed when it fails to meet our admittedly high standards. Of course, we celebrate our successes, but we naturally want to understand how we can do better and never repeat awful mistakes, like a $1,000,000,000 USD write-off of malfunctioning Xbox 360 units. It is our nature to be critical and call for accountability. If you want an honest assessment of where Microsoft is making mistakes and needs to do better, forget the frothing hate-zone of Slashdot. Find yourself a Microsoftie.

Microsoft is not a huge collection of factories spitting out widgets staffed by hapless workers. Microsoft, at its core, is about the expression of intellect typed into code that manipulates bits on your hard disk, your network, and your screen. Everything we do comes down to the people we are.

And we want that meritocracy back. We want leadership. And we're kind of wondering. … Who's going to be in charge?

Microsoft is at a leadership inflection-point. Bill Gates is reducing his role at Microsoft. Perhaps when you thought of Microsoft, you thought of Bill Gates and his wealth and his foundation, and your respect for Microsoft was mostly based in your respect of what Bill Gates has accomplished. What does a Microsoft without Bill Gates mean to you?

I look at our post-Bill Gates executive leadership, and I see a variety of characters: some ill-fitting in their jobs, some leaving me with a dim sense of revulsion, one as a complete mystery, and a few truly impressing me with how they've managed their organization and demonstrated sterling leadership for their part of Microsoft. Yet I certainly don't see another Bill Gates arising from within the company. There is no replacement for Bill.

So what's the plan for Microsoft as it recovers from Vista and finally expands enough to have room for all these new hires? Are we too big now for there to be one leader to inspire and represent us, and—as Steve Ballmer proposed in a recent Microsoft Company Meeting—do we become a *collection* of Microsofts, each with its own distinct culture and leadership?

It's a huge problem. Microsoft has so much raw potential, but it needs extreme leadership to break out of the bureaucratic morass it encumbered itself with during the hiring explosion and that derails it from consistently shipping great software.

As part of managing my public conversation on Microsoft, I've learned far more about my own company than I ever could have from my day-to-day corporate duties. And yet I still have just a slice of understanding about Microsoft.

As I've researched news and perspectives on Microsoft, I've come to rely on Mary Jo Foley's expert writing on Microsoft to help me keep track of developments in the company. Ms. Foley has taken on a huge undertaking to wrap her mind around the whole corporation. She does a fabulous job of tracking the pulse of Microsoft, and what new developments are on the horizon (there's been more than one meeting I've called because of something new I discovered via Ms. Foley).

She knows the competitive threats that Microsoft faces, and what kind of strategies and successes the various teams and leaders can be expected to produce. Sometimes Microsoft can be a competitor's worst enemy, and sometimes Microsoft can be its own worst enemy. Microsoft, in my opinion, is on the edge of great renewed potential, and it's either going to have a fantastic revival or slip into the tar pit of obsolescence.

I'm betting that there will be a Microsoft 3.0 discussion one day, and I'm going to grab on hard and enjoy the ride between here and there.

—*Mini-Microsoft*
May 2008, Redmond, Washington

Acknowledgments

Thanks to the people, places, and things that kept me sane while trying to write a book about the future while living in the present: Elsa Ferguson, Marilyn Foley (thanks, mom!), dedicated reader dkt (Darryl K. Taft), the folks at Om Yoga, the tea aficionados at the T Salon, and my editors at Wiley.

Also thanks to my Microsoft blogging colleagues who have been and continue to be a daily inspiration to me: Kip Kniskern, Robert McLaws, Mini-Microsoft, Chris Overd, Josh Phillips, Bob Stein, and Long Zheng. I'm also indebted to other members of the Microsoft Featured Communities and Most Valuable Professional programs who've helped me along the way.

Finally, thanks to the many sources, tipsters, Microsoft Corporate Shuttle drivers, and others who've helped me with my coverage of Microsoft over the years. Thanks, too, to those individuals (who asked not to be named) who read parts of this manuscript before publication. Any mistakes are mine. The kudos are yours.

Introduction
Microsoft 2.0: Welcome to the New (Post-Gatesian) Microsoft

He [Bill Gates]'s kind of like the pope of our industry. And as the pope, he always draws a crowd and people follow every word he says. You either go to heaven or you don't, if you have the Microsoft blessing.

> —Gary Shapiro, chief executive of the
> Consumer Electronics Association,
> The Seattle Times, December 31, 2007

*A*t 5:00 a.m. on July 1, 2008, Microsoft CEO Steve Ballmer's Zune alarm clock will buzz him awake—and into a new reality.

Today will be the first day that Chairman Bill Gates won't be officially large and in charge of Microsoft. As announced two years ago, Gates decided to relinquish his day-to-day responsibilities to focus more on his Bill and Melinda Gates Foundation work. Gates still will be Chairman of Microsoft, but won't be a fixture in code reviews, industry tradeshows, and in the daily decision-making process.

"Yet again, Bill gets all the glory, and I get left with the mess," Ballmer sighed as he rolled over, burying himself in his Halo 3 print sheets. "Customers and our partners are revolting against Vista. Then there's the lunatic Linux fringe and their patent-violating ways. And don't even get me going about the Google. I might throw not just a chair, but my La-Z boy!"

For once, the usually bombastic Ballmer didn't want to seize the day. Microsoft was starting to drift into irrelevance, and Ballmer didn't really have a clue about *how to get the good ship back on course. Software as a service is supplanting the high-margin software business at a faster and faster clip. Apple—the company Microsoft bailed out not so long ago, lest anyone forget—has evolved into the new darling of the press and Generation X/Y/Zers. And thanks to Neelie Kroes, Colleen Kollar-Kotelly, and those other meddling antitrust busters, Microsoft can't add squat to Windows any more without being sued every way to Sunday!*

Cut!

That's how some of my colleagues wanted me to start this book on what will be the next chapter of Microsoft's new, post-Gatesian life. They wanted me to make the case that Microsoft has lost its Evil Empire crown and soon will become nothing but a footnote in the tech industry. And they wanted me to go the trite "narrative nonfiction" route, putting "likely" dialogue in Softies' mouths, to do so.

> *"Gates still will be Chairman of Microsoft, but won't be a fixture in code reviews, industry tradeshows, and in the daily decision-making process."*

I can't do it. I find that style of writing affected and offensive, for one. But more importantly, that's not how I see things evolving.

Yes, Microsoft is at a crossroads. But to me, *crossroads* isn't synonymous with *dead*. I know not everyone agrees. Major Wall Street firms claim that the old gray Soft just ain't what it used to be. Many are predicting that Microsoft might need to empty its huge cash coffers in order to compete with Google and other Web 2.0 companies.

Cutting-edge technologists claim that Microsoft has lost its way and evolved into a company whose operating systems are loved only by "grandmas" (Programmer Paul Graham's words, not mine).[1]

---

[1] In 2007, programmer Paul Graham set out to insult Microsoft, but ended up enraging many grandmothers and those who love them. In an April post that started out with "A few days ago I suddenly realized Microsoft was dead," Graham made a series of generalizations that enraged everyone from Windows backers to feminists. His most memorable and controversial quote: "All the computer people use Macs or Linux now. Windows is for grandmas, like Macs used to be in the 90s. So not only does the desktop no longer matter, no one who cares about computers uses Microsoft's anyway." To read the post in full, go here: www.paulgraham.com/microsoft.html.

Up until now, Microsoft *was* Bill Gates. The guy who stood up to the U.S. Department of Justice lawyers and insisted in his deposition that he didn't know the meaning of the word "we."[2] The CEO famous for breaking the will of company employees during code reviews with a single dismissal. The college dropout who became the world's richest and one of technology's most powerful and feared leaders.

Gates' stamp was and is everywhere on Microsoft—from how other executives dress, part their hair, and rock in their chairs, to the "friends of Bill" management slate that traditionally has ruled the Redmondian roost.

> *"Yes, Microsoft is at a crossroads. But to me,* crossroads *isn't synonymous with* dead.*"*

When Gates founded Microsoft, the Internet was not something with which average users interacted the way they do today. Google didn't yet exist. The PC software industry was largely a packaged-product (not a services) business. And no one had yet heard of Ajax or Google or open source.

With the emergence of these new forces, many industry watchers have come to feel Microsoft was even slower than usual to understand and react to the new trends. Consequently, they characterized Microsoft as a has-been that would never be able to regain the same level of industry dominance it once enjoyed—even if it went so far as to try to buy a major Web 2.0 powerhouse like Yahoo. On the opposite end of the spectrum, others believed that Microsoft could never be toppled from its perch, simply because of its size and its monopolistic history.

I fall somewhere in between these extremes. I know that it often simply takes a strong competitor—and acknowledgement of it by the cautious Microsoft top brass—to galvanize the Redmond software maker. I know that Microsoft has no pretenses of following any kind of Google-like "Do No Evil" platform. After all, Microsoft didn't get to the position in the tech business

---

[2] In the late 1990s, it was Bill Gates vs. David Boies—or who's zooming whom. As part of the U.S. DOJ/States vs. Microsoft antitrust trial, Boies, who was the lawyer representing the prosecution, conducted several hours' worth of depositions involving Microsoft Chairman Gates. While Gates's lawyers allegedly warned him to be on-guard, Gates's evasiveness was all anyone remembered from his taped grilling. *Businessweek*, like many other pubs, captured Gates's (non) performance here: www.businessweek.com/1998/48/b3606125.htm.

that it has enjoyed for the past couple of decades by being kind and equitable. "All's fair in love and business" is Microsoft's credo. And even if it's not fair, if you can get away with it and it helps the bottom line, go for it, is Microsoft's more likely motto.

I've spent just about all of my 25 years as a journalist watching and writing about Microsoft. I've never been interested in writing a book about the company, as I'm not one who spends a lot of time looking back. And who writes business books about the future?

Well, you're holding in your hands an attempt to do just that.

> *"It often simply takes a strong competitor— and acknowledgement of it by the cautious Microsoft top brass— to galvanize the Redmond software maker."*

This is a book about Microsoft's next chapter. It's going to be an unpredictable one, as Microsoft's purchase of Yahoo earlier this year makes evident. In the not-too-distant future, many of the execs currently leading the Microsoft charge are likely to go their own way—especially if the company's stock stays as stagnant as it has been over the past few years. Technology will continue to advance at a breakneck pace. Microsoft will forge deals of a size and scope it never previously envisioned in order to keep pace. The fear that the Redmond software juggernaut traditionally inspired will be replaced with the foolish (in my assessment, at least) tendency to count Microsoft out.

I can't and won't claim to possess a crystal ball, allowing me to predict flawlessly what Microsoft plans to do in the next few years … or even few months. But based on the many Microsoft executives, partners, customers, and competitors with whom I converse regularly, I feel I'm sitting in a good spot to make some fairly educated guesses.

This book, *Microsoft 2.0*, describes the Microsoft people, products, and strategies that I believe will be key for the next-gen Microsoft. I realize that my attempt to describe the future of the company's handful of business units is a bit like that of the proverbial blind men who tried to describe an elephant. Just because you know the Windows trunk might look and feel like a snake, and the Office tusk, a spear, doesn't mean you'll be able to discern how the 80,000-employee-and-growing Microsoft is shaping up.

That said, there are some good clues out there, as to what Microsoft is likely to do next. Piecing them all together, you've got a reasonable, educated guess as to what Microsoft 2.0 will look like as it enters the next decade and beyond. I hope my attempt to connect the dots helps the customers, partners, and other Microsoft-watchers out there make better informed decisions in 2008 and beyond.

> *"Microsoft 2.0 describes the Microsoft people, products, and strategies that I believe will be key for the next-gen Microsoft."*

Microsoft's Next Chapter: It's Not All Roses

Before you write off this book as an apology from a Microsoft apologist—as some no doubt will—let me explain why I think Microsoft has some formidable challenges ahead.

- Ray Ozzie won't be the same kind of Chief Software Architect (CSA) that Gates was. While Ozzie may keep the CSA title he inherited in 2006, insiders and outsiders are skeptical he will want or be able to be Microsoft's main technology-strategy figurehead. Microsoft will be scrambling to find a new public persona to serve the role as lead technologist. And there will be plenty of political infighting inside Microsoft among those who believe they're best suited to assume the role.
- The bureaucracy that entangled the Windows team and resulted in a late, unfinished, and poorly received Vista release already is threatening to ensnare the Windows Live team. Unless something changes, Windows Live services will become mired in the processes and procedures that made the Windows Client unit bloated and slow-moving. And that regimentation will end up hurting Microsoft's attempt to beat Google, Salesforce.com, and other more agile services players.

- Microsoft will continue to circle the wagons around its most important franchise—Windows—in the hopes that the Web 2.0 bubble will burst before it has to abandon Software + Services for services alone. It takes Microsoft years to decide to take what look like baby steps to try a new software-delivery scheme or license code under a more permissive software license.
- Microsoft is a bit player in several of the fastest-evolving and most strategic arenas in the tech world: mobile phones, Web search, online advertising, and online music/video delivery, to name just a few. Almost every time Microsoft has delivered an "innovation"—think Tablet PC, SPOT watches, "Mira" smart displays—it has gone nowhere. Microsoft is casting about for ways to institutionalize innovation, with initiatives like corporate Quests, Live Labs, Office Labs, and adLabs, to name but a few, but so far, to no avail.

> "Microsoft will continue to circle the wagons around its most important franchise—Windows."

Microsoft has wielded its monopoly power profitably up to this point in its history. But a Gates-less Microsoft is going to be a direction-less Microsoft—at least in the near term. The existing set of top managers is too mired in old thinking and old ways to turn the Redmond ship quickly. Luckily for Microsoft, the company's Windows and Office cash cows will keep fueling the Microsoft ship for the next two to three years. But unless Microsoft brings in/promotes some new blood that isn't so vested in maintaining the status quo, the Redmondians are going to have a tough time fending off the many and varied competitors springing up around it.

All that said, I am less dire about Microsoft's prospects for continuing to be a major force in the tech world than are many other industry observers. (And it's not just because of my status as a full-time, paid Microsoft watcher. I always could switch gears and become Ms. "All About Facebook" or "All About Google," if need be.)

> "A Gates-less Microsoft is going to be a direction-less Microsoft—at least in the near term."

Why do I think it's wrong to count Microsoft out?

- Microsoft sales in fiscal 2007: $52 billion. Number of employees: 80,000 and counting. Number of companies Microsoft plans to acquire: twenty a year for the next five years. Microsoft's multimillion-dollar data centers with thousands of servers for Web hosting are under construction and/or operational in Chicago, Dublin, Quincy (Wash.), San Antonio, Santa Clara, Siberia, and other locales. Microsoft is not some smoke-and-mirrors Web 2.0-come-lately. There's a lot of *there* there.
- Microsoft's decision to bet on Software + Services—and not just services only—is a smart (albeit, roundly criticized) one. Think about it: How often do you want to build a spreadsheet from inside a browser only? Will you be creating a lot of PowerPoints from an Internet kiosk somewhere, rather than from a laptop/desktop?[3] Until uptimes for completely Web-ified office products are a lot more reliable, the majority of information workers aren't going to bet on them.
- A large, profitable, and surprisingly loyal Microsoft ecosystem continues to thrive. In spite of all the antitrust suits, class-action lawsuits, and "Microsoft sux" Twitter messages, there are a lot of Microsoft fans out there. Microsoft has helped lots of consultants, VARs, and system integrators earn a nice living. Even though Microsoft continues to carve away at the niches around which its channel partners have built their businesses, lots of folks have made and continue to build businesses based on their symbiotic relationships with the Redmondians.
- It's going to take a long time to unseat Microsoft from industry dominance. For example, even with all the mistakes Microsoft made in the Web browser space, it still has more than 75 percent market share.

---

[3] Pundits continue to lament Microsoft's decision not to release a Web-ified version of its Office suite. But why such a move would make sense for Microsoft is seldom examined. Not only would a completely Web-based version of Microsoft Office cut severely into Microsoft's Office profits, but also it would serve the needs of a relatively small segment of the population. Who is really interested in creating PowerPoint presentations from a Web kiosk or working on Excel spreadsheets without their laptops? I explored this disconnect more here on my ZDNet "All About Microsoft" blog: http://blogs.zdnet.com/microsoft/?p=1030.

Ditto with Windows, which still is installed on more than 90 percent of all PCs. Yes, Apple has won somewhere between 3 percent and 7 percent of consumer PC market share, and is becoming a more beloved brand than Microsoft among the younger demographic (as well as among many press folk, though not yours truly). But Microsoft has the rest, including the lion's share of the more lucrative business market.

> *"It's going to take a long time to unseat Microsoft from industry dominance."*

Too many pundits, venture capitalists, bloggers, and enthusiasts have been too hasty in writing off Microsoft. A good battle—especially when David(s) beat Goliath—is a great story. But the reality is that even if Microsoft completely botched every marketing/strategy decision from here forward, it would still take multiple years for the giant to be toppled.

Microsoft's Comment on Its Future: No Comment

Before going any further, I should make it clear that this is an *unauthorized* book about Microsoft's future. I asked Microsoft executives—through both official (public-relations) and non-official (unsanctioned, direct contact via e-mail) channels to talk to me about the company's plans for its future for this book. I even went so far as to offer to go under non-disclosure agreements (NDAs), which would last until this book was published, so company execs would feel free to share with me, as much as possible, their strategies and thinking about what's next for the company.

After several weeks mulling my request, Microsoft made an official decision against talking to me about the future or anything pertaining to this book.

Here's the official denial (courtesy of a company spokesman): "Microsoft has made the decision to not participate in any books about BillG [Bill Gates's] transition, future of Microsoft etc. This means that as it stands now, we will not be able to provide Bill/Ray/Steve et al. for your Book either."

Skeptics will conclude, no doubt, that Microsoft officials wouldn't talk to me about the future because they have no concrete and definable plans for the future. As much of a Microsoft realist as I am, I don't believe this to be the case. Microsoft's various divisions have lots of one-, two-, and even 10-year plans for the future. (I've even seen a few of them, as you'll see in Appendix A, "Memos, Letters, and e-Mails.")

Instead, there are other reasons I think Microsoft officials decided against participating in this book.

First and foremost, Microsoft wants to make sure no one panics about the fact that Gates is passing the torch, as of July 1, 2008. Microsoft's sanctioned message is that nothing will change: It's business as usual. Nothing to see here, folks. But sorry, guys, I just don't buy it. No matter how much Microsoft Kool-Aid you guzzle, it's not realistic to say that Microsoft, as of July 1, sans Gates involved on a daily basis, will be the same old Microsoft with Gates involved intimately in day-to-day activities.

> *"Skeptics will conclude, no doubt, that Microsoft officials wouldn't talk to me about the future because they have no concrete and definable plans for the future."*

There's also growing pressure inside Microsoft to be more "translucent," rather than "transparent," about the company's strategies and plans. (If you're confused about the distinction, think *translucent* as in shower curtain, as one Microsoft spokesman explained to me. Check out excerpts from Windows and Windows Live Engineering Chief Steven Sinofsky's internal blog post, which I've included in Appendix A for more.)

Microsoft's public justification for its increased secrecy is that customers and partners don't want to be led astray about what Microsoft plans to deliver, when. While this may be true to an extent, the bigger reason Microsoft is encouraging translucency over transparency is to avoid embarrassment and stock-price dings when product timelines slip and features get

> *"Microsoft wants to make sure no one panics about the fact that Gates is passing the torch, as of July 1, 2008."*

axed. There's probably a bit of Apple CEO Steve Jobs's envy mixed in here, too.[4] If Microsoft could keep more of its products and plans a secret up until it is ready to ship, the "gee-whiz" factor would rise, exponentially, some Softies argue.

Disclosures (No Shower Curtain Required)

While Microsoft's brass may not be big on transparency these days, I am. I am a freelance journalist turned blogger. I have no investments in Microsoft stock and have done no consulting gigs—paid or free—for the company. My primary source of livelihood these days, my ZDNet blog, "All About Microsoft" (blogs.zdnet.com/Microsoft), is in no way connected to Microsoft, other than by its subject matter.

I've written about Microsoft since 1984, which was the first time I met and interviewed Gates. Since that time, I've followed closely the company's business/Enterprise-focused strategy and products. While you can't write about Microsoft these days without covering the company's growing number of consumer-focused products and strategies, I touch only lightly on Xbox, Zune, IPTV, and games in this book. In part, this is because of my expertise. I am not a gamer or a gadgeteer.

> *"While Microsoft's brass may not be big on transparency these days, I am."*

Microsoft's Ozzie has gone on record saying he believes tech companies need to have a strong consumer focus in order to stay up-to-date, as the consumer market is where tech innovations are getting their start these days.[5] At the end of 2007, there was

---

[4] Can and should Microsoft try to create an Apple-like reality-distortion field (RDF)? It's tempting to think if someone at Microsoft simply would don a black turtleneck and answer all inquiries about product futures with "no comment," Microsoft might capture an iota of Apple's cool. While appealing, assuming Microsoft can create an RDF on the par of the force-field surrounding Apple is a tad simplistic. I made a case for why this was the case in my blog: http://blogs.zdnet.com/microsoft/?p=590.

[5] Microsoft CSA Ray Ozzie went on record in 2007 claiming that the most exciting innovations in tech these days are coming from the consumer, rather than the Enterprise market. For context, here's a transcript of Ozzie's remarks from Microsoft's annual Financial Analyst Meeting: www.microsoft.com/msft/speech/FY07/QAFAM2007_2.mspx.

quite a debate among tech bloggers as to whether consumer technologies are "sexier" than Enterprise/business ones.[6] The vocal majority seem to believe this is the case.

Me? I think tech vendors have come to realize that consumer products are easier to get press coverage for than Enterprise software. Consumer products are easier to understand and explain—and more likely to end up on Page 1 of newspapers, magazines, and web sites than Enterprise software ever will be. Will we see the *Wall Street Journal* review a new Microsoft Zune? Yes. Microsoft Exchange Server software? No.

The reality is that Microsoft still makes the bulk of its money from Enterprise software sales and looks poised to continue to do so for years to come. Microsoft is continuing to pour money into new and consumer-aimed business arenas in the hopes of diversifying its portfolio, as well as to find new ways to connect with customers who use technology not just in their 9-to-5 jobs, but at home, too. The thinking: If a user likes Xbox and Zune, s/he is more likely to consider Microsoft products and technologies at work, too.

> *"To me, the only real 'innovation' that is happening first in the consumer space is around user interfaces, or, as Microsoft prefers to call them,* user experiences.*"*

In early 2008, Microsoft began stepping up its consumer marketing/advertising campaigns, earmarking $300 million for a new consumer-products ad-blitz. Expect even more money to go toward the company's consumer-focused development and marketing strategies in the coming months and years.

However, to me, the only real "innovation" that is happening first in the consumer space is around user interfaces, or, as Microsoft prefers to call them, *user experiences*. Making software easier to use, update, deploy, and maintain is the new Holy Grail, not just for Microsoft, but for all software vendors. Users are coming to expect PCs and mobile phones to be as easy to use as TVs

---

[6] A debate with no real resolution in site: Which is sexier: consumer or Enterprise software? Former Softie Robert Scoble kicked off the contest with a late December 2007 blog posting, entitled, "Why Enterprise Software Isn't Sexy," which can be found here: http://scobleizer.com/2007/12/09/why-enterprise-software-isnt-sexy/.

and digital-media players. User experiences are where consumer technologies and vendors are leading—and informing—Enterprise ones. So that's the other reason that I focus more on Microsoft's business products and strategies than its consumer ones, both on my blog and in this book.

About This Book's Title (or, the Multiple Meanings of 'Microsoft 2.0')

I had mixed feelings using the "2.0" nomenclature in the title of this book to describe the next chapter in Microsoft's history.

For one, *Web 2.0* is one of the most overused and meaningless terms in the tech business. It's also a loaded term, with many in the industry ascribing to the theory that Web 2.0 is a panacea for all that's wrong with the tech world as we know it. Many use *Web 2.0* as a shorthand differentiator for companies, ideas, and technologies that are not espoused by the current tech power-houses like Microsoft, IBM, SAP, Oracle, and the like.

But over the past year or so, Microsoft officials finally began glomming onto Web 2.0 branding and concepts. And Ozzie seemingly believes Web 2.0 is the future. Microsoft, a company that once ridiculed Web 2.0, has become one of its biggest proponents. The growing family Windows Live services, in all their mapping, blogging, RSS, and social software glory, are all examples of Web 2.0 at its best/worst. Other Microsoft teams have been finding ways to relabel and reposition their products as "mash-ups," "virtual worlds," and "user-generated content."

> "Microsoft, a company that once ridiculed Web 2.0, has become one of its biggest proponents."

If Microsoft is willing to start talking Web 2.0—better late than never—then I feel my choice to use "Microsoft 2.0" to refer to the company's next-generation strategy/products/people is fair game. So *Microsoft 2.0* is my shorthand for the next chapter(s) in Microsoft's history. *Microsoft 2.0* implies the new, Web 2.0-centric Microsoft. It also encompasses all the other non-Web-2.0 products, services, strategies, and technologies that will carry Microsoft into the coming decades.

Microsoft 1.0: It Was All about Bill

1

Bill Gates earns $250 every SECOND; that's about $20 million a DAY and $7.8 billion a YEAR! If he drops a thousand-dollar bill, he needn't even bother to pick it up because in the four seconds it would take him to pick it up, he would've already earned it back.

"Little-Known Facts about Well-Known Leaders—Bill Gates," a June 22, 2007 post from the AchieveMax blog

Given that this is a book about Microsoft's future, and not the past, this chapter is short and to the point. However, as it's impossible to look at where Microsoft is going without looking back on where it's been in the past 30+ years, I can't just skip over the past altogether. So consider this a whirlwind tour of Microsoft up to the point of Chairman Bill Gates's retirement from his daily duties at the company.

If you want the short and sweet version of Microsoft's history, there's no need to look further than Chairman Bill Gates. More than almost any tech company, Microsoft has been identified with its founder and leader since the get-go. As Gates went, so, too, did Microsoft.

An immeasurable amount of change has happened in the industry and inside Microsoft since Gates launched the company in 1975. I am not going to re-document the history of Microsoft as so many others have done (both well and badly) before me. Instead, I'll point you to the annotated reading list of some of the best known and loved books on Microsoft that appears in the Appendix. There you'll find everything from choice biographical tidbits about Gates, to blow-by-blow coverage of Microsoft's strategy in the 2004 U.S. antitrust trial against the company. (The reading list is not meant to be exhaustive, by any stretch—there have been hundreds of tomes written about and by the Softies—but it represents what I regard as an essential introduction.)

> "If you want the short and sweet version of Microsoft's history, there's no need to look further than Chairman Bill Gates."

There are a few things I do want to note about Microsoft's first chapter—the period I've christened "Microsoft 1.0." Sometimes it's easy to forget that Microsoft didn't just emerge overnight into the tech world as a big, bad monopolist. The following timeline[1] of some of the most important milestones in the company's climb to its current status is a reminder that Microsoft's climb has been a methodical one:

1975—Microsoft founded. By year end, it had three employees: Bill Gates, Paul Allen, and Rick Weiland.

1978—Microsoft's sales exceed $1 million.

1980—Steve Ballmer hired.

1981—IBM PC debuts, running Microsoft Disk Operating System (MS-DOS).

1983—Microsoft introduces Windows 1.0, an extension to DOS.

1985—Microsoft turns 10. Sales for the year: $140 million. Employees: 900.

1987—Windows 2.0 debuts.

1990—Windows 3.0 is born.

1993—Windows NT launches.

1995—Microsoft launches a slew of new products, including Windows 95, Internet Explorer, Microsoft Bob. Microsoft turns 20. Sales for the year: $5.9 billion. Employees: 17,800.

1998—Ballmer is named President and Gates, Chairman and CEO.

2000—Microsoft launches Windows 2000.

2001—WindowsXP and Xbox gaming console debut.

---

[1] For an easy-to-digest and succinct view of Microsoft's history, check out http://www.thocp.net/companies/microsoft/microsoft_company.htm.

2005—Microsoft comes to terms with EU over antitrust violations and agrees to create SKUs of Windows that don't bundle Windows Media Player.

Ray Ozzie pens his "Internet Services Disruption" memo, and Microsoft launches its "Live" Software + Services strategy.

2006—Microsoft announces Gates's plan to relinquish day-to-day duties in July 2008 and passes the Chief Software Architect torch to him, effective immediately.

2007—Microsoft launches Windows Vista and Office 2007.

The latest tally (from Microsoft's FY 2007 year-end Securities and Exchange filing): As of June 30, 2007, Microsoft employed approximately 79,000 people on a full-time basis, 48,000 in the United States and 31,000 internationally. Approximately 31,000 were employed in product research and development, 24,000 in sales and marketing, 13,000 in product support and consulting services, 3,000 in manufacturing and distribution, and 8,000 in general and administration.[2] Sales for fiscal 2007 hit $51.12 billion.

> *"Sometimes it's easy to forget Microsoft didn't just emerge overnight into the tech world as a big, bad monopolist."*

The Cult of Bill

As Microsoft has morphed and spread into new markets over the years, Gates has remained the constant star by which everything and everyone connected with the company has navigated. In short, up until this point, Microsoft has been all about Bill.

I remember the first time I heard someone who worked for Microsoft refer to Gates as "Bill." It surprised and shocked me. Did he mean Bill Gates, the big kahuna? Was everyone on a first-name basis with the Chairman?

While everyone at Microsoft knew that any reference to "Bill" meant the one and only Bill Gates, there was no buddy-buddy Billism inside the company. Gates was famous for his tirades, berating employees of all levels whom

---

[2] Microsoft's end of fiscal 2007 SEC statement can be found here: http://www.sec.gov/Archives/edgar/data/789019/000119312507170817/d10k.htm.

he deemed unprepared for meetings or suggesting product or strategy questions he considered irrelevant. He was the same with the press. I was at the wrong end of Gates's wrath more than once for asking "the stupidest question I ever heard," among other pleasantries.

So how do we reconcile the Gates we see these days donating billions to help eradicate childhood diseases in Africa with the tyrant Gates? A mellowing with age? The humanizing influence of his wife Melinda and his three kids? Ya got me….

> *"Up until this point, Microsoft has been all about Bill."*

It's worth noting that Gates was never a hands-off, figurehead-type leader. He set the tone for the company. To pay homage, managers started rocking in their chairs like Gates, parting their hair likes Gates, wearing the same kinds of glasses and shirts as the Chairman. They peppered their speech with Gatesisms like *super*, as in "super excited."[3]

The Softies both respected and feared Gates. Employees took their kids out of school to bring them to company shareholder meetings to get Gates's autograph. They were proud to say they'd had a chance to meet Gates themselves or—for some lucky few—visit his palatial mansion on Lake Washington. If he personally commented on a paper they submitted for consideration for one of Gates's annual ThinkWeek retreats, they wore that fact like a badge of honor.

> *"The Softies both respected and feared Gates."*

Because he owns and has run Microsoft, Gates has had nearly unquestioned power to do what he wants. If Gates chose to champion a technology or an idea, it got love and seemingly unlimited funding. Some of Gates's pet projects turned into successes for the company. Others have not. IPTV, Tablet PCs, SPOT watches, speech input—all Gates-backed projects that allegedly are still top priorities for the company—still have not gained traction.

There've been some company watchers who've opined that, given the new dynamics in the IT industry, Gates is passing the torch to a new leader at the right

---

[3] For more on Gates's—and the rest of Microsoft's—obsession with the word "*super*," read this post by RedMonk analyst James Governor: http://redmonk.com/jgovernor/2004/11/12/six-degrees-of-super-ation-closer-to-bill/.

time.[4] At 52, Gates is no longer (if he ever was) a trendsetter. The company needs new blood—leaders who aren't so mired in the past, the reasoning goes.

That said, it's hard to imagine Microsoft without Gates. Microsoft's image makers have been careful in orchestrating the transition,[5] making sure to emphasize repeatedly that Gates isn't really going away on July 1, 2008, and will still have a hand in a number of projects at the company even though he won't have day-to-day duties there any more. Instead of just springing the idea of a Gates successor on the public months or even a year before Gates relinquishes his management responsibilities, the Microsoft public-relations squad has been slowly and carefully painting an image of a team of chief technology officers taking over where Gates is leaving off.

(It's been interesting to watch how Microsoft originally played up the idea of all three of its CTOs—Ray Ozzie, Craig Mundie, and David Vaskevitch—running the company together when they first floated the plan for Gates to move on. The mentions of Vaskevitch quickly fell off. Shortly thereafter, Ozzie was elevated to the Chief Software Architect role, with Mundie being pushed to the side as the head of research and policy.)

> *"Microsoft's image makers have been careful in orchestrating the transition, making sure to emphasize repeatedly that Gates isn't really going away."*

A Microsoft sans Gates is going to be a very different Microsoft. Regardless of what you think of the "three presidents" and other top managers (I'll talk about this motley crew at length in Chapter 3), at least for the next few years, "2.0" Microsoft is going to be run by more "adults" than Microsoft 1.0 was. This year, Ballmer will be 52. Business Division chief Jeff Raikes will be 50 (and his replacement taking over

---

[4] From a June 7, 2007 article entitled "Bill Gates Goes Back to School" in *Time* Magazine: "Gates is probably getting out of technology at the right time. Funnily enough, it's not really a business for nerds anymore. Gates was at the center of the personal-computer revolution and the Internet revolution, but now the big innovations are about exactly the things he's bad at. The iPod was an aesthetic revolution. MySpace was a social revolution. YouTube was an entertainment revolution. This is not what Gates does. Technology doesn't need him anymore."

[5] Microsoft's June 2006 press release announcing Gates's plans to transition out of his day-to-day role at Microsoft by July 2008 can be found at http://www.microsoft.com/presspass/press/2006/jun06/06-15CorpNewsPR.mspx.

later this year, Stephen Elop, is 44); Platforms and Services Chief Kevin Johnson, 47; and Entertainment and Devices honcho Robbie Bach, 46; according to the latest SEC year-end filing.

While Microsoft is still a leader in operating systems and desktop business applications, it is a follower in the other main markets in which it is playing. And lawsuits figure a lot more prominently in Microsoft's existence these days than they did when the company got its start.

Inside the Borg House

Microsoft always has been a company of paradoxes. It has grown and thrived on dichotomies. And it is these dichotomies that have shaped Microsoft into the company that it is today. In the following sections I discuss some of those that have struck me most over the years I've been covering the company.

The "We Rule" versus "We Suck" Culture

It's not too surprising that arrogance and success often go hand-in-hand. At Microsoft, that's been the rule, not the exception. Many Softies believed and continue to believe that Microsoft employees are smarter than everyone else and that the company is a magnet for the brightest, most ambitious tech and marketing experts (in spite of the well-proven recruitment capabilities of adversaries like Google and Facebook).

> *"Microsoft always has been a company of paradoxes."*

At the same time, I've seen Microsoft employees be quite introspective, self-deprecating...and, some might even say, insecure. When inviting rivals, developers, and customers to campus or other events, among the first questions the Microsoft minions pose is "Where are our blind spots?" and "What could we be doing better?" Good Softies want to know their own weaknesses so that they can address them and fare better against the competition.

Case in point: In March 2007, Microsoft invited a bunch of "non-fanboys"—Java, Linux, and PHP developers—to campus as part of a Tech Summit. Microsoft wanted critical feedback on everything from its Ajax platform to its

---

[6] To read more about one of many Microsoft events in which the company's competitors are invited to campus so that the Softies can pick their brains—I mean, talk partnership opportunities—check out my All About Microsoft blog posting here: http://blogs.zdnet.com/microsoft/?p=358.

open-source strategy (or lack thereof). It got what it bargained for—and more. But it also got the answer to the question that the event organizers posed repeatedly to attendees: "How do we suck?"[6]

Another related instance: Microsoft's human-resources team, as well as plenty of other employees, were fascinated in mid-2007 with an e-mail message that made the rounds inside Microsoft that portrayed—from a former Google employee's perspective—what "Life at Google" was really like. (The employee who provided Microsoft with a brain dump on what was

> *Microsoft wanted critical feedback on everything from its Ajax platform to its open-source strategy (or lack thereof).*

and what wasn't working at Google was a former Microsoft employee who returned to the Redmondian fold.) The e-mail was dissected and analyzed at length for possible lessons Microsoft could glean from what was and wasn't working for Google, in terms of hiring and maintaining its workforce.[7] Not so coincidentally, in late 2007, Microsoft announced plans to make its Entertainment & Devices campus more Google-like, with an on-site health-care clinic, fast-food restaurants, and a bar.[8]

"Frat Boys" versus the Bootstrappers

In the mid-1990s, there was palpable tension inside Microsoft between the "privileged" Ivy Leaguer hires and the bootstrapped local (many times Northwestern born-and-bred) employees, some of whom went to less prestigious local colleges and universities—as well as several others who never attended college at all. Many of the locals felt the private-college boys (and small number

> *"Surprisingly, the fact that Chairman Bill Gates is both a Seattle local and a college dropout didn't seem to reduce the friction."*

---

[7] I covered the whole ugly blow-up involving the former Softie who turned Googler, who went back to being a Softie in this blog post: http://blogs.zdnet.com/microsoft/?p=541.

[8] Microsoft's plans to revise its Entertainment and Devices campus are detailed in this *Seattle Post-Intelligencer* story from November 8, 2007 ("Feel Like a Beer? Let's Stop Off at Microsoft"): http://seattlepi.nwsource.com/business/338776_msftcampus08.html.

of girls) got a lot more appreciation and opportunities. There was a definite privilege schism inside the hallowed Redmond halls. (Surprisingly, the fact that Chairman Bill Gates is both a Seattle local and a college dropout didn't seem to reduce the friction.)

There's still some of the old "us versus them" and "local versus outsider" undercurrent there, from what I've seen and heard. The dichotomy is less visible than it might have been a decade or two ago, but there's no denying there are two camps of Softies, right up until this day—the privileged and the bootstrapped.

> *"It's definitely not one, big, happy melting pot."*

If you're looking for concrete examples, consider the case of two Windows execs. Bill Veghte, Senior Vice President, Online Services & Windows Business Group, and Iain McDonald, Director of Product Management for Windows Server, could not come from more different places.[9] Veghte graduated with honors from Harvard, with a B.A. in East Asian studies. "He joined Microsoft directly out of college drawn by the people, the impact that software could have in helping people realize their potential, and the Northwest," according to his bio on Microsoft.com. McDonald got his start as a busker in his native Australia. He dropped out of university and did, in his words "this kind of little computer schools course that a friend of mine had recommended. And I did a bunch of software contracts where you go and work for three months."

With Microsoft becoming more of an international company than ever before—in terms of its hires and office locations—there's less of a "frat boy" versus bootstrapper divide. Now there are "subcontinents" within Microsoft Redmond.

It's definitely not one, big, happy melting pot. But one thing's for sure: Microsoft is further, not closer, from being a homogeneous company and culture than ever before.

The Kids versus the Old Guard

In spite of all the stories you read about Microsoft attrition, there remains a sizeable contingent of 10-, 15-, and 20+-year veterans at the company. Many

---

[9] A tale of two Windows guys. For more about Bill Veghte, check out his biography page here: http://www.microsoft.com/presspass/exec/veghte/default.mspx. And for more on Iain McDonald's colorful background, check out this blog posting: http://blogs.zdnet.com/microsoft/?p=551.

of these old-school Softies remember happier Microsoft times, pre-antitrust lawsuits, pre-Linux, and pre-Web 2.0. They liked working at a company where software was developed in a predictable way, on a relatively predictable schedule, with (mostly) predictable results. They never cottoned to the government ruling that found Microsoft a monopolist that abused its power. And, wherever they've been able, many of the old guard have brought their old-guard ways with them as they've climbed the corporate ladders.

Then there's the new guard—the 20- and 30-somethings who have come to Microsoft more recently and with a different perspective. The newer blood wasn't there for the Windows 95 launch and the U.S. DOJ trial against Microsoft. (Heck, some of them were toddlers when Microsoft launched Windows 95.) Several of these folks joined Microsoft over the past few years straight out of college and grad school, picking Microsoft over Google, Facebook, and other hipper, get-rich-quick-promising Web 2.0 companies. The Microsoft they joined was vastly different from the one in which their now-graying predecessors enrolled. The Windows Live team is full of these fresh-faced new recruits.

(There's also a core group of not-so-young but brand-new Softies—some of whom joined the company after fending off recruitment attempts for years, and others who've defected or been lured from other companies, inside the software business and not.)

Microsoft has been ratcheting up its pursuit of the younger Generation X/Y types, especially to fill its growing number of consumer-focused jobs on the Xbox, Zune, Windows Live, and Windows Mobile teams. In 2007, Microsoft created several new recruitment sites aimed specifically at this demographic, emphasizing openings on cool/new teams over more traditional business-focused development and marketing jobs.

> "There's the new guard—the 20- and 30-somethings who have come to Microsoft more recently and with a different perspective."

As the Boomers and near-Boomers continue to drift away, whether via retirement or other means, and Microsoft becomes more dominated by employees with shorter memories and more itchy stock-trading fingers, it will be interesting to see how Microsoft's culture changes.

Bill's Guys versus Steve's Guys

Ballmer is from Mars and Gates is from Venus. Bill Gates is a nerd. Steve Ballmer is a salesman. Gates has nurtured a group of hand-picked managers, as has Ballmer. Gates's picks, not surprisingly, have tended to be techies; Ballmer's are more in the category of "consummate salesmen."

The result? Two distinct camps formed inside Microsoft: Bill's guys and Steve's guys. Techies like Chief Technology Officer David Vaskevitch, Chief Research and Strategy Officer Craig Mundie, and Senior Vice President of Technical Strategy Eric Rudder are all examples of Bill's guys. Chief Operating Officer Kevin Turner, Platforms and Services chief Kevin Johnson, and Mobile and Entertainment President Robbie Bach and new Microsoft Business Division chief Stephen Elop (a former Chief Operating Officer with Juniper Networks) are Steve's guys. There are a few execs who have managed to straddle the fence and are favored by both Bill and Steve, including Chief Software Architect Ray Ozzie yet even Ozzie is more of a Bill guy than a Steve guy..

> *"Gates's picks, not surprisingly, have tended to be techies; Ballmer's are more in the category of 'consummate salesmen.'"*

But in the end, it's all about nerds versus sales when it comes to categorizing who's who inside the Borg House. And with Gates on his way out, it is going to be interesting to see what happens to Bill's Guys in the aftermath. Will they hang on and carve out new niches for themselves (like Rudder seems to be doing, with his latest rumored project—devising an operating system that ultimately could supersede Windows)? Will they be *riffed* once Gates leaves the building?

With Ballmer running the show, sales pedigrees and MBA degrees are likely to be more valued as Microsoft builds its leadership team for the next decade-plus. While a lot of lip service is and will be given to wanting to hire and cultivate technical thought leaders like Ozzie, there will likely be more COO Turner-types gaining power in the post-Gates Microsoft regime. This might not be an entirely bad thing, as Computer Science/Electrical Engineering degrees don't prepare individuals to run teams of thousands. But for a company that's always been by, for, and about geeks, a sales-heavy culture and management structure will be unsettling to more than a few inside and outside Redmond.

Microsoft's Scarlet "A": Antitrust

More than the exponential growth in processor speeds, the rise in popularity of open-source software, or the skyrocketing market cap of Google, the external event that had the biggest impact on Microsoft in the past 30 years has been the ongoing antitrust scrutiny to which the company has been subject.

That's not just me talking. In speaking with several Microsoft insiders, antitrust suits and oversight were mentioned, time and again, as having changed irrevocably the course of the company.

No doubt, some of Microsoft's insistence on the strong influence of antitrust oversight on the way the company does business these days could be pure posturing. When the European Court of First Instance came down hard on Microsoft in September 2007, refusing to overturn the European Commission's 2004 antitrust ruling against Microsoft, Microsoft officials were a little too ready to proclaim publicly and privately their fears of further antitrust scrutiny on a variety of fronts. If the EU frowned on Microsoft for bundling technologies and withholding documentation others needed in order to make their products interoperable, just imagine what the courts might do to Google or Facebook, the Softies whispered.

Whether intentionally exaggerated or not, past antitrust suits and the threat of potential new ones have had an increasingly strong influence on how Microsoft builds and positions its products. In part, Microsoft has been making fewer and fewer moves that could be construed as anticompetitive because several of the managers who seemed to believe the company was above the law have moved on (some-

> *"Antitrust suits and oversight was mentioned, time and again, as having changed irrevocably the course of the company."*

times with a little encouragement from the top brass). The bulk of those who stayed—including a handful of company representatives who were rewarded with more visible and likely more lucrative jobs for "taking one for the team" during the U.S. Department of Justice antitrust trial—seemingly have gone to charm school. Those who were impervious to charm seem to have been persuaded that some of Microsoft's old ways of doing business needed to be left by the wayside. (See Chapter 5 for more on Microsoft's old modus operandi.)

It's important to remember that in the United States, at least, it's not illegal to be a monopolist. It's illegal to abuse one's monopoly power. Microsoft was found guilty of abusing its desktop operating-system monopoly power. As Microsoft posited in its August 2007 self-examination regarding whether antitrust oversight in its case warranted a five-year extension:

> *Microsoft did not achieve its position in the PC operating sys-*
> *tems market unlawfully; rather, the Court found that Microsoft*
> *maintained that position by specific anticompetitive means.*
> *Having prohibited Microsoft from further employing those or*
> *similar means, and having created mechanisms to facilitate*
> *competition with Microsoft, the Final Judgments created an*
> *environment in which market forces can determine the relative*
> *success and thus the market shares of participants. Measured*
> *by that standard, the Final Judgments have been a success.*[10]

Whether or not you agree that Microsoft has been punished enough for its abusive ways (and is really and truly sorry and won't ever do it again, as the company contended via the list of "Voluntary Principles" it published in 2006),[11] you'd be hard-pressed to argue that the company hasn't had to change as a result of current and potential antitrust suits.

The "cut-off-their-air-supply" Microsoft just ain't what it used to be. If today's Microsoft were the same unbowed and unbridled company it was back in the 1990s, there would be some very different business practices in place.

A more cutthroat Microsoft would have been so bold as to try strategies like bundling SQL Server with Windows Server, or integrate and preload one or, most likely, more Windows Live services with Windows bundled on new

---

[10] This passage comes from Microsoft's report on Final Judgments from August 2007: http://www.microsoft.com/presspass/download/legal/SettlementProceedings/08-30MSFTReportConcerningFinalJudgments.pdf.

[11] In July 2006, right in the midst of its attempts to prove to U.S. and international regulatory authorities that Microsoft was a good company that was sorry for any antitrust laws it had broken, as a gesture of goodwill, Microsoft announced a set of "Voluntary Principles." These 12 "guiding principles for development of the Windows desktop operating system" were all about ensuring that "Windows continues to foster competition and innovation in the marketplace." They espoused everything from interoperability, to open APIs. The principles got a lukewarm reception from the press and many Microsoft "partners." The full list of the principles is here: http://www.microsoft.com/about/corporatecitizenship/citizenship/businesspractices/windowsprinciples.mspx.

PCs. In the good old pre-antitrust days, Microsoft would have had few qualms about tightening the screws on system vendors who dared to preload Linux on new systems by charging them more per copy for Windows licenses, intentionally withholding Windows beta releases, or levying other punishments against vendors who dared show their "disloyalty" by

> *"You'd be hard-pressed to argue that the company hasn't had to change as a result of current and potential antitrust suits."*

cavorting with anyone other than Microsoft. But constant scrutiny—and/or threats of scrutiny—by the U.S. authorities, the European Commission, and representatives from other U.S. and international regulatory bodies has led Microsoft to be a lot more cautious than it used to be.

Public exposure of Microsoft's antitrustworthy ways also has made its existing and potential partners more leery of how they work with the software giant. Independent software vendors and services companies have become more careful about sharing product details and roadmaps, which, going forward, should lessen the Redmondiands' long-favored practice of "borrowing" cool concepts and features to incorporate in their own wares.

That said, the European Court rules won't change significantly the market dynamics in place. Whether or not new antitrust cases are lodged against Microsoft—which they undoubtedly will be—Microsoft execs have been forced to realize that they always have to operate with an assumption of illegal

> *"Don't be surprised to see Microsoft to make more 'proactive' changes to its products."*

monopolistic behavior working against the company. Microsoft brass know that every product development and marketing decision Microsoft makes for the rest of the time it is in existence will be scrutinized for possible lawsuit opportunities.

Don't be surprised to see Microsoft make more "proactive" changes to its products—like it did when it changed Vista's built-in desktop search technology to head off a likely antitrust suit from Google. But don't put too much stock in antitrust concerns completely crippling Microsoft's business practices, nor (contrary to what its executives love to claim) its ability to innovate.

Enter the New Kids on the Block

While Microsoft is a desktop operating-system monopolist, it's not the run-away leader in several other categories in which it's playing (search engines, digital-media players, game consoles, mobile operating systems). To assume that Microsoft can wield its desktop OS power to unfair advantage in these areas just because Microsoft is Microsoft is a big leap of faith.

The competitive landscape the Microsoft of 2008 is entering without Gates in a day-to-day supervisory role is very different from the one in which the company played in 1978, 1988, or 1998. While Microsoft always has had competitors with which to contend, it's now facing not just its usual stable of relatively well-understood adversaries (IBM, Oracle, SAP, Intuit, etc.), but a whole raft of additional, less-predictable ones (Google, Facebook, Salesforce.com, etc.).

To appreciate just how much Microsoft's competitive landscape is changing, as of late, check out Microsoft's annual 10-Ks from 2002 and 2007.[12] Just a few years ago (in 2002), the Softies explained the playing field in this way:

> The Company's competitors include many software application vendors, such as IBM, Oracle, Apple, Sun Microsystems, Corel, Qualcomm, and local application developers in Europe and Asia....A number of Microsoft's most significant competitors, including IBM, Sun Microsystems, Oracle, and AOL-Time Warner, are collaborating with one another on various initiatives directed at competing with Microsoft.

> The Linux open source operating system has gained increasing acceptance as well. Several computer manufacturers preinstall Linux on PC servers and many leading software developers have written applications that run on Linux....Microsoft's online services network, MSN, faces formidable competition from AOL-Time Warner, Yahoo!, and a vast array of Web sites and portals that offer content of all types and e-mail, instant messaging, calendaring, chat, and search and shopping services, among other things.

---

[12] Todd Bishop from the *Seattle Post-Intelligencer* analyzed Microsoft's lists of its competitors from 2002 and 2007 on his blog post last year: http://blog.seattlepi.nwsource.com/microsoft/archives/119449.asp.

Cut to 2007. While many old-time Softies would doubtless rank IBM as still being Microsoft's No. 1 competitor, there are a lot of other new contenders who belong on Redmond's list of rivals. Add Mozilla, Google, VMWare, Nintendo, Sony, Nokia, Symbian, and a raft of other new competitors to the existing list of Apple, Red Hat, Oracle, and the like.

> *"Microsoft is now playing in several markets outside of its traditional areas of core competency."*

The result? Microsoft is now playing in several markets outside of its traditional areas of core competency. The company has been hiring folks with expertise outside of development tools and Windows—former Electronic Arts Studios President Don Mattrick, who is now Senior Vice President of Microsoft's Interactive Entertainment Business, for example. Until recently, Microsoft hasn't had to pour a lot of effort or money into recruitment; Microsoft was a hot commodity for the software-savvy. But management is going to have a tougher time convincing big-name hires to join a company that is not a leader in a number of key, hot markets—that they should join a behemoth like Microsoft.

Past Microsoft Truisms: Will They Hold in the Future?

Just because Microsoft clung to a strategy or behavior in its first 30+ years doesn't mean that the company will continue to follow the same patterns in its next 30. But there are a handful of "truisms" I've noticed about the Soft's past strategies that I am hard-pressed to believe they'll try and/or succeed in changing.

1. Outsiders Never Become Insiders at Microsoft

Microsoft has had a disastrous—there's really no other word for it—record in hiring from the outside. I've lost track of how many highly touted managers Microsoft has hired, only to be forced to acknowledge their hasty retreats. A few examples:

- **Rick Belluzzo**—In 2002, just 14 months after taking the President and Chief Operating Officer reins, Rick Belluzzo resigned from Microsoft. Belluzzo was the former CEO of Silicon Graphics Inc., a long-time Hewlett-Packard exec, and touted as a Ballmer buddy when he was brought on board.

- Robert Herbold—Chief Operating Officer of Microsoft from 1994 to 2002, joined the company from Procter & Gamble (Ballmer's former employer). While eight years is a good amount of time to put in at any job these days, Herbold's tenure was rocky. Many company watchers considered him odd man out, despite his longevity.
- Steve Berkowitz—The former Ask.com CEO who joined Microsoft in 2006 to help fix the Online Services Business (OSB) is, for a couple more months, the Senior Vice President of the Online Services Group. Since he joined Microsoft, Berkowitz repeatedly was rumored to be on his way out.

Outsiders just never seem to make the transition to Microsoft insiders. In spite of this fact, the Microsoft brass continues to look outside to bring in new blood to supervise the troops. (And former Digital Equipment Corp. execs, many of whom have thrived inside Microsoft, don't really count as "outsiders" in my book, given that DEC West was practically an extension of Microsoft before it was shut down.)

> *"There are a handful of 'truisms' I've noticed about the Soft's past strategies that I am hard-pressed to believe they'll try and/or succeed in changing."*

Granted, there are a few exceptions to the "Outsiders Not Welcome" rule. When hiring a new Live Search chief, Microsoft decided to award the position to an insider and chose Dynamics ERP veteran Satya Nadella, for example. (One caveat: Some say that Nadella won out over outsiders because no one wanted to take on the task of trying to turn the distant No. 3 search player into the market leader.) And so far, at least, Chief Operating Officer Kevin Turner is an outsider who is still, as of this writing, managing to carve out for himself a spot as one of Microsoft's most influential insiders. (And then there's Chief Software Architect Ray Ozzie...but more about him and his prospects of becoming a permanent Microsoft fixture in Chapter 3.)

Do the Nadella and Turner cases show that Microsoft is turning over a new leaf? Maybe. But as a general rule, veteran Softies are not optimistic about outsiders' potential for success.

2. All Strategies Must Start (and End) with Windows

Microsoft's biggest and most successful franchise is Windows. That isn't a coincidence.

Nearly every strategic move Microsoft has made to date has been designed to protect the Windows business. When Microsoft faced a choice between promoting itself as a Web company or a Windows company back in the mid- to late-1990s, it went with Windows. The result? Microsoft bundled its Internet Explorer (IE) browser into Windows (and got in deep legal hot water in the process) rather than porting IE to other platforms and building itself into a Web powerhouse. Because Gates, former Platforms Chief Jim Allchin, and other influential Softies feared that an emphasis on IE could erode its Windows stronghold, Microsoft decided against betting big on the Web until its competitors started eating its lunch.

Former *Wall Street Journal* reporter David Bank wrote an entire book about the war inside Microsoft between Windows and the Web, entitled *Breaking Windows: How Bill Gates Fumbled the Future of Microsoft*, which was published by The Free Press in 2001. As a *BusinessWeek* review of Bank's book succinctly explained:

> *The Web and its open standards were the future, Microsoft's Internet faction contended. Perhaps, replied the software experts inside the company, but Windows was the wellspring of the company's success and would remain the key to its financial future. The Internet forces had been in the ascendancy since December, 1995, when Gates publicly embraced the Net as the future of the company. But the move turned out to be more of a tactical feint designed to thwart upstart Netscape Communications than a strategic reorientation.*[13]

Microsoft almost waited until it was too late to try to fix the error of its Windows-centric ways. For five years—between 2001 and 2006—Microsoft let IE remain dormant because it was trying to prove its contention that the browser was an inextricable part of Windows. Microsoft's argument nearly cost

---

[13] To read the full *BusinessWeek* review of Bank's book ("The Uncivil War Inside Microsoft," August 16, 2001, by Steven Wildstrom), go here: http://www.businessweek.com/bwdaily/dnflash/aug2001/nf20010816_910.htm.

the company a loss in the U.S. Department of Justice antitrust case, and did allow Mozilla to come in and steal a good chunk of Web-browser market share.

Given this history, you might think that Microsoft had learned its lesson about trying to make the world bend around Windows. Right now, that doesn't look to be the case.

> *"Microsoft almost waited until it was too late to try to fix the error of its Windows-centric ways."*

After former Windows chief Jim Allchin retired in 2007, Microsoft appointed as the new head of Windows and Windows Live Engineering, Steven Sinofsky. While Sinofsky is credited as one of the executives who helped convince Gates and other Microsoft managers of the importance of the Web, he also has a vested interest in maintaining Windows as it exists as one of the company's core franchises—regardless of how the market changes. Windows 7, the next version of Windows, sounds from early tips and feedback like a continuation of Windows Vista. And Internet Explorer 8, the next version of Microsoft's Web browser, has been slow out of the gate—much slower than Gates promised it would be back in 2006.

3. The Third Time's the Charm

Smart—and risk-adverse—customers never buy first- or second-generation Microsoft products. By the time it rolls out the third release of a new technology, Microsoft finally gets it right, according to industry lore and legend.

> *"Unfortunately, customers' experiences have not jived with the scenarios Microsoft has painted."*

Microsoft's contention is that this "truism" is no longer true. Customers don't need to wait around for service packs or new versions of software because Microsoft can continuously fix/update its products by pushing the latest patches and updates over its Windows Update/Automatic Update patching mechanism, the Softies claim. And when a product is "released to the Web," as opposed to shipped on disks or on new PCs, Microsoft can update that product regularly and often over the Web, as well, officials say.

Unfortunately, customers' experiences have not jived with the scenarios Microsoft has painted. Microsoft emphasized during the first year of availability of Windows Vista that users didn't need to wait around for Service Pack (SP) 1 before upgrading, since the company planned to push any and all fixes and updates over Windows Update as soon as they were ready. That didn't stop many, if not most, businesses from waiting at least for SP1, which shipped in early 2008, before getting serious about planning their Vista deployments.

It takes more than just hundreds of thousands of beta testers to get a product right. It takes hours and hours of everyday people running every possible permutation and combination of software, hardware, and services to make a product rock-hard. (And this isn't true for Microsoft products only, as Apple and other companies are discovering as their wares are gaining greater market share.) Yet every time Microsoft changes substantially the inner workings of its software, the countdown toward the magic Version No. 3 starts all over again for many long-time Microsoft users. And that scenario doesn't look like it is going to change any time soon.

4. You Don't Have to Be First to Win

Microsoft has spent an awful lot of time and energy in recent years trying to prove that it is just as innovative, if not more so, than its competitors. But the reality is quite different.

Microsoft is far better at copying, building on, and "perfecting" existing innovations than it is at coming up with brand-new ones. Microsoft studies its competitors and finds their weak spots. And it has the time, the cash, and the people to be very thorough in its studies.

> *"Microsoft is far better at copying, building on and 'perfecting' existing innovations than it is at coming up with brand-new ones."*

It's hard to dispute that Microsoft didn't copy Apple when developing Windows Vista. But so what? Instead of feigning outrage, why not admit that Microsoft took the best of a number of Apple's "Tiger" Mac OS X concepts and ended up one-upping Tiger on several fronts. Ditto with Zunes and iPods; Xbox consoles and Sony Playstations; Live Search and Google Search; C# and Java; and Internet Explorer 7 and Mozilla.

When Microsoft strikes out on its own and tries something new/different, its track record is far less stellar. Microsoft's Surface multi-touch tabletop is my favorite whipping boy when talk turns to Microsoft as innovator. Going further back, the Microsoft Bob interface is another oft-cited example of Microsoft's failure to innovate. More examples: SPOT watches, Tablet PCs, ultra-mobile PCs and plenty of other much ballyhooed Microsoft innovations.

Sure, there are some instances in which Microsoft was first to market with an innovation that turned into revenue gold for the company. Xbox Live, Microsoft's gaming service, comes to mind here. But as a general rule, Microsoft has built itself up by being more of a strong follower than a thought-leader. Microsoft should embrace its "extend and embrace" strategy rather than fight it.

5. If You Can't Beat 'Em, Wait 'Em out

Microsoft—even the old, more ruthless, pre-antitrust-tamed Microsoft—often gets painted as more diabolical than the company actually is.

> *"Did the vendors of each of these products end up making so many missteps that Microsoft was able to wait them out and capitalize on their failures?"*

While Microsoft has been credited with putting more than a few companies out of business, it's often the ineptitude of its competitors that ends up eliminating Microsoft adversaries. Was Microsoft Office really better than WordPerfect? NT superior to OS/2? Internet Explorer a noticeable advance over Netscape? The Xbox a killer compared to Sony's Playstation? Or did the vendors of each of these products end up making so many missteps that Microsoft was able to wait them out and capitalize on their failures?

I am not trying to excuse Microsoft here. Microsoft abused its desktop operating-system-monopoly powers to squeeze out unfairly some of its competitors and to hurt some of its supposed PC and software allies, as various antitrust regulatory bodies around the world have ruled. Withholding protocols and documentation required for interoperability; creating onerous licensing terms—Microsoft was found to have done all of these things and more in its quest to be No. 1 in its various markets.

However, Microsoft also has benefited and is continuing to benefit from its deep pockets that enable the company to wait out its rivals. Microsoft was able to get Novell to sign a patent cross-license agreement because Novell was hurting financially and needed Microsoft as an ally to continue to do business. When selling databases, mail servers, and systems-management suites, Microsoft has been able to wait months, if not years, for lengthy (and lucrative) enterprise sales to close—a luxury that many of its less-well-heeled competitors and/or single-product vendors do not have.

Microsoft has time to keep trying to crack new markets (see Truism No. 4 above). If at first it doesn't succeed in gaming consoles, hosted CRM software, or healthcare services, Microsoft has time to try and try again. And more time means more chances for other vendors to make wrong moves.

The bottom line: Time is on Microsoft's side. And even with more and more technologies, especially on the consumer side, being developed "in Internet time," Microsoft still is going to be able to wait out its rivals, customer fads, and the vagaries of the market for a good number of years.

Enough about the past. It's onto the topic of Microsoft's future from here on out....

Microsoft 2.0: The Buzzwords

2

Perception becomes reality, if left unchecked....

*—Frank Shaw, head of Microsoft PR
at Waggener Edstrom, in a June 20, 2007
posting on his "Glass House" blog*

The adage "actions speak louder than words" is true, and especially true in the Microsoft context. But there's also a whole lot about Microsoft's current and future intentions that can be gleaned by analyzing the words that execs have chosen to define the company and its strategies.

I'm not talking about MicroSpeak here. *MicroSpeak* is the specialized lexicon that's sprung up inside Microsoft, which sometimes makes it tough for non-Softies to follow the gist of a conversation. (Prime examples of MicroSpeak are *forcing function, ring-fencing, business decision maker, aka BDM*.) Over the years, several "Gates-isms" have crept into the MicroSpeak canon, including gems like "that's so random" and "super" (as in, "I think blogging is super-important").

Instead, this chapter will focus on some of the strategic and marketing catch phrases upon which Microsoft currently is relying to shape its policies and products. I've selected eight buzzwords that any Redmond watcher looking for clues about what's next for Microsoft should keep in mind when analyzing the company's next-gen products and strategies.

In no particular order, here are the eight:

1. Innovation
2. Quests
3. eXperiences
4. Common codebase

5. Interoperability
6. Open
7. S+S (Software Plus Services)
8. People-Ready

Microsoft: Innovators Я Us

Ever since Nicholas Carr published his oft-quoted "IT Doesn't Matter" article in the May 2003 edition of the *Harvard Business Review*, Microsoft officials have been hell-bent on proving him wrong. The quest continues and looks likely to continue for the foreseeable future.

Every top executive at Microsoft makes one or more mentions of how much money Microsoft is spending on R&D when discussing the company's future. In fiscal 2007 that total hit more than $7 billion.

> *"There's also a whole lot about Microsoft's current and future intentions that can be gleaned by analyzing the words that execs have chosen to define the company and its strategies."*

But here's the Catch 22: More R&D spending doesn't equate automatically to more or better innovation. In fact, there remains a widespread perception—a good part of it well-earned—that Microsoft is much better at copying/borrowing/taking others' ideas and parlaying them into moneymakers than it is at creating new technology innovations from scratch. While several Microsoft research projects have ended up as commercial products and/or elements of commercial products, many others have not.

Microsoft has been actively seeking ways to bring more of its innovations (and perceptions of innovation) to the fore. On the "perception side," the company launched in the mid-part of this decade its "Innovative Integration" campaign. After *bundling* became an officially "banned in Redmond" term, Microsoft launched its "Better Together" campaign. Then came Better Together's natural complement, "Integrated Innovation."[1]

---

[1] Microsoft dropped a press release in 2004 attempting to explain coherently what it meant by "Integrated Innovation." The full text of it is here: www.microsoft.com/presspass/features/2004/jul04/07-12IntegratedInnovation.mspx.

Integrated innovation became shorthand for Microsoft's strategy for integrating more and more previously stand-alone technologies and products into Windows, Office, and other core products. The Softies also occasionally used *Innovative Integration* to refer to cross-platform integration—the old "Better Together" concept that the Windows client and server don't need to be used in tandem, but doing so will make for an even better, more feature-rich experience.

In the latter half of 2006, the popularity of Integrated Innovation began to wane. CEO Steve Ballmer went on record saying that Microsoft's new, official plan of record had changed to "Innovate, Then Integrate." No one seems quite sure what Ballmer's new slogan means. My best guess? Make sure a new technology is cooked before committing to make it part of a core product and before making dependencies on it when coding.

> *"Every top executive at Microsoft makes one or more mentions of how much money Microsoft is spending on R&D when discussing the company's future."*

Terms change, yet innovation still remains a hot button for the Redmondians. On its Innovate-On portal,[2] which the company launched in 2007, Microsoft makes a case for why its reseller, solution-provider, PC maker, "white box" system builder, and other channel partners should build on top of Windows Vista, Windows Server 2008, Office 2007, SQL Server 2005, Dynamics, and Windows Live wares. (Exactly what this has to do with "innovate" is rather amorphous.)

> The INNOVATE ON initiative provides you with a full range of technical and business resources as you develop your solutions on our technologies. In each product portal, you'll find the steps you need to build your product and take it to market faster.

---

[2] Microsoft's Innovate-On portal: Although partnering seemingly has little to do with innovation, Microsoft has glommed onto the "innovate" buzzword most recently via this web site: www.innovate-on.com/Default.aspx?LangType=1033.

Incubating and Greenhousing Toward Innovation

But back to the question of alchemy. Microsoft has grappled for years—actually, decades—with how best to turn "innovations" into products. In Microsoft's earlier years, management often pitted internal teams against one another and let the "best" product win. That strategy eventually fell out of favor, one might assume, because of inefficiencies and resignations by "sore losers." Going forward, Microsoft is trying other tactics—including more formal methods and processes for moving research creations into the product groups.

Microsoft Research (MSR) has never been a pure "research for research's sake" kind of organization. The fruits of MSR have found their way into a variety of products, from the Surface multi-touch tabletop to Windows Vista. That said, there is also a larger group of MSR products and technologies that never saw and most likely never will see the light of day, at least not inside Microsoft. In 2005, Microsoft decided to make available for licensing some of these out-in-left-field MSR technologies—things like the MSR-developed "Wallop" social-networking application and LaunchTile, a navigator for mobile devices.

> *"Microsoft has grappled for years—actually, decades—with how best to turn 'innovations' into products."*

In some recent cases, Microsoft assigned members of the Microsoft Research staff to product teams to help facilitate the transition of specific technologies and ideas into groups designated to "productize" them—take, for example, the assignment of Lili Cheng and other members of the social computing group team at MSR to the Windows Vista development team. (Cheng ended up playing a key role in helping develop the Vista user interface.) In other cases, Microsoft has simply grabbed an MSR-developed technology, like the "RingCam" panoramic video-camera technology from MSR, and moved it into the commercial channel (albeit, several years later). It took more than five years, but in late 2007, RingCam, now known officially as "RoundTable," finally hit the market.

The RoundTable example gets to the very heart of why research doesn't correspond, one-to-one, with innovation at Microsoft. That reason is agility.

Microsoft has been seeking that special sauce that will allow it to bring newly developed technologies quickly—and quietly—to market. Recent experiments include the formation of LiveLabs, SearchLabs, and adCenter Labs. As their names suggest, LiveLabs is a combination of Windows Live and Microsoft Research staffs; SearchLabs is an amalgamation of Microsoft Search experts and Microsoft researchers. And adCenter Labs is a joint project between the adCenter online-advertising-platform team and MSR.

Projects emanating from these joint-incubation teams so far have been primarily proof-of-concept designs. The ultimate goal of all of these new labs remains the creation of commercialized products, however.

The adCenter Labs team, for instance, was known to be working on the following laundry list of projects in 2007:

- Video-display ads that use JavaScript for highlighting and commenting. They also allow for authentication using Windows Live ID, "So users can choose to view comments from their friends only."
- Video hyperlinks, "the first stand-alone product developed by adCenter Labs," lets marketers embed video hyperlinks within online video ads.
- Large display feedback, which is vision-based technology that creates interactive public displays—using a computer-vision algorithm that tracks hand movements—that consumers can remotely control.
- Keyword optimization for paid-search and content ads.
- Contextual advertising tools, which classify web sites and keywords into hierarchical taxonomy in order to help increase relevance of contextual ads. (Microsoft has been testing its "ContentAds" capabilities with selected advertisers since fall 2006.)

Microsoft also is continuing to hone its incubation processes and procedures, borrowing, when applicable, from others in the process. In 2003, Microsoft's Information Worker division was cultivating greenhouse incubators to nurture various projects, including what became known as Microsoft's *Knowledge Network*. More recently, the Microsoft Business Division (the unit that superseded the Information Worker unit) was housing Officelabs, a new incubator.

Officelabs is a fledgling group aimed at functioning more like a Windows Live team than the Office one. Microsoft brass has been encouraging the

Officelabs team to make use of open-source concepts in order to make better use of developers across different divisions within the company. They've been pushing the Officelabs team not to think inside the traditional Microsoft box by encouraging practices like:

- Releasing fixes more quickly.
- Getting new innovations into the hands of testers and users before they've been tested for months/years.
- Releasing products and updates early and often, instead of waiting for orchestrated mega-launches like the Vista/Office 2007 one that finally happened, after five long years of development, at the end of January 2007.

In case those management strategies don't wow you, it's worth noting that those kinds of concepts are very non-Office-like. The Office team tradition-ally has prided itself on the lengthy, rigorous, closely controlled testing that versions of Office undergo.

> *"Microsoft also is continuing to hone its incubation processes and procedures, borrowing, when applicable, from others in the process."*

Another example of a Microsoft innovation incubator at work is the "virtual team" created by the Developer Division, the Windows divi-sion, and the official Technology Incubation units to work together on operating-system and programming-language futures. As Microsoft officials have noted repeatedly, many-core, or massively multi-core, PC and server systems are going to require changes in every level of the computing stack. This virtual incubation team is work-ing on prototypes of an operating-system–hypervisor combo. (It could possi-bly take the form of the "Viridian" hypervisor, combined with Microsoft Research's non-Windows-based microkernel OS, known as *Singularity*.)

There's also an entity inside Microsoft known as the "Microsoft Experimentation Platform Team" that has been dabbling with ways to test and launch services more effectively. The team is relying on scientific methods in the area of randomized experimental design to learn how new features affect users, as well as how to get new functionality more quickly into users' hands. Microsoft has been starting to rely on these methods to roll out enhancements and additions to its own family of Windows Live, Xbox Live, and MSN services. Allegedly, the Experimentation Platform Team is looking to allow third-party developers to make use of the techniques and processes Microsoft is honing—for a hefty fee, no doubt—to add their services to Microsoft's various online properties.

On the home and entertainment side of the business, Microsoft is test-driving yet another way to turn product concepts more rapidly into products. There's been a considerable amount written about how Corporate Vice President, Design and Development, Entertainment and Devices Division, J. Allard, and his team sequestered themselves in separate buildings—away from the main Redmond campus—in order to develop the Xbox and accompanying Xbox Live subscription service. Microsoft pursued an almost identical near-spinoff type of strategy in creating and launching the Zune.

> *"There's also an entity inside Microsoft known as the 'Microsoft Experimentation Platform Team' that has been dabbling with ways to test and launch services more effectively."*

Now that it is fully formed, the Entertainment and Devices unit is continuing to seek ways to continue to foster an innovation-centric vibe. One way they're attempting this is by the creation of a multi-disciplinary team of designers and creatives, working hand-in-hand with the Xbox and Zune software developers and marketers. Microsoft refers to this group as *The Studio*. The goal of the group is to build and maintain a sticky design/brand that Microsoft will apply across all of its consumer devices, current and future.

Innovation Doesn't Preclude Imitation (or Does It?)

Are there other places Microsoft should be looking to take innovation cues? With the company's obsession on Web 2.0 poster children—FaceBook, Socialtext, del.icio.us, ad nauseum—there's no shortage of "get innovative quick" schemes that various folks at Microsoft are advocating.

> *"And then there's archrival Google, which gets all kinds of credit for being innovative."*

And then there's archrival Google, which gets all kinds of credit for being innovative—with everything from its "Don't Be Evil" moniker, to its fabled 20 percent policy (encouraging employees to spend 20 percent of their time working on new projects—which may or may not ever amount to anything marketable).

Taking a page out of Google's innovation book might not be the worst idea in the world, blogged Dare Obasanjo, a program manager with the Windows Live Platform group:

> My advice is to look at companies within your industry that are considered innovative and see what you can learn from them. One such company is Google which is widely considered to be the most innovative company on Earth by many in the software industry. A number of Google's competitors have several internal groups whose job is to "incubate ideas" and foster innovation yet it seems that Google is the company most associated with innovation in the online space.

Among the ideas from Google worth a look, according to Obasanjo[3]:

1. **Everyone Is Responsible for Innovation**—Obasanjo mentions the 20 percent principle, as well as Google's decision to work from a single code base for all of its projects.

   > Google has a single code base for all of their projects and developers are strongly encouraged to fix bugs or add features to any Google product they want even if they are not on the product team. This attitude encourages the cross pollination of ideas

---

[3] Lessons on Innovation from Google: Microsoft Program Manager Dare Obasanjo blogged in July about some Google innovation plays that Microsoft would do well to adopt. See Obasanjo's full post here: www.25hoursaday.com/weblog/2007/07/09/LessonsOnInnovationFromGoogle.aspx.

*across the company and encourages members of the various prod-
uct teams to keep an open mind about ideas from outside their
particular box.*

2. **Good Ideas Often Come from Outside Your Box**—Innovation
   through acquisition—whether it's Google, Microsoft, or any other
   vendor doing the acquiring—is no sin, Obasanjo noted.

3. **Force Competition to Face the Innovator's Dilemma**—Challenge
   pre-existing notions of what works, in terms of software, in any and
   all categories, Obasanjo said. Disruptive technologies win, he said.

*It is quite clear that Google will move to address the gaps in time
(see Google Gears) so we are likely on the cusp of a multi-billion
dollar software category [that will] undergo upheaval in the next
few years.*

The bottom line when it comes to innovation, according to Obasanjo, is
"Change the Game. Do not play by the rules that favor your competitors."

Microsoft's Vision Quests: Flights of Fancy or Folly?

For the past couple of years, various Microsoft executives have made mention
of a somewhat intangible set of goals, or "quests," that Microsoft is honing for
future planning purposes.

These quests have been championed by Microsoft's top managers, from
Chairman Bill Gates on down. Currently, however, they sound like they're the
province of David Vaskevitch. Vaskevitch is a 22-year Microsoft veteran with
the current somewhat strange title of Senior Vice President, Chief Technical
Officer for Business Platform. Vaskevitch has been reporting directly to Gates
for years. His mission, according to his Microsoft bio page: "To develop a
focused and unified strategy and architecture for future Microsoft platforms."

With that info as a backdrop, there is a bit of public information on the
quests. Microsoft maintains the list of detailed quests and employee comments about them on an internal SharePoint wiki. (And no, I haven't seen this
wiki—or the full list of quests.) By capturing and preserving this "corporate
knowledge," Microsoft's goal is to make the company less dependent on particular high-placed individuals (like Gates).

Microsoft CEO Steve Ballmer has described the corporate quests that Microsoft is using internally as a long-term planning tool. Ballmer said that there are 70 areas that the Microsoft executive team has identified as important to the company's future. The 70 quests are subdivided into six buckets: Productivity, entertainment, business works, IT in the data center, software development, and "the future of Windows," meaning both the user interface and the computational computing models enabled by the platform. Each of these quests will manifest in different ways for Microsoft's different audiences (consumer, IT professional, and developers).

> *"By capturing and preserving this 'corporate knowledge,' Microsoft's goal is to make the company less dependent on particular high-placed individuals"*

Not every Microsoft employee is enamored with the quests approach. Some—in particular, a handful of vociferous posters on the anonymously written Mini-Microsoft blog—have been particularly harsh about whether the identified quests are the right ones, as well as whether this quest exercise is anything more than tilting at windmills.

But Microsoft's execs are trying anything and everything they can to get and stay "innovative." You can only "miss" the wholesale move to the Web once and survive it. In 2006, Ballmer told News.com:

> *Two years from now ... the commitment I made to Bill is that we're going to be in the position where hopefully we would anticipate anything he would suggest to us. ...That's part of getting the company to the place where it can have this broad, big agenda and it's got to be driven by not only guys like me, but the next generation of leaders.*[4]

---

[4] Ballmer and Gates talk "quests." In a June 19, 2006 interview with News.com (the subject of which was what's next for Microsoft after Gates retired in two years), the pair talked a bit about Microsoft's quests as a method for preserving corporate knowledge. The full story is here: http://news.com.com/Microsoft+looks+beyond+Gates+for+new+ideas/2100-1014_3-6085030.html.

eXperiences: More Than Just Another Pretty UI

For the past few years, I've struggled to understand the nuances of Microsoft's use of the word *eXperiences* (yes, written just like that). I used to consider eXperiences synonymous with "user interfaces." And in large part, that over-simplified definition is not far off the mark.

But in Microsoft's big-picture view, eXperiences are more than interfaces. They are immersive activities. Basically anything with which a user might directly interact seems to be considered part of the "eXperience." The two teams that most heavily rely on the word *eXperience*—in everything from job titles to mission statements—are the Windows Client and Windows Live teams.

On the Microsoft executive roster, look at how many executives, as of mid-2007, had the word *eXperience* in their titles:

- **Tom Gibbons**—Corporate Vice President, Productivity and Extended Consumer Experiences Group
- **Kathleen Hogan**—Corporate Vice President, Worldwide Customer Service, Support and Customer and Partner Experience (CPE)
- **Chris Jones**—Corporate Vice President, Windows Live Experience Program Management
- **Julie Larson-Green**—Corporate Vice President, Windows Experience Program Management
- **Steve Liffick**—Corporate Vice President, Windows Live User Experience Group

Trying to pin any Softie on exactly how an eXperience differs from a user interface is a challenging task. One of the few to take the challenge was Steve Berkowitz, the senior vice president in charge of Microsoft's Online Services Group. Berkowitz's definition of *eXperiences*: "ways to enter the Internet," (specifically) search, commerce, entertainment portals (such as MSN.com), and community.

> *"In Microsoft's big-picture view, eXperiences are more than interfaces."*

The Windows folks talk of eXperiences in a slightly different way: a photo and imaging experience; a gaming experience. UX (User Experience), in the

Windows sense, includes toolbars, sounds, warnings, confirmations, and a host of other branding/design elements. As former Windows chief Jim Allchin described the experiences concept a few years back:

> *Experience computing is solution-centered, person-minded, and focused on experiences. It's about sites and sounds, feel, and emotion. Today, the devices that are evoking the most emotion in people are the most popular ones.[5]*

The UX drum is only getting louder inside Microsoft's hallowed halls. On the "Design for Innovation" blog,[6] three "Microsoft user experience evangelists" discuss topics around interface design. Marketing seems to be part of what Microsoft means by UX, as well. If you scratch the surface of anything to do with Microsoft's Silverlight "Flash killer" and the Expression Studio tools designed to build applications for Silverlight, user experience isn't far behind.

> *"Microsoft is slowly but surely becoming more attuned to the importance that design plays in product development, reception, and loyalty."*

Bottom line: Microsoft is slowly but surely becoming more attuned to the importance that design plays in product development, reception, and loyalty. Instead of relegating design to an afterthought, Microsoft is finally taking a page out of the books of Apple and other major tech and non-tech companies by realizing that non-geeky elements are key to software and services' success, too.

The Holy Grail of the Common Codebase

Across many different Microsoft business units, a common codebase is the holy grail worth sacrificing almost anything to obtain.

---

[5] Allchin on "eXperiences": During his Windows Hardware Engineering Conference 2004 keynote, former Windows chief Jim Allchin turned up the volume on Microsoft's "experience computing" concept. Read a report of his speech here: www.windowsitpro.com/articles/print.cfm?articleid=42548.

[6] Design for Innovation blog: Three "Microsoft User Experience Evangelists" tackle the thorny topic of "UX" at Microsoft in their regularly updated blog, available here: http://design-for-innovation.com/.

In Windows, the desire for a common codebase took decades to realize. Until Windows Vista and Windows Server 2008, Microsoft was building the Windows client on one codebase and the Windows server on another. Once Microsoft took the plunge and decided to build both client and server atop the same core codebase, the company was able to reduce one element of complexity that has plagued Windows from the beginning of its life.

Microsoft seemingly has given up on trying to ship Windows client and server simultaneously. Nonetheless, the two make use of many of the same core elements. Microsoft's Core Operating Systems Division (COSD)—a group created in 2003 to advance "engineering excellence" across the Windows groups—works on the common kernel, I/O (input/output) system; virtualization; core devices; setup; and all the build properties. As of mid-2007, about three-quarters of the Windows code was shared by the client and server teams.[7] COSD builds the bits at the bottom of the Windows stack, and the client and server teams add the custom elements to their respective products.

Maintaining a common codebase isn't only a Windows-unit goal. Other divisions at the company are working on their own renditions of this concept.

The Microsoft Business Solutions (MBS) team, which is part of the Microsoft Business Division, has been going back and forth over how, when, and if it would be able to unify its four different ERP products under a common codebase. Originally, the MBS team talked about unifying its four different product families (Great Plains, Navision, Axapta, and Solomon) into a single Microsoft-branded ERP product that would meld the best features of the four. That initiative was code-named *Project Green*. But the MBS team scrapped that goal back in 2006 and instead decided to roll out "waves" of its existing ERP products that shared more and more of a common look and feel, common workflow engine, and similar business-intelligence tools.

The Windows Live team also has been moving toward its own version of a common codebase concept. From the get-go, Microsoft's online services business seemingly was committed to developing a common back-end

[7] Windows Server Program Manager Iain McDonald shared more on the whole "shared-code" concept in a Redmond Developer News article in June 2007, entitled "Building the New Server." An online version of the article can be found here: http://reddevnews.com/features/article.aspx?editorialsid=736.

infrastructure/platform that would support all of its Live services. And increasingly, starting last year, the various Microsoft Live services were starting to integrate more seamlessly with one another—that is, the same Live Messenger instant-messaging service was implemented across a variety of different Live services.

> *"Maintaining a common codebase isn't only a Windows-unit goal."*

Additionally, as of mid-2007, the team acknowledged publicly that Microsoft's current strategy of rolling out Windows Live services willy-nilly may have seemed a tad convoluted. (That's an understatement!) Going forward, the Windows Live team is focusing on delivering a core set of Windows Live services that will share a common installer and updater. There is no firm commitment on when this kind of unification of the core services might become a reality, however.

Interoperability: Where the PR Rubber Meets the Customer Road

What does Microsoft mean by "interoperable"? Anything that can run on multiple versions of Windows, the old saying goes.

Microsoft has been trying to change this public perception for years in order to convince its partners, customers, and even competitors that the company is serious about interoperability. Microsoft's campaign has met with mixed results, at best.

In Europe, the European Commission (EC) has been all over Microsoft for allegedly failing to provide sufficient documentation to enable its competitors to interoperate with Windows and other Microsoft products. Microsoft's competitors claimed repeatedly that the Redmondians dragged their feet on delivering the interoperability documentation required under the terms of the European Union's 2004 antitrust ruling regarding Microsoft.

Meanwhile, the EC has been investigating Microsoft's willingness or lack thereof to provide its competitors with necessary information for Office-suite interoperability. In July 2007, the European Commission sent a second questionnaire to Microsoft rivals, seeking information on whether the Redmond vendor has been withholding technical data on Word and Excel that others require in order to interoperate. The Commission launched an official probe on behalf of Microsoft's rivals regarding Office interoperability (and the alleged lack thereof) in January 2008.

In spite of public perceptions, Microsoft is continuing to beat the interoperability drum publicly on a variety of fronts. And it's showing no signs of abating.

Microsoft has created several interoperability alliances and groups, such as the Interop Vendor Alliance. The company is turning up the volume on the rather obscure Windows Rally, a set of networking protocols and licenses designed to simplify the connection of peripherals to Windows. It is making a subset of its Common Language Runtime (CLR) technology—that not so long ago was tied

> *"What does Microsoft mean by 'interoperable'? Anything that can run on multiple versions of Windows, the old saying goes."*

exclusively to Windows—available on non-Microsoft platforms running Mozilla's Firefox and Apple's Safari browsers. It is stepping up its efforts to enable Office Open XML (the document file format built into Office 2007) to be able to interoperate with the rival Open Document Format (ODF) backed by IBM, Sun, and other rivals. And Microsoft has been signing interoperability pacts with various leading Linux vendors, including Novell, Linspire, and Xandros.

As some of Microsoft's Linux competitors have noted, Microsoft's Linux interoperability pacts come with strings attached. Novell, Linspire, and Xandros all signed patent-protection clauses as part of their interoperability agreements with Microsoft. Under terms of these clauses, Microsoft has agreed not to sue these companies' Linux users—as long as they are running software that is not licensed under the GNU General Public License version 3. GPLv3, approved by the Free Software Foundation in late June 2007, included a provision of which Microsoft is leery—specifically that all GPLv3 software will be covered by the patent-protection afforded to Novell and other Microsoft partners.

While most Linux vendors all have claimed publicly that they don't believe their software infringes on Microsoft patents, Microsoft has said that it has found Linux and other open-source software to infringe on 235 of its patents. Microsoft has continued to refuse to provide publicly any specific examples of infringements or to offer more detailed charges. It's not clear what—if any-thing—Microsoft is showing to Linux vendors to convince them to sign patent-protection/interop agreements. Officials with Red Hat, the biggest of the Linux vendors, have said that Red Hat has been in on-again/off-again negotiations with Microsoft regarding an interop deal but has no intentions to sign a patent-protection deal.

(As of the time I submitted this manuscript, Red Hat and Microsoft had not signed an interop/patent-protection deal. Make of that what you will.)

> *"As some of Microsoft's Linux competitors have noted, Microsoft's Linux interoperability pacts come with strings attached."*

If you listen to Microsoft's competitors and the strong base of die-hard open-source/Linux customers, many, if not all, of these interoperability initiatives are nothing but publicity campaigns. While Microsoft has trotted out happy customers willing to provide quotes expressing satisfaction with Microsoft's interoperability work, it's hard to measure how much or how little these initiatives have done to make customers' lives easier.

Let's be real here. Yes, interoperability is like motherhood and apple pie. But why would Microsoft genuinely want to make it easier for its customers to run a mix of Linux and Windows, or Unix and Windows—even if that's what customers are clamoring to do? Microsoft's real goal is to convince users that running an all-Windows environment is easier/better/cheaper. If it can't persuade users to follow the Windows-only path, the company needs, at the very least, to polish up its interoperability story. And if Microsoft can convince open-source-software vendors that they should port their wares to Windows (as Microsoft is having increasing success in doing), it's a double win for the Redmond software maker.

Some companies, who are cognizant of (and/or victims of) Microsoft's legendary strong-arm tactics, have been understandably gun-shy when it comes to signing alliances with the Soft. Has Redmond really conceded that if you can't beat 'em, you might as well partner with them? Or does Microsoft simply want more of a chance to study competing technologies up close so that it can better emulate and ultimately kill off non-Microsoft products?

Some companies do believe that there's been a genuine change of heart at Microsoft (or maybe they are convinced that they can beat Microsoft at its own game). They've seen Microsoft's willingness to hire individuals with real open-source chops to staff the Microsoft Linux Labs. They've witnessed the Internet Explorer team bring on as a consultant Molly Holzschlag, an internationally recognized standards expert. And they've accepted invitations from various Microsoft teams to come to the belly of the Borg and have lived to tell about it.[8]

Microsoft's aforementioned decision to trumpet its patent-infringement counts definitely resulted in the company losing some of the goodwill it had started to build up among its rivals. But as Microsoft employees love to say, they are among the most paranoid folks out there. They want to know where, why, and how "they suck." And they'll go so far as to bring some of their staunchest critics to the Redmond campus to hear the harsh truth directly.

All that said, I'd still say hardware makers, independent developers, services firms, and other potential Microsoft *coopitors* (competitors + cooperators) still are generally more distrustful of Microsoft than not—and often with good reason.

In spite of this perception, Microsoft has had decent success getting companies, including several of its competitors, to sign on as participants in the aforementioned Microsoft-backed Interoperability Vendor Alliance. BEA (now part of Oracle), Citrix Systems, SugarCRM, Software AG, and a handful

> *"Some companies do believe that there's been a genuine change of heart at Microsoft (or maybe they are convinced that they can beat Microsoft at its own game)."*

---

[8] "The non-fanboys descend on Redmond": On my ZDNet "All About Microsoft" blog, I covered the visit to Microsoft headquarters by a bunch of invited open-source experts in March 2007. The post is here: http://blogs.zdnet.com/microsoft/?p=358.

of others are part of the group. Other than lots of philosophical commitments and shared goodwill, however, it's not entirely clear what members of the alliance—or their customers—get by signing on the dotted line. Yet to Microsoft, growing the ranks of participants in this group has obvious marketing and public-relations value.

Open, as in "Source" and "Standards"

The way Microsoft uses—and doesn't—the "O" (*open*) word also is worth further exploration.

The most common use of the word *open* in the software world is "*open* as in *open source*." In spite of the latest interoperability rhetoric, Microsoft still views open source as a force to be combated. Sure, the company has dabbled with open sourcing a couple of smaller niche products, like its Windows Installer (WiX) and FlexWiki and the Active Template Library. And every now and again, certain teams make noise about emulating open-source development models to become more agile in product development, testing, and updating Microsoft code. But until quite recently, Microsoft insisted that the best way for it to license its technologies "openly" was by using the company's own Shared Source licenses, as opposed to bona fide Open-Source-Initiative (OSI)-approved ones.

> "In spite of the latest interoperability rhetoric, Microsoft still views open source as a force to be combated."

In July 2007, something suddenly changed. Microsoft announced that it planned to submit two of its Shared Source licenses—the Microsoft Permissive License and Microsoft Community License—to the OSI for approval as certified "open source" licenses. (The company submitted them to the OSI in early August.) Reaction to Microsoft's move was all over the map. Several company watchers noted that there was no reason Microsoft couldn't have submitted its licenses ages ago for OSI certification. Others warned the OSI to watch out for a wolf in sheep's clothing. Microsoft officials didn't help calm the skeptics by being vague in explaining why the Redmond software maker had a change of heart and now decided to go the OSI-certified route.

Microsoft Port 25 blogger Jon Rosenberg offered a partial explanation[9]:

> *IT professionals told us they wanted both platform choices and platform interoperability. Developers told us that they wanted more open collaboration and that the language of that collaboration is code. In response, Microsoft has reached interoperability agreements with several key vendors of open source software, CodePlex is now supporting 2,000 collaborative development projects, and the features of CodePlex itself are largely driven by the votes of the community.*

It sounds like there might have been one or more open-source vendors who dragged their feet at partnering with Microsoft until there was more of a semblance on Microsoft's part of making nicer with the open-source community. (Perhaps Microsoft interop partner SugarCRM, which recently got OSI certification itself, requested Microsoft to get the "official" open-source OK. ...)

What's less clear is whether Microsoft's behavior/tactics toward the open-sourcers will change commensurately. Allowing Microsoft lawyers to trumpet still-publicly unsupported claims, like the aforementioned "Open-source software violates 235 Microsoft patents," undid a lot of goodwill. And Microsoft's backtracking, regarding whether its patent-protection deals with Novell, Xandros, and others will extend to software covered by the GNU General Public License version 3, didn't improve the increasingly hostile interpretations of Microsoft's intentions vis-à-vis the open-source community.

> *"What's less clear is whether Microsoft's behavior/tactics toward the open-sourcers will change commensurately."*

While there's a chance that OSI certification of Microsoft's Shared Source licenses might go some way toward repairing the damage done, there's no

---

[9] Microsoft Port 25 blogger Jon Rosenberg explained Microsoft's philosophy behind seeking OSI approval for its Shared Source Licenses in his inaugural blog post, published in July 2007, here: http://port25.technet.com/archive/2007/07/26/intelligent-design-the-osi-and-microsoft.aspx.

question that distrust of Microsoft by open-source vendors and users remains and will remain for the foreseeable future.

One final point: *Open* doesn't refer solely to code released under an OSI-approved license. It also can be used in a broader sense, as in "open standards."

Open standards is another catch phrase that Microsoft has come to know all too well. As previously mentioned, Microsoft and its lobbyists have been fighting "open standard" tyranny in states and other countries around the globe. Fearful that its proprietary OOXML technology that's baked into Office 2007 wouldn't qualify for government requests for proposals that called for open-document-formatted products, Microsoft has spent countless hours to get its Office Open XML (OOXML) through the ECMA and ISO standards processes. To increase the perceived openness of OOXML, Microsoft also partnered with several vendors, including Novell, Sun, and Linspire, to develop converters that will allow OOXML users to read documents making use of the rival Open Document Format (ODF).

The ODF camp, led by IBM and Sun, has shown no signs of wanting a truce with Microsoft around file formats. They were counting on OOXML not qualifying as a real, open standard to give Open Office, StarOffice, and other Office rivals a boost in their battle against Microsoft Office.

S+S: Just a Lot of Sass?

Microsoft was admittedly late in coming to the software services party. Chief Software Architect Ray Ozzie made that abundantly clear in his infamous October 2005 "Internet Disruption" memo—the note credited as the official kickoff of Microsoft's current and future services push. (Excerpts from Ozzie's memo can be found in Appendix A.)

Ozzie painted an ambitious, company-wide services strategy for Microsoft. At the heart of his plan—designed to ensure that Microsoft would avoid being left behind as Google, Yahoo, Salesforce.com, and a variety of startups rocketed to the top of the tech food chain—was the concept of ad-supported services and software.

> *Most challenging and promising to our business, though, is that a new business model has emerged in the form of advertising-supported services and software. This model has the potential to fundamentally impact how we and other developers build, deliver, and monetize innovations.*

Ozzie didn't waste time ensuring that his vision statements moved past being nothing but ideals. Shortly after Ozzie's memo hit, Microsoft launched a raft of new properties under the Live banner. In addition to nearly two-dozen services branded as "Windows Live," there's also Office Live, CRM Live, a hosted version of Microsoft's CRM 4.0, Silverlight Streaming, a hosting service for video and other rich-media content, and more.

Starting in 2007, Microsoft officials began describing Microsoft's services strategy as "Software + a Service," rather than "Software as a Service" (SaaS). Rather than move to a completely cloud/service-centric set of offerings, Microsoft is advocating an approach via which fat-client software is "extended" with services. Microsoft isn't alone in this approach, as Ozzie told members of Microsoft's sales team last year. Skype, Pownce, and Joost are all examples of S+S offerings, not pure services-only plays, Ozzie claimed.[10]

In Microsoft's S+S taxonomy, there are three tiers of services:

- **Building Block**—The raw building block capabilities to enable developers to build interesting services (or composite apps)
- **Attached**—Services that feed into the premise software, for example, Exchange Hosted Services (security, anti-spam, archiving), Windows Live Update
- **Finished**—Services built for delivery over the Internet, such as Dynamics CRM Live

All of Microsoft's live and managed services will make use of a common back-end set of servers, programming interfaces, and software. In July 2007, Ozzie outlined the Live platform layers upon which Microsoft is building. Ozzie's layer cake looked like this (from the bottom up):

- **Global Foundation Services**—This is the physical infrastructure that powers the cloud, including data centers, racks of disks, networks, and the people building and monitoring this infrastructure.

---

[10] Ozzie on S+S: In a blog post entitled "Ray Ozzie Is a Big Stud Part 2," Jeremiah Jamison reports on Microsoft's Chief Software Architect's talk at the 2007 Microsoft Global Exchange Conference. See Jamison's full post here: http://jeremiahsjamison.wordpress.com/2007/07/23/ray-ozzie-is-a-big-stud-part-2/.

- **Cloud Infrastructure Services**—The computing, networking, and storage software layer. This is the "utility computing fabric on which all of our online services run," Ozzie said. It also includes application frameworks for "horizontal scaling" and the storage, file systems, databases, and searchable storage.
- **Live Platform Services**—These are identity and directory, device management and security, adCenter ad platform, communications, rendezvous, and presence.
- **Applications and Solutions**—These are the services that will run on top of the infrastructure—things like connected entertainment, document sharing and collaboration, hosted and Microsoft-managed services, and so forth.

> *"As many critics (including yours truly) have noted, there are still a lot of pieces missing from Microsoft's S+S puzzle."*

As many critics (including yours truly) have noted, there are still a lot of pieces missing from Microsoft's S+S puzzle. The next few years will be ones in which Microsoft attempts to categorize and prune its existing set of Live services, moves the many Live services currently in alpha or beta to final, and gets into a rhythm of regularly updating its Live stable. Microsoft will also launch a few brand-new live services—think "ERP Live" (which could take the form of a Microsoft-managed service), Office Live Enterprise (aka, Microsoft's growing collection of Microsoft-hosted "Online" services), and more Windows Live services designed to complement and update Windows Vista and Windows 7.

Are Your People Ready for "People-Ready"?

Microsoft, like most big companies, wants and needs a catchy marketing catch phrase. For a while, it was "A PC on Every Desk and in Every Home." Next up was "Information at Your Fingertips." There was the era of "Where Do You Want to Go Today?" And who can forget "Your Potential. Our Passion"? None of these campaigns has gone completely by the wayside. After all, old marketing slogans almost never die; they just keep going and going. ...

In March 2006, Microsoft ushered in a new slogan around which it has been building its most recent market campaigns: "People-Ready." Since that initial launch, Microsoft has issued People-Ready press releases, built a People-Ready web site, written People-Ready white papers, and attempted to

> *"Old marketing slogans almost never die; they just keep going and going. ..."*

"start a conversation" in exchange for ad dollars around what People-Ready means to A-list bloggers who advertise via Federated Media.

Does People-Ready have any real meaning? I say no. You decide. From Microsoft's People-Ready web site[11]:

> *In an era where some see technology as a force that promises to make people subservient to highly structured or automated processes, Microsoft sees a better way to unlock the potential of every person. Systems can only create efficiency: It is people who create value. And the more people can do in their roles, the more value they can create. When Microsoft looks ahead, we see a world where organizations succeed by empowering people to harness information, expertise and the possibilities of complex networks with tools that give them insight, reach and opportunities.*

Meaningless or not, Microsoft is pumping hundreds of millions of dollars into the "People-Ready" branding and concepts. In 2007, nearly every Microsoft executive speech that focused on Microsoft products aimed at enterprises in 2007 mentioned, at least in passing, Microsoft's goal of ensuring that its customers are "People-Ready," thanks to Microsoft's various technologies.

> *"Meaningless or not, Microsoft is pumping hundreds of millions of dollars into the 'People-Ready' branding and concepts."*

---

[11] Microsoft's People-Ready web site: Are you ready for Microsoft's People-Ready rhetoric? Here it is, in all its glory: www.microsoft.com/business/peopleready/default.mspx.

It looks like the People-Ready campaign isn't going away anytime soon. In fact, if 2007 was any indication, it's picking up steam as Microsoft rolls toward the end of this decade. By the start of the next, there will be yet another new Microsoft slogan in place, no doubt.

A Final Note: Microsoft Codenames Just Ain't What They Used to Be

Until late 2006/early 2007, I'd have suggested that Microsoft codenames would be the perfect antidote to the mindless marketing-speak represented by "People-Ready" and its ilk. But something happened on the way to Vienna, Blackcomb, and Fiji. (In case you aren't a student of Microsoft codenames, I am referring to "Windows 7," Windows 2010, and the next version of Windows Media Center, respectively.)

Microsoft codenames used to provide useful clues and information about what was in the Microsoft product and strategy pipelines. If you knew a Microsoft codename—for example, *Macallan*—you automatically knew you had some good info on something having to do with Windows CE, as the CE team favored naming its new releases after single-malt Scotches.

For a while, the Windows team was on a U.S. cities codename kick (*Memphis, Chicago, Cairo*). The SQL Server team was betting on national parks (*Yukon, Acadia, Jasper*).

But around the time that Microsoft decided to stop using *Longhorn* as Windows Vista's codename, the bottom fell out of Microsoft's codename universe. On the Windows and Office sides of the house, fun, descriptive codenames got the boot. The next version of Windows is Windows 7. Period. Ditto with Office. Office 14 is next. That's that.

There are still a few teams at Microsoft, especially those within the Developer Division, who love a good codename theme. But more often than not these days, Microsoft teams that decide to assign codenames to their forthcoming wares take the easy way out and just go with a place name. Among some of the recent Microsoft codenames that fall into that category: *Greenland* (WS-Management protocol version 1.1), *Monaco* (Microsoft's alleged competitor to Apple's GarageBand music-production software), and *Hawaii* (a set of future concepts pertaining to Visual Studio).

These caveats aside, there are still some worthy clues about Microsoft's future to be found in codenames. Codename themes make it easier to figure out how an evolving set of products and strategies is meant to fit together.

For example, the cloud-services team seemed (and still seems) to be on a "fathers of electricity" kick, with *Tesla* (a project involving compiling the Common Language Runtime intermediate language to JavaScript) and *Volta* (an incubation project exploring how to extend the .Net programming model to the cloud). Nikola Tesla and Alessandro Volta were both pioneers in the electricity field.[12]

> *"Microsoft codenames used to provide useful clues and information about what was in the Microsoft product and strategy pipelines."*

OK. Enough of the marketing promises. It's on to what Microsoft actually is likely to deliver on the near- and longer-term product fronts.

---

[12] The (Definitive) Microsoft Codename Collection (at least I like to think so). On my ZDNet "All About Microsoft" blog, I maintain a running list of interesting Microsoft codenames and their (possible) meanings. See the full list here: http://blogs.zdnet.com/topic/ Microsoft+Codenames.html.

Microsoft 2.0: The People

3

Of course I'm living within the shadow of my predecessor. Clearly, within Microsoft, there will never be another Bill Gates.

—Ray Ozzie, Microsoft's Chief Software Architect, quoted by the Seattle Post Intelligencer *in a May 1, 2007 story entitled "Software Architect Ozzie Has Blueprint for Microsoft"*

A company's products and strategies are obvious indicators of its future plans. But so are its people. Leadership—or lack thereof—is the single best measure of success. Indeed, a transition in leadership at Microsoft is what spurred me to write this book now and to assess who will be leading the company at this critical juncture in its history.

But with the constant reorgs, shufflings, hirings, and firings that have characterized Microsoft throughout its corporate history, it's challenging to try to create a "Microsoft 2.0: Who's Who" list that won't be obsolete before this book even gets out the door. However, that doesn't mean it's completely impossible to provide some guidance about where the real seats of power are inside the Redmond software company. But before digging into this chapter, here are a few points worth pondering.

The past few years have been among the most turbulent in Microsoft's personnel history, for many reasons, including:

1. **A Maturing Workforce**—Several of the most familiar faces in Redmond are now rich and/or old enough to move on or retire. Many are doing so.

2. **Hungry Rivals Poaching from Microsoft's Executive Ranks**—Google, Facebook, Amazon.com, and other vendors are picking off Softies (in some cases right in Microsoft's own backyard).

3. **A Stagnant Stock Price**—Despite a brief, buoyant period in which Microsoft's stock price finally moved beyond $30, it's nowhere near Apple's, Google's, and other tech vendor's levels. The days when Microsoft employees were almost guaranteed to leave the company as millionaires are over.

4. **Lots of Housecleaning as Microsoft Rethinks Its Core Missions**—Microsoft almost never says publicly that it has canned employees—especially its most visible faces. (There've been a few very public exceptions to that rule, including former Corporate Vice President Martin Taylor, former CIO Stuart Scott, and former HR manager Ken DiPietro, all of whom were rumored to have been let go for company policy violations.) Instead, Microsoft typically helps ease out those it doesn't want—as part of its "bottom five-percent" staff reduction or via other means. Microsoft's Live Search team did a lot of this kind of pruning in 2007. And Microsoft's purchase of aQuantive resulted in more than a few Softies getting squeezed, if not out of the company completely, at least into new roles.

5. **Lots of Acquisitions in the Pipeline**—CEO Steve Ballmer has said to expect Microsoft to make, on average, about 20 acquisitions of companies worth between $50 million and $1 billion each year over the next five years.[1] And then there's the matter of that little $40+ billion acquisition target, Yahoo ....

Going into the next decade, Microsoft will need people with some very different skill sets than those it has traditionally sought. Sure, the Redmondians will still need plenty of coders, testers, product marketing managers, and the like. But Microsoft is going to be seeking employees with more of a design sense, more social-networking savvy, more gaming-industry prowess—and more consumer electronics expertise, in general.

Another factor that will influence Microsoft's future hirings, firings, promotions, and demotions: With Chairman Bill Gates's retirement from day-to-day

---

[1] The prediction that Microsoft will buy about 20 companies a year for the next five years came from CEO Ballmer during the Web 2.0 Summit in October 2007. The citation can be found here: http://blog.seattlepi.nwsource.com/venture/archives/123983.asp.

involvement at the company in July, there will likely be more turmoil, as "Bill's guys" and "Steve's guys" (as mentioned in Chapter 1) wrestle for turf.

Microsoft has more than 80,000 employees worldwide. The market researchers at the Kirkland, Washington research firm, Directions on Microsoft, provide a poster-sized reference chart (which they update multiple times a year) that provides an organizational chart listing the top 700-plus executives at the company.[2] Obviously, I can't hope to begin to provide this level of completeness.

> *"Going into the next decade, Microsoft will need people with some very different skill sets than those it has traditionally sought."*

In addition, as noted in the Introduction of this book, Microsoft declined my request for interviews with the people profiled in this section. The company's public-relations team asked its executives not to talk with me about this book and the general topic of Microsoft's future. As a result, I was not able to get new or additional information about these people and their views on what's next for the company directly from them.

Fortunately, that doesn't mean others inside and close to the company declined to speak to me, however. Consequently, this chapter is an amalgamation of my own opinions with those of others I know and trust to be knowledgeable about Microsoft.

The Public Face of Microsoft 2.0: Sales Triumphs Over Tech

Up until July 2008, Microsoft was a company where science mattered more than sales. Specifically, Chairman Gates valued technology more than marketing and built Microsoft to reflect his priorities. Gates's tech vision was evident through the people Microsoft hired and promoted, the projects that got funding, and the amount of commitment the company put behind various initiatives.

---

[2]For a sample of the detailed (but intentionally outdated) Directions on the Microsoft org chart, go to their web site here: www.directionsonmicrosoft.com/sample/DOMIS/orgchart/sample/orgchart.html.

The balance of power is set to change. Microsoft CEO Steve Ballmer will be taking even more of a leadership role, with his pal Bill Gates out of the day-to-day picture. And while Ballmer is no technical slouch, he himself also acknowledges that "one of the biggest mistakes I've made over time is not wanting to nurture innovations where I either didn't get the business model or we didn't have it."[3]

America's Top Sales Guy: Steve Ballmer

Ballmer won't be new to the CEO role in the post-Gates era. He was named CEO way back in January 2000. But until now, Ballmer has ruled the Microsoft roost alongside Gates. The two have been perfect foils who've worked side by side almost since Day 1 of Microsoft's existence. (Gates hired Ballmer in 1980 to be the company's first manager.)

> *"Microsoft CEO Steve Ballmer will be taking even more of a leadership role, with his pal Bill Gates out of the day-to-day picture."*

I won't repeat much about Ballmer's background, as it has been documented numerous times in authorized and unauthorized forms. Ballmer was raised outside of Detroit, where his father worked for Ford Motor Co. He graduated from Harvard with a B.A. in mathematics and economics and attended the Stanford Graduate School of Business. Before joining Microsoft, he worked for two years at Procter & Gamble as an assistant product manager, repping products like Duncan Hines cake mixes.

Ballmer's always had a larger-than-life personality and is well-known for everything from his "monkey-boy dance" at a company sales event, where he chanted his famous "I love this company" rallying cry, to allegedly throwing a chair at a former company executive who defected to Google. (For the

---

[3] Ballmer's self-critique is part of a profile of Ballmer by Steve Lohr, entitled "Preaching from the Ballmer Pulpit," that ran in the January 28, 2007 *New York Times*. The full article is here: www.nytimes.com/2007/01/28/business/yourmoney/28ballmer.html?pagewanted=print.

[4] Former Microsoft exec turned Googler, Mark Lucovsky, relayed quite a vivid account of Ballmer's alleged reaction when he told him he was leaving Microsoft for its archrival. Ballmer has denied that he threw a chair, as well as other parts of Lucovsky's story. Ballmer

record, Ballmer has denied the chair toss.[4]) He's great with names, amazing with numbers,[5] and, from what I've heard from Microsoft employees and partners over the years, not one to suffer fools gladly.

With Gates out of the day-to-day picture, Ballmer's tendency to favor sales over tech will likely become even more pronounced—especially given that there is no one who can or will fill Gates's technology-champion shoes.

> "If neither Gates nor Ballmer was at the helm, Microsoft would carry over next-to-nothing of the old Microsoft culture."

There is a small but vocal contingent of Microsoft shareholders who have been advocating for Ballmer to step down—now, not in another ten years or so (the timeframe Ballmer has stated publicly as his retirement timeframe goal). The fact that Microsoft's stock price has barely moved for years (and there's still little hope for a spike in the picture) is the primary reason for their discontent. The fact that nearly every time Ballmer blurts something about open source or other pet peeves of his, he sets back any kind of progress that Microsoft has made in working with its partners doesn't help matters, either. And Microsoft's bid to buy Yahoo for $44 billion gave Ballmer's critics even more fodder. The anti-Ballmer camp's take: Microsoft's CEO is doing more harm than good as Microsoft's chief cook and bottle washer. It's time for new blood in the top spot, the Ballmer critics argue.

The anonymous blogger at MSFTextrememakeover encapsulated the wave of anti-Ballmer feelings quite succinctly in a late 2007 blog post:

> *Can Ballmer pull it (a revitalization of Microsoft) off? I'm doubtful—he's had eight years so far and we've seen the results. Who does that leave? Raikes? He'd seemingly get the nod if Ballmer and Gates have a say, and it's likely the main reason he's stuck around. Is he up to the task? Again, I doubt it. He's simply too*

told *BusinessWeek* that Lucovsky's account is "a gross exaggeration of what actually took place." The full back and forth on Lucovsky's exit is here: `www.businessweek.com/magazine/content/05_39/b3952001.htm`.

[5] More interesting tidbits from Steve Lohr's aforementioned profile of Ballmer, available at `www.nytimes.com/2007/01/28/business/yourmoney/28ballmer.html?pagewanted=print`. Ballmer got a perfect 800 in math on his SAT and allegedly has a near photographic memory, which he applies often to spreadsheets.

invested in what used to work but no longer does. Who does that leave? One of the hip earring-adorned geniuses from H&E that can't figure out basic ROI? Pass, thanks. One of the former CEO's from companies MSFT has acquired like AQNT (aQuantive)? That strikes me as the best choice—or of course an outsider. The problem? I don't seen any signs that Ballmer is planning on giving up his chair.[6]

I, too, haven't detected any rumblings about Ballmer actually leaving any time soon. And I believe that is a good thing. If neither Gates nor Ballmer was at the helm, Microsoft would carry over next-to-nothing of the old Microsoft culture. Yet that culture is something the company needs to perpetuate in order to carry it into its next chapter. To some, a Microsoft without Ballmer would be a positive. To me, it would leave Microsoft rudderless at a crucial juncture.

Ballmer's Inner Circle: The Three Tenors (Johnson, Raikes, and Bach)

Bar any unforeseen executive departures—the presidents at Microsoft today are likely to continue to comprise the seat of executive power at the company for at least the next few years. Even though some shareholders (including some of Microsoft's own employees) believe a change in leadership is what's needed to keep the company relevant in the next five-plus years, it doesn't seem as though the bulk of Ballmer's "inner circle"—aka the "Senior Leadership Team"—is going anywhere. The obvious exception to this is Microsoft Business Division chief Jeff Raikes, who is retiring in September, 2008. Raikes is passing the torch to Adobe/Macromedia and Juniper Networks veteran Stephen Elop. Elop will become the third Microsoft president as part of the transition. Meanwhile, there's some speculation that Microsoft could add a fourth president, who most likely would be Server & Tools Chief Bob Muglia,

---

[6] There are lots of "Ballmer should retire now" posts at the anonymously penned Microsoft Extreme Makeover blog. The author, who identifies himself as a Microsoft shareholder, has been tireless in his advocacy for replacing Ballmer in order to jump-start Microsoft's near-stagnant stock price. The passage I quote in this chapter is part of the "Will This Dog Ever Hunt Again?" msftextrememakover post from December 2007: http://msftextrememakeover. blogspot.com/2007/12/will-this-dog-ever-hunt- again.html.

to the corporate structure in the near term. So far, there's been no confirmation from Corporate on that, however.

Not surprisingly, given Ballmer's background and priorities, all three of Microsoft's presidents are strong sales guys. These are the execs who will shepherd Microsoft through the next few years, as the company repositions itself as a player in the brave, new software-as-a-service (SaaS) world.

Online Advertising Champion: Kevin Johnson

If you want evidence of the extent to which Microsoft 2.0 is going to value sales vis-à-vis tech, look no further than Kevin Johnson.

Johnson, the president of Microsoft's Platforms & Services Division, runs two of the most critical elements of Microsoft's business: The Windows team and the up-and-coming Live unit. The fact that Ballmer charged Johnson, a guy who—until a few years ago, was the Group Vice President in charge of Microsoft's Worldwide Sales and Marketing—with overseeing these two core components of the company's business says volumes about where Microsoft's priorities are in 2008 and beyond.

Johnson, to put it bluntly, is not a tech guy. Until last year, when Johnson shared the Platforms & Services leadership role with former Windows chief Jim Allchin, that fact didn't really seem to matter. Johnson could worry about sales strategies, and Allchin about product-specific details. And there was no doubt that Johnson was well-equipped to oversee the sales and marketing side of the house. As stated on his bio page on Microsoft's web site:

> In his tenure as head of sales, marketing and services, Johnson led a transformation in the field. He organized subsidiary leadership teams in more than 80 countries and regions and orchestrated their efforts to better align with product development and company priorities. His re-engineering of the field operating approach and the sales compensation system contributed to an $11 billion increase in sales from 2002–2005. Johnson also led a cross-company initiative focused on emerging markets, positioning the company as a trusted partner for future growth.[7]

---

[7] Microsoft provides bios for nearly all of its top execs on a centrally located site, which can be found here: www.microsoft.com/presspass/exec/default.mspx?group=A-D. President Kevin Johnson's page is here: www.microsoft.com/presspass/exec/kjohnson/default.mspx.

Johnson grew up in New Mexico and earned a B.A. in business adminis-tration from New Mexico State University. As of 2008, he has been with Microsoft for 16 years. Between 1986 and 1992, Johnson worked for IBM in its Systems Integration and Consulting Business unit.

> *"Johnson, to put it bluntly, is not a tech guy."*

In 2007, Microsoft's Platforms & Services unit encompassed more than 14,000 people worldwide who han-dled product development, marketing, and strategy. Yet in spite of Allchin's retirement, Johnson seemingly hasn't increased his focus on the platforms side of the house. In fact, during the few public speeches he gave in 2007, Johnson talked up Microsoft's online adver-tising plans to the exclusion of almost any other topic.

You could argue that Johnson's near-total attention to online advertising and services is necessary, as it's a business that is critical to the future success of Microsoft, and one that its partners, customers, and cadre of company watchers don't know as well as they do the traditional Microsoft strongholds. Or perhaps Johnson's one-pointed focus on the online advertising market can be attributed to the fact that a sales guy naturally feels more comfortable talk-ing about advertising than the Windows file system.

Regardless of the reasons, Johnson's services obsession makes it feel as though no one is really minding the Microsoft platform store. Yet Windows, .NET, and other "platforms" are Microsoft's bread and butter, and will be for the foreseeable future.

The Old Mr. Business: Jeff Raikes

Jeff Raikes has been a rare combination at Microsoft: He's a business guy who isn't intimidated by the prospect of doing his own tech demos.

Slowly but surely over the past couple of years, Raikes has amassed quite the collection of divisions under his Microsoft Business Division domain. He has been overseeing the Information Worker, Server and Tools, Unified Communications, and Business Solutions (CRM/ERP) units.

Raikes has continued to squeeze profits from all of his domains in a tough market. As of a few years ago, Microsoft had nearly saturated the market for desktop productivity suites. With more than 95 percent market share—and more and more customers who felt older versions of Office fulfilled their needs—Raikes needed to find a way to grow the information-worker business at the company. While pushing his team to continue to add more and more features to the already feature-crammed (or, as some prefer, "bloated") Microsoft Office product, Raikes also looked for ways to grow the definition of the "office"/productivity market in new ways. Under Raikes's watch, Microsoft started pushing into the PBX, services, document-management, and back-end server applications spaces in a major way.

While Raikes has had several senior execs reporting directly to him about all of the facets of the Business Division business, none of these individuals ever rose to much of a level of power and prominence. It's rare that Raikes's lieutenants, such as Kurt DelBene (Senior Vice President, Office Business Platform Group), Ted Kummert (Corporate Vice President, Data and Storage Platform Division), or Lewis Levin (Corporate Vice President of Office Business Applications Strategy), were empowered to speak about their various units or

> *"Raikes has made no bones about his interest in and the importance he has given to unified messaging, presence, audio/video/Web conferencing, and overall productivity futures."*

products. Instead, the Microsoft Business Division has been an "all Raikes, all the time" show. It's not surprising that many Microsoft watchers expected Raikes to end up as the next CEO of Microsoft, a role that Ballmer didn't seem ready to cede quickly enough for Raikes's liking, according to insider gossip.

Raikes, a former Apple software developer, has done a little bit of everything since joining Microsoft in 1981 as a product manager. He helped drive the company's applications-marketing strategy, its Apple business, and pen-computing forays. He has been very focused on the concept of measuring and improving information-worker productivity. Lately, he has spent a lot of cycles championing the unified communications concept at Microsoft and pushed the company into competing head-on with PBX, VOIP, and other telecommunications vendors.

Raikes has made no bones about his interest in and the importance he has given to unified messaging, presence, audio/video/Web conferencing, and overall productivity futures. "The amount of R&D investment that we're putting in with unified communications and voice over IP is the largest R&D investment beyond what we do in the core of Office," Raikes told News.com in an interview last year.[8]

Nebraska native Raikes got his bachelor's degree in engineering and economic systems from Stanford University. He also is part owner of the Seattle Mariners baseball team.

The New Mr. Business: Stephen Elop

Microsoft's announcement in January 2008 that Raikes would be retiring in September caught just about every Microsoft watcher by surprise. And the appointment of a relatively unknown exec from the outside to take Raikes's spot as the head of the division that is the biggest revenue-generator (the Microsoft Business Division) for the company really sent them reeling.

> *"Elop definitely fits the mold of one of 'Steve's guys.'"*

Elop has been the head of two of Microsoft's rivals: Macromedia (bought by Adobe in 2005) and Juniper Networks. Given that both Adobe and Juniper are in Microsoft Business Division's sights, the choice of Elop isn't as out-of-the-blue as it might first appear.

(And Ballmer & Co.'s decision to bring in an outsider, rather than promote one of Raikes's long-time Office lieutenants, to become one of the three Microsoft presidents also wasn't universally panned. Some see Elop as bringing new blood into a business unit that needs some new ideas.)

Elop definitely fits the mold of one of "Steve's guys." While he has a degree in computer engineering and management from McMaster University in Ontario, and in a previous life was a Chief Information Officer (for Boston Chicken Inc.), more recently, he's been honing his sales pedigree.[9] Elop was Macromedia's CEO in 2005 and Juniper's Chief Operating Officer in 2007. While some have questioned his lack of longevity in any one job, various

---

[8] News.com's profile of Jeff Raikes, which ran on March 6, 2007, and is entitled "Newsmaker: Microsoft Turns to Telephony," includes several quotes from the Microsoft Business Division chief on the importance to Microsoft of a unified inbox/VOIP and other "unified communications" technologies. The profile is here: http://earthlink.com.com/ Microsoft-turns-to-telephony/2008-1035_3-6164871.html?tag=st.nl.

reports have claimed that Elop's ambition is to ultimately become CEO of a major corporation. Make of that what you will, in Microsoft's case. ...

The Entertainer: Robbie Bach

Of the three presidents, Robbie Bach, head of Microsoft's Entertainment & Devices Division, is the one most squarely focused on the consumer marketplace, rather than the business one.

Bach has a wide charter, spearheading the divisions in charge of everything from Xboxes and games, to Zunes, to Windows Mobile smartphones. He also manages Microsoft's relationships with worldwide retailers and entertainment-focused media partners, as well as Microsoft's "specialized devices and applications"—which encompasses PC hardware, Microsoft's automotive business, Mac Office, and even Microsoft's Surface tabletop system.

> *"Bach's uber-mission is to create and deliver on the constantly morphing Microsoft vision for 'Connected Entertainment.'"*

Bach has a bachelor's degree in economics from the University of North Carolina at Chapel Hill and an MBA from Stanford University. He joined Microsoft straight out of Stanford in 1988—doing a stint as a financial analyst at Morgan Stanley & Co. in between undergrad and graduate schools.

Bach still looks and sounds like a stereotypical college guy—the sports-minded, video-game-playing type who made good. It's not hard to believe the Milwaukee-born, Winston-Salem, N.C.-bred Bach was a tennis champion as a kid, in spite of having to wear a full head/neck brace for five years to correct a curved spine.[10]

---

[9] *ComputerWorld* provided a good backgrounder on Elop following the Microsoft January 2008 announcement of his appointment, "Who Is Microsoft's New Business Division Leader, Stephen Elop?" in its January 11 issue here: www.computerworld.com/action/article.do?command=viewArticleBasic&articleId=9057001. *ComputerWorld* reporter Eric Lai noted that Elop's nickname at Macromedia was "The General" because of his buttoned-down, corporate ways.

[10] Everything you wanted to know about Robbie Bach but were afraid to ask can be found in this glowing profile that ran in *BusinessWeek* in November 2005: www.businessweek.com/magazine/content/05_48/b3961094.htm.

Bach's uber-mission is to create and deliver on the constantly morphing Microsoft vision for "Connected Entertainment." Bach explained his latest view of that concept at the Microsoft Mix '07 conference in the spring of 2007:

> Connected entertainment is a simple premise that people are going to want to be able to get their entertainment experiences whenever, and wherever they want, on whatever device. So, whether they're in the living room, the family room, the kids' bedroom, in a car, at work, they have a set of entertainment experiences they want, whether it's video, gaming, music, communications services, these are things that they want to tie together. And our job in building out our services and products in this area is to make sure we can deliver that connected entertainment experience.[11]

With the growing emphasis at Microsoft on the consumer market, Bach and his teams' products are likely to get a lot more visibility and marketing dollars in Microsoft 2.0 than they did in Microsoft 1.0. Bach's call for Microsoft to attract (via customization), engage (via interactivity), and excite (via social-networking) its consumer audiences already has begun to spill over into Microsoft's other business units. Bach's Entertainment and Devices unit has been at the forefront of the try-and-buy push for which Chief Software Architect Ray Ozzie has been agitating. Expect Microsoft's other divisions to take more and more pages out of Bach's playbook in the coming months and years.

The Private Face of Microsoft 2.0: Mystery Man Ray Ozzie

Gates has said in several interviews that he had been interested in hiring now-Chief Software Architect Ray Ozzie for years.[12] In 2005, Gates finally got him, as part of the agreement forged when Microsoft bought Groove Networks. I

---

[11] The full transcript of Bach's Mix '07 speech is available here: www.microsoft.com/presspass/exec/rbach/05-01-2007MIX07RobbieBach.mspx.

[12] From a March, 2006 *Boston Globe* story, entitled, "How Microsoft Got Its Groove": "I had said to Steve for a long time that Ray was the best guy in the industry who didn't work for us," Gates, the Microsoft cofounder, chairman, and chief software architect, said in an e-mail. "And Steve would always respond, 'Well, let's get him.'" The full story is here: www.boston.com/business/technology/articles/2006/03/13/how_office_got_its_groove/.

wonder if Gates and Ballmer have since thought about the old adage "Be careful what you wish for. ..."

I don't say this because Ozzie isn't up to the tasks with which he's been charged. Or because he isn't a gentleman and a scholar. Ozzie is seen inside and outside the company as a solid technical guy. There's no doubt about that. Some go so far as to consider the inventor of Lotus Notes a tech visionary.

But since joining Microsoft, Ozzie has been swallowed by the Borg. It's not clear whether it's Ozzie himself who wants out of the limelight or if it is Microsoft's public-relations squad encouraging Ozzie to make himself scarce in order to perpetuate a mystique around him. Perhaps it's a little of both. Regardless, Ozzie—a champion of all things Web 2.0/social networking/collaboration—has become a recluse. Even Softies with whom I've chatted have characterized Ozzie as someone who much prefers a quick, informal hall chat to a bona fide "meeting."

Ozzie started with Microsoft in April 2005, right after Microsoft bought Groove Networks, a collaboration software vendor Ozzie founded that was having some tough financial times. While Microsoft and Groove played up the synergies of their respective collaboration products, Groove seemed to have little appeal outside of the government sector. Some industry watchers believed Microsoft paid $120 million for Groove simply to bail out a flailing partner and—more importantly—to finally get Ozzie to become a Softie.

Ozzie started out as one of three Microsoft Chief Technology Officers, alongside David Vaskevitch and Craig Mundie. But in 2006, Gates and Ballmer elevated Ozzie to Gates's own "Chief Software Architect" level, setting him up to be Gates's successor in the role of chief technologist at the company.

Ozzie's charter is far-reaching, at least on (virtual) paper. According to his bio on Microsoft's web site, Ozzie is "responsible for oversight of the company's technical strategy and product architecture."[13] He also is directing development of Microsoft's various services platforms.

---

[13] Fittingly, there isn't a lot of biographical information about mystery man Ozzie that is publicly available. Microsoft's bio of Ozzie is available on the company's corporate web site: www.microsoft.com/presspass/exec/ozzie/default.mspx. A *Software Magazine* profile on Ozzie from his pre-Microsoft days (February 1996) contains some good tidbits: http://findarticles.com/p/articles/mi_m0SMG/is_n2_v16/ai_17856249/pg_1. Ozzie's own bio on his Live Spaces blog (to which he hasn't posted in a couple of years) is here: http://spaces.live.com/editorial/rayozzie/pub/pages/who.html.

Prior to Groove, Ozzie founded Iris Associates, where he led the development of Lotus Notes. Before Iris, he was part of the development teams for Lotus Symphony and Software Arts' TK!Solver and VisiCalc, and was involved in early distributed operating-systems development at Data General Corp. Ozzie, an Illinois native, got his bachelor's degree in computer science from the University of Illinois Urbana–Champaign.

> *"Since joining Microsoft, Ozzie has been swallowed by the Borg."*

With such a solid technical pedigree, how could Ozzie be anything but the ideal candidate to follow in Bill Gates's footsteps?

To date, Ozzie has been careful not to look as if he's trying to usurp Gates's power, even with Gates being a "lame duck" Chief Software Architect the past few years. But Ozzie's taking a back seat has backfired.

Unlike other tech leaders, Ozzie is not a regular speaker on the conference circuit. He has yet to step up and take charge. All this might change once Gates retires from day-to-day duties at the company in July 2008. But many folks I talk to inside and outside the company aren't optimistic about Ozzie's willingness or interest in moving into a more visible, strong leadership role. The general perception from Microsoft insiders is that Ozzie is guiding Microsoft in the right direction, but that he is not the right guy to be the public face of Microsoft.

> *"As Ozzie himself has said, he is no Gates."*

It's hard to know exactly how much of Microsoft's Software+Services direction Ozzie is creating or enforcing. Ozzie's Internet Services Disruption memo back in late October 2005 was the last major strategy pronouncement from Chief Software Architect Ozzie. There are lots of rumors about exactly what Ozzie is doing on a day-to-day basis.

Some close to the company claim it's Ozzie (and not Windows development chief Steven Sinofsky) who has been pushing Microsoft to be less transparent in its roadmap and goals than previous Softies were. Given how cryptic the bicoastal commuter Ozzie has been about his plans for Microsoft, it could be that Ozzie is one of the main forces behind Microsoft's newfound favoring of "translucency" over "transparency."

As Ozzie himself has said, he is no Gates. And Microsoft employees, partners, and customers used to a very public and surprisingly accessible Gates are having trouble adjusting to "OzzieSoft."[14]

My prediction, as I stated in the Introduction to this book, is: Ozzie is going to stick around for a while. Microsoft would lose way too much face if Ozzie were to bail after the company made so much of hiring him. But don't be surprised to see Ozzie become

> *"If Ozzie isn't going to rise to the occasion and lead Microsoft, who is?"*

even more of a behind-the-scenes manager than a public figurehead. Ozzie is not going to be the one to lead Microsoft into the next decade; instead, he'll back the play of Ballmer and others who will set Microsoft's course in the coming years.

The Baby Bills: Where Are They Now?

If Ozzie isn't going to rise to the occasion and lead Microsoft, who is? Who else is on the fast track at Microsoft these days? Who are the up-and-coming superstars who will likely lead the company during its next 10-plus years? I've asked various Microsoft watchers, partners, customers, and employees these questions, and the fact that few could come up with immediate suggestions says volumes.

Just because a Microsoft exec has a big title or a prominent spot on the organizational chart doesn't mean that s/he is likely to emerge as one of Microsoft's big guns in its next decade. The clip at which Microsoft managers fall in and out of favor makes predicting the future slate of top Softies even trickier.

Five years ago, back in 2003, *Business 2.0* magazine compiled a list of the 10 most promising rising stars at Microsoft, a group the publication dubbed

---

[14] A couple of Softies—Steve Clayton and James Senior—dropped the term *OzzieSoft* into blog posts in 2007, as I noted here: http://blogs.zdnet.com/microsoft/?p=475. To date, the term has gained little traction—but perhaps that's because Ozzie has (yet) to do much to put his personal stamp on Microsoft.

"The Baby Bills."[15] Indicative of how quickly things change, that list looks obsolete today. Some of the Gates potential heirs-apparent have left (or been forced out of) the company; several others have been pushed into less visible jobs at Microsoft. The Softie who many thought would be a shoe-in successor to Gates—Eric Rudder—has retreated from a visible position running Microsoft's Server and Tools business, to working in a research incubator while plotting his next move.

A couple of the 2003 Baby Bills are on my list of up-and-comers. Before I get to that roster, here's a snapshot of the *Business 2.0* Baby Bill Class of 2003 and what each of these execs is doing today:

- **Eric Rudder**—*Then:* Senior Vice President, Servers and Tools. *Now:* Allegedly working on a secret distributed operating-system project under Chief Research Officer Craig Mundie.
- **Chris Jones**—*Then:* Corporate Vice President, Windows Client Group. *Now:* Corporate Vice President of Windows Live Experience Program Management.
- **J Allard**—*Then:* Corporate Vice President, Xbox Platform. *Now:* Corporate Vice President, Design and Development, Entertainment and Devices Division.
- **Yusuf Mehdi**—*Then:* Corporate Vice President, MSN Personal Services and Business Division; and later, Chief Advertising Strategist. Edged out of advertising management as a result of the aQuantive purchase and subsequent Microsoft realignment. *Now:* Senior Vice President of Strategic Partnerships.
- **Steven Sinofsky**—*Then:* Senior Vice President, Office. *Now:* Senior Vice President of Windows and Windows Live Engineering.
- **Martin Taylor**—*Then:* Platform Strategist (and Ballmer Chief of Staff). Fired by Microsoft allegedly for a company policy violation. *Now:* Operating Principal, Vista Equity Partners.
- **Tami Reller**—*Then:* Corporate Vice President, marketing and strategy, Business Solutions. Passed over for job running Microsoft Business Solutions unit. *Now:* Chief Financial Officer, Platforms & Services Division.

---

[15] The original "Baby Bills" list that appeared in the now-defunct *Business 2.0* magazine still can be found here: http://money.cnn.com/magazines/business2/business2_archive/2003/10/01/349469/index.htm.

The Baby Ballmers: Who Will Matter at Microsoft in the Near Term?

From the original Baby Bills short list, Allard, Jones, and Sinofsky remain among the core group to whom Ballmer is looking for ideas for Microsoft 2.0. I'd add a few new names to a 2008 version of the "Baby Ballmers," too.

Along with the three presidents and Ozzie, there are a handful of Microsoft managers whose strategies and thinking will help Microsoft make—or miss—a transition into its next phase as more of a software *and* service provider.

> *"Are any of these individuals the heir apparent to Ballmer?"*

Are any of these individuals *the* heir apparent to Ballmer? Many Microsoft watchers are doubtful that Ballmer and the board will go inside to find the next Microsoft leader. I tend to agree. Next time Microsoft needs a CEO—which could be at any time the 52-year-old Ballmer decides he's finally had enough— the company might look outside, rather than inside, for fresh top-management blood. (For the record, Ballmer has said he plans to stick around at Microsoft for close to a decade or longer—at least until his youngest son is in college.)

That said, here are some of the young (and not so young) Turks likely to influence Microsoft's near-term, post-Gates directions, in alphabetical order.

J Allard: The Next Best Thing to a Black-Turtlenecked Steve Jobs

J Allard is the corporate vice president of Design and Development for the Microsoft Entertainment and Devices Division. In that role, Allard oversees the Xbox gaming console business, the Zune digital-music player, and other as-yet-unannounced consumer offerings.

> *"Before becoming Microsoft's public face for the hipster generation, Allard contributed to Microsoft's Internet strategy. ..."*

Before becoming Microsoft's public face for the hipster generation, Allard contributed to Microsoft's Internet strategy, Windows NT, and TCP/IP products. He has a bachelor's degree in computer science from Boston University.

Allard—the closest thing that Microsoft has at the executive level to a hip exec able to appeal to the all-important 16-to-34-year-old mountain-bike-riding, gaming-savvy geek demographic—is a 15-year Microsoft veteran. A profile from *BusinessWeek* captured the Allard image:

> *Never afraid to speak his mind, Allard started pushing buttons way back in 1994, when, as an eager 25-year-old programmer only three years on Microsoft's payroll, he penned a sea-changing memo titled "Windows: The Next Killer Application on the Internet," which found its way to Gates. The note, now part of Microsoft lore, helped awaken Gates to the potential and threat of the Web. "I'm a pain-in-the-ass change agent," Allard says.*[16]

Craig Mundie and the Multicore Madness

Although Microsoft image makers have attempted to position Chief Software Architect Ray Ozzie and Chief Research and Strategy Officer (CRSO) Craig Mundie as co-leaders of technological-direction setting for the company, neither Microsoft insiders nor outsiders perceive the Ozzie–Mundie relationship as a sharing by equals.

Mundie definitely is seen as the No. 2 technology guy at Microsoft. (According to some recent rumors, Mundie is none too happy about this and is looking for a way to climb his way up the corporate ladder.)

Whether Mundie manages to get ahead, he currently is charged with overseeing the company's research and technology incubation efforts. Mundie also works hand-in-hand with Senior Vice President and General Counsel Brad Smith to help guide Microsoft's intellectual-property and technology-policy initiatives, including security, technology policy, privacy, telecommunications regulation, intellectual property protection, and software-procurement standards.

Before taking on the CRSO role, Mundie was Microsoft's Chief Technology Officer for advanced strategies and policy, and worked closely with Gates to help carve out Microsoft's positions on key technical, business, and policy issues.

At the start of his Microsoft career, Mundie helped build and run the Consumer Platforms Divisions at Microsoft since the time he joined the company in 1992. That unit developed Windows CE, software for the Pocket PC, and

---

[16] *BusinessWeek*'s December 4, 2006 cover story, "The Soul of a New Microsoft," focused on Allard as the epitome of the Web 2.0-savvy Microsoft. The full story is here: www.businessweek.com/magazine/content/06_49/b4012001.htm.

Auto PC and "early console-gaming products," according to Mundie's bio on the Microsoft.com site. Mundie also is behind Microsoft's continued push into digital TV, having helped acquire and manage WebTV Networks.

Mundie has a bachelor's degree in electrical engineering and a master's in information theory and computer science from Georgia Tech. He's been part of the tech world since 1970, when he was working on operating-system development for Data General minicomputer systems.

In the past year, Mundie seemed to have two favorite topics. At the low end, he was heavily focused on championing technologies aimed at improving the lives of those in developing nations (not WindowsXP Starter Edition—more like Fone+, the cell-phone-hooked-up-to-TV combo that Mundie has demonstrated a few times in recent years). At the high end of the market, Mundie has been talking up the need for Microsoft and other companies to invest in tools, operating systems, and other software that will take advantage of the 8-, 16-, and 64-core client machines that are on their way to becoming commonplace.

> *"Mundie definitely is seen as the No. 2 technology guy at Microsoft."*

Satya Nadella: Around the Empire in 16 Years

Sixteen-year Microsoft veteran Satya Nadella has trod a long and winding road inside Microsoft.

Nadella currently is Senior Vice President, Search, Portals and Advertising Platform Group—aka, the Windows Live Search, Microsoft adCenter, and subscriptions/points/billing platforms.

Nadella was appointed to his latest role in the spring of 2007, after leading, starting in 2006, the Microsoft Business Solutions ERP, CRM, and Office small-business products teams. Before that, Nadella is credited as having founded and led the Microsoft bCentral small-business services team and was a general manager for commerce platforms, where he helped run the Microsoft Commerce Server and BizTalk units. And before that, Nadella

> *"In his current role, Nadella faces more than a few challenges, starting with growing Microsoft's Web-search share."*

worked on Microsoft's interactive TV, digital rights management, and Windows Developer Relations.

To some, Nadella's wide breadth of experience inside the company is a positive; to others, his meandering career path is a sign that Nadella has yet to find his niche.

Nadella got his start in the business with a master's degree in computer science from the University of Wisconsin, a master's degree in business administration from the University of Chicago, and a stint at Sun Microsystems, where he was a member of the technology staff.

In his current role, Nadella faces more than a few challenges, starting with growing Microsoft's Web-search share. Throughout most of 2007, Microsoft's Web-query share was stuck at around 11 to 12 percent of the total worldwide market. Microsoft officials have been quoted saying they believe Microsoft can grow its search share to 30 percent in the next three-to-five years.[17]

Nadella also will need to find a way to hang on to his adCenter responsibilities given the infusion of advertising specialists Microsoft received in 2007 when it bought aQuantive. Microsoft is in the midst of incorporating aQuantive's people and products—like its Atlas ad platform and DRIVEpm services—into its own advertising repertoire.

Steven "Clockwork" Sinofsky: Making the Trains Run on Time

Steven Sinofsky runs engineering for two key teams at Microsoft: Windows client and Windows Live. He was moved into this role in 2006 for a reason—Microsoft's top brass were tired of being hurt and embarrassed by Microsoft's ongoing failure to release products on a timelier basis. And ways to keep the trains running on time—or, at the least, of maintaining a public perception that the trains were punctual—was something Sinofsky knew how to do quite well, as he had proven in Microsoft's Office organization.

Sinofsky has held several positions on Microsoft product teams, and also was Gates's technology assistant (TA). Before taking on his current position, Sinofsky oversaw the development of the Microsoft Office system of programs, servers, and services, responsible for the product development of the 2007 Microsoft Office system, Microsoft Office 2003, Microsoft Office XP, and

---

[17] Microsoft's 30 percent share goal is part of Platform and Services Chief Kevin Johnson's stated 10-20-30-40 plan, which is explained in full here: www.reuters.com/article/ousiv/idUSN1534354920071116?pageNumber=1.

Microsoft Office 2000. Before that, he was part of the Development Tools Group.

Sinofsky has been with Microsoft since 1989. He has an undergraduate degree from Cornell University and a master's in computer science from the University of Massachusetts Amherst.

Sinofsky isn't in charge of everything to do with Windows and Windows Live. He does not oversee Microsoft's Core Operating Systems Division (COSD), the group established by former Windows chief Jim Allchin to improve the processes via which Microsoft's thousands of Windows programmers build the subsystems that are part of Windows. Sinofsky also is not in charge of Live Search; he was stripped of that role in the spring of 2007, when Microsoft created a unified Search and Advertising Platform Group and appointed Satya Nadella to head it.

Nonetheless, Sinofsky is charged with nothing short of remaking the very image of Windows. That is why he is overseeing both the Windows client and Windows Live teams. Sinofsky's so-called Windows Experience fiefdom is "an integrated system of programs, services and solutions that largely make up the Windows Client Experience,"[18] according to a description on the Microsoft web site. And it's these different components that are being "designed to work together to address a broad array of customer problems and needs."

To deliver on this more integrated goal, Sinofsky has been cleaning and reorganizing the Windows Client unit for the past couple of years. As one anonymous poster on the Mini-Microsoft site described these changes as early as 2006:

> I'm in the Windows Client org, and I can attest to the changes that are going on with Steve Sinofsky in charge. He is completely restructuring and redesigning the way Windows works. While time will tell how successful he is, I can honestly say in the decade I've been at Microsoft I've never seen more radical changes take root.[19]

[18] Microsoft's definition of the "Windows Experience" is here: www.microsoft.com/presspass/exec/george/default.mspx.

[19] The post from an anonymous commentor about the changes Sinofsky began instigating a couple of years ago can be found on the Mini-Microsoft blog here: http://minimsft.blogspot.com/2006/09/rebuilding-microsoft-in-wired-magazine.html#c115951827172172388.

Sinofsky has made a key component of his Windows campaign the idea of *translucency* versus *transparency*. His reasoning: Customers and partners only need to know product and roadmap details once they are nearly set in stone. Keeping them abreast of information that might change leads to dissatisfaction when ship dates slip, features are cut, and so on. While former Windows chief Jim Allchin was a big believer in transparency, Sinofsky is not. (For more, see excerpts from Sinofsky's internal blog post on his views on translucency vs. transparency in Appendix A.)

> *"Sinofsky is charged with nothing short of remaking the very image of Windows."*

Since taking on the role of head Windows engineer, Sinofsky has surrounded himself with several of his former Office colleagues. Sinofsky made Grant George the Corporate Vice President of Testing and Operations. George used to be test manager for Office, starting back when he joined the company in 1994. Julie Larson-Green, the Vice President of Program Management who is overseeing the design of Windows, is another of Sinofsky's Office chums. Starting in 1997, Larson-Green was instrumental on the Office team. She is credited as one of the main forces behind the user-interface design teams for Office XP, Office 2003, and Office 2007.

The Evangelist: Kevin Turner

If you've ever heard Microsoft Chief Operating Officer Kevin Turner give a speech, you'll immediately understand the "evangelist" reference. When he speaks publicly on behalf of Microsoft—which he is doing increasingly at a variety of internal and public events—Turner is big on charismatic one-liners, complete with the perfectly orchestrated pauses for effect.

> *"Before joining Microsoft in 2005, Turner worked for Wal-Mart for almost 20 years."*

Turner's style seems to have won some converts. He currently runs field sales and marketing, product support, customer support, branding, advertising, public relations, marketing research, corporate operations, and internal IT at Microsoft. In short, he's one of Microsoft's chief ambassadors to the outside customer world, as well as the uber-boss of nearly 40,000 of Microsoft's 80,000 or so employees.

Before joining Microsoft in 2005, Turner worked for Wal-Mart for almost 20 years. He filled a variety of roles there, with the most recent being president and CEO of Sam's Club. He also worked in Wal-Mart's IT department and served as the company's CIO.

Turner obtained his bachelor of science in management from East Central University in Ada, Oklahoma. He started his Microsoft tenure by creating "a common definition of success through our subsidiaries." As he explained to News.com in 2007:

> *I feel really good about the fact that we have a common scorecard,*
> *a common goal sheet, that people are on the same page as it*
> *relates to both how they're compensated as well as how their per-*
> *formance review is [done]. That sounds like a trivial thing, but*
> *with 80,000 people scattered around the world, if you don't have*
> *that common framework that people are working under, then they*
> *see things through a different lens.*[20]

Not everyone is fond of Turner's rah-rah style, however. More than a few have interpreted his zealotry as insincerity and said so on Mini-Microsoft and other blogs. Turner's Wal-Mart background hasn't endeared him to some of the rank and file, either, given Wal-Mart's reputation in some circles for its alleged union-busting, low-paying, labor-standards-defying practices.

Ten More Softies You May Never Have Heard of (But Will Soon)

Looking out beyond the next three-to-five years, the list of whose star is rising at Microsoft gets a bit tougher to anticipate. It's safe to wager that execs leading the services charge at Microsoft are likely to become more visible in the future—ditto with those leading Microsoft's continuing war on open-source and IP protection programs and its online advertising push.

---

[20] The Q&A with Turner from which this quote comes ran in July 2007 on News.com. The full Newsmaker profile, "Kevin Turner: No Longer the New Guy," is here:
www.news.com/kevin-turner-no-longer/2008-1012_3-6196637.html.

If I were to choose the 10 Softies whose names currently aren't household ones but who are likely to become increasingly prominent and powerful, this would be my list (in alphabetical order):

Jon DeVaan, Senior Vice President, Windows Core Operating System Division

Another of Windows Chief Steven Sinofsky's protégés, Jon DeVaan is in charge of the engineering team that develops the core components and architecture of Windows. DeVaan doesn't report to Sinofsky these days, but he works hand-in-hand with him to ensure consistency in standards and directions for software engineering.

Microsoft's web site credits 23-year veteran DeVaan with having managed the TV division at Microsoft, co-managed Microsoft's Consumer and Commerce Group ("where he helped design and initiate the turnaround strategy for MSN"), and having led Microsoft's Desktop Applications Division.

Alexander Gounares, Corporate Vice President, adCenter and Commerce Platforms

> *"Like many Microsoft execs before him, Alex Gounares served as Microsoft Chairman Bill Gates's technology assistant during his stint at the Redmond software giant."*

Like many Microsoft execs before him, Alex Gounares served as Microsoft Chairman Bill Gates's technology assistant during his stint at the Redmond software giant. Most recently, Gounares has been leading the engineering efforts for Microsoft's core advertising and commerce platforms, helping to oversee payments, points, subscriptions, and more. Given the increasing importance that adCenter and online advertising in general have to Microsoft's future corporate strategy, Gounares is likely to be even more of a central fixture in Microsoft's management hierarchy.

Before that, Gounares worked as a development manager on one of Gates's pet projects, the Tablet PC, as well as on the Microsoft Office team.

According to his Microsoft bio, "Gounares has been involved with many initiatives across the company, covering everything from search to workflow technologies to new Internet services such as Microsoft Virtual Earth and a number of yet-to-be announced products."[21]

Scott Guthrie: Corporate Vice President, .NET Developer Division

Scott Guthrie is a newly-minted Corporate Vice President in Microsoft's Developer Division. But don't let Guthrie's modest public demeanor fool you. The guy runs a lot of teams that are going to become increasingly important to Microsoft and its developer constituency.

Guthrie runs the development teams that build Silverlight, Windows Presentation Foundation, Windows Forms, the Common Language Runtime (CLR), ASP.Net, IIS 7.0, Commerce Server, the .Net Compact Framework, and Visual Studio Web

> *"Don't let Guthrie's modest public demeanor fool you."*

and Visual Studio Client development tools. As I'll explain more in the conclusion of this book, Silverlight, in particular, seems to be one of the keys to the future Microsoft kingdom. Guthrie will likely become even more of a crowned prince as the importance of Microsoft's Flash-competitor evolves and emerges.

Bill Hilf: Corporate Vice President, .NET Developer Division

Corporate Vice President Bill Hilf has had a tremendous amount of influence inside and outside Microsoft on how the Redmondians relate to open-source vendors and customers.

Hilf joined Microsoft around 2004 from IBM, where he helped drive Big Blue's Linux technical strategy for its emerging and competitive markets organization. Before that, he was the senior director of engineering at eToys, where he helped build the company's Linux-based eCommerce business infrastructure.

In his early years at the Empire, Hilf said he was spending a lot of time making Linux more transparent to Microsoft managers, doing a lot of educating around the open-source development, testing, deployment, and licensing models.

---

[21] Alex Gounares's bio on the Microsoft web site is here: www.microsoft.com/presspass/exec/gounares/default.mspx.

> *"Hilf will no doubt be the eye of the Microsoft hurricane."*

After running Microsoft's Linux Lab for a few years, Hilf was promoted in 2007 to General Manager of Platform Strategy. In that capacity, he worked on Windows Server and Tools long-term planning, as well as interacting directly with field sales and customers to get their feedback, especially in the arena of Microsoft's strategy vis-à-vis open-source software.

As Microsoft continues to swing between the two poles of cooperating with and beating the pants off Linux and other open source, Hilf will no doubt be the eye of the Microsoft hurricane.

Chris Jones: Corporate Vice President, Windows Live Experience Program Management

One of the original "Baby Bills," Corporate Vice President Chris Jones is still seen as a golden boy at Microsoft.

Currently, Jones is Corporate Vice President of Windows Live Experience Program Management. In that role, he does planning, design, usability research, and more for the amorphous entity known as the *Windows Live Experience*.

> *"Chris Jones is still seen as a golden boy at Microsoft."*

Jones used to be, until a couple years ago, Corporate Vice President of Windows Client Core Development. There, he was charged with "driving for excellence" in user interface, Internet Explorer, graphics, digital media, and presentation. In short, Jones was the go-between liaison between Windows Client and the Windows Core Operating System Division (COSD). And before that, he was a key exec on the Internet Explorer program management team.

Given his experience on both the Windows Client and Windows Live sides of the house, 17-year Microsoft veteran Jones is the perfect candidate to help Microsoft increasingly tie its Live services to the Windows platforms. The Microsoft brass are counting on Jones's Windows-client experience to help rein in the free-for-all Windows Live development/deployment strategy that dominated in 2006 and early 2007. Jones already is putting a lot of Windows-like policies and procedures in place. But if Jones ends up over-regimenting a group that needs to be agile to succeed, he might end up hurting the Windows Live effort more than helping it.

Don Mattrick: Senior Vice President of Interactive Entertainment Business

Don Mattrick, Senior Vice President of Microsoft's Interactive Entertainment Business, joined Microsoft at a key juncture for its gaming unit. Days before Mattrick joined Microsoft, long-time Microsoft Xbox veteran Peter Moore announced he was leaving the company to join Mattrick's alma mater, Electronic Arts. At EA, Mattrick was most recently president of EA's worldwide studios.

Microsoft had a mixed year on the gaming front in 2007. While Halo3 broke all kinds of sales records, Microsoft's $1 billion charge it took for fixing faulty Xboxes undid much of the revenues from the fast-selling Halo. And right after Mattrick stepped into his new role, Microsoft's Halo3 subsidiary, Bungie, announced that it would be seceding from the Microsoft mothership and going out on its own.

> *"Like Chief Software Architect Ozzie, Mattrick has kept a very low profile since joining Microsoft."*

Mattrick is in charge of the Xbox and Games for Windows businesses. His team also is in charge of games development at Microsoft Games Studios. Word is that Mattrick's on a massive house-cleaning campaign inside his various Windows gaming units and that more veteran Softies are likely to be forced (or encouraged) to move on from Microsoft's various entertainment properties in the 2008+ timeframe. Like Chief Software Architect Ozzie, Mattrick has kept a very low profile since joining Microsoft. It will be interesting to see if that changes anytime soon.

Brian McAndrews: Senior Vice President, Advertiser and Publisher Solutions Group

Brian McAndrews came to Microsoft as part of the 2007 aQuantive acquisition. He is in charge of Microsoft's newly minted Advertiser and Publisher

Solutions Group, which is charged with building and marketing all of Microsoft's myriad ad platforms, including Atlas, DRIVEpm, MSNDR, Microsoft AdCenter, and PubCenter, plus "emerging media," like the Atlas On Demand, Massive, and ScreenTonic businesses.

> *"There is going to be a lot of pressure on McAndrews to maintain and grow the customer relationships."*

McAndrews, former CEO of aQuantive, is definitely Microsoft's most experienced online advertising staffer. He headed aQuantive since January 2000. Before that, McAndrews worked for close to a decade for ABC and held executive positions at ABC Sports, ABC Entertainment, and ABC Television Network.

Given that Microsoft officials have said they consider online-advertising marketshare as more important to Microsoft than even search share, there is going to be a lot of pressure on McAndrews to maintain and grow the customer relationships Microsoft needs to fulfill its goal of being No. 2 in the online ad business in the next few years. If Microsoft ends up taking over Yahoo, McAndrews should have a starring role in leading MicroHoo.

Marshall Phelps: Corporate Vice President and Deputy General Counsel for Intellectual Property

Marshall Phelps joined Microsoft in 2003. His importance has been on the upswing ever since.

Phelps is the Corporate Vice president and Deputy General Counsel for Intellectual Property (IP). As such, he oversees all of Microsoft's IP groups—trademarks, trade secrets, patents, licensing, standards, and copyrights. He has been building for Microsoft an IP portfolio for licensing, as he did for IBM during his 28 years there.

Under Phelps, Microsoft has amassed more than 3,000 U.S.-issued patents, their "foreign counterparts," and more than 11,000 trademark registrations. Before Phelps joined the company, there was no concerted effort at the company to build up its patent and trademark arsenal into a revenue-contributing bulwark.

Phelps is considerably older than the up-and-comers on this list. It's not clear how much longer he'll stay at Microsoft before he retires. But for as long as he's there, he'll be helping Microsoft build a patent arsenal to rival those amassed by any of the corporate tech giants—including even his former employer IBM.

> *"He has been building for Microsoft an IP portfolio for licensing, as he did for IBM during his 28 years there."*

Eric Rudder: Senior Vice President of Technical Strategy

Just a few years ago, Eric Rudder seemed destined to become the new Bill Gates. As Senior Vice President of Microsoft's lucrative Server and Tools unit, Rudder was in the catbird seat. Before leading that division, Rudder worked directly with Gates as one of Gates's famed technology assistants.

Around 2006, when Microsoft elevated outsider Ray Ozzie to the Chief Software Architect slot, something happened. Rudder suddenly disappeared. There were rumors that he was poised to leave the company, as more and more of Steve B's guys (of which

> *"Just a few years ago, Eric Rudder seemed destined to become the new Bill Gates."*

Rudder was not one) were gaining in power. Rudder continued to report directly to Gates, but few seemed to know exactly what he was doing, other than biding his time to see if he'd be able to climb the corporate ladder again.

Last I heard, Rudder was working on a project under Craig Mundie to design and develop a distributed operating system that might or might not be built on the Windows core. The new Rudder project sounds a lot like the BigTop/BigWin distributed operating-system project[22] Microsoft attempted to get off the ground earlier this decade (but supposedly killed). I've included

---

[22] Microsoft never publicly discussed its BigTop/BigWin project. Luckily, some anonymous person knowledgeable about the project tipped me to it. BigTop was designed to allow developers to create a set of loosely coupled, distributed operating-systems components in a relatively rapid way. Lots more BigTop/BigWin details can be found in my 2004 post about the project here: www.microsoft-watch.com/content/operating_systems/a_peek_under_microsofts_secret_bigtop.html.

more about Rudder's new project, which is codenamed *Midori*, in the Conclusion.

David Treadwell: Corporate Vice President, Live Platform Services

Nineteen-year Microsoft veteran David Treadwell has been focused on honing Microsoft's various "platforms" throughout his career.

> *"Treadwell also helped start the 'Windows Live Core' incubation project."*

Treadwell used to run the .NET Developer Platform team. These days, he is Corporate Vice President of Live Platform Services, the group at Microsoft charged with building the common back-end platform upon which all of Microsoft's future "Live" and other Web services will be built. Live Platform Services include unified identity and directory, data synchronization, transport, and presence.

Treadwell also helped start the "Windows Live Core" incubation project, which Microsoft describes as a "key component of the company's services platform that will allow the creation of compelling applications by making deep use of network-based information."[23] A more layperson-like explanation of Windows Live Core is that it is the back-end fabric, plus front-end set of core cloud services that will allow users to access their data any time, any place, and from any device.

Treadwell is one of the leaders of an all-star team that Microsoft has built to create the Windows Live Core.[24] Other members include:

- **Dave Cutler**—Yes, that Dave Cutler—the guy who is credited as the father of the VMS and Windows NT operating systems. He's currently a "senior technical fellow" at Microsoft.
- **Amitabh Srivastava**—A Microsoft technical fellow, formerly with the Core Operating System Division (COSD), who, according to one of

---

[23] This description of Windows Live Core—an initiative that Microsoft still is not discussing publicly—comes from Microsoft's web site (Treadwell's bio page, in particular): www.microsoft.com/presspass/exec/treadwell/default.mspx.

[24] The roster of the Windows Live Core team was first unearthed by the independent LiveSide.Net blogging team. I annotated LiveSide's post on my "All About Microsoft" ZDNet blog here: http://blogs.zdnet.com/microsoft/?p=349.

his bio pages on the Microsoft web site, "was responsible for the development of core operating system components such as the kernel, operating system architecture, definition of development processes, and development of advanced tools to automate the development processes."

- **James Hamilton**—An architect on the Windows Live Core team "interested in multi-tenant hosted systems, the management of very large scale systems, massively parallel data management systems, database security, and unstructured data management."

- **Abolade Gbadegesin**—An architect for both the Windows Networking Division and the Windows Live Core Datacenter Services team. Gbadegesin "was responsible for leading the redesign and implementation of the networking stack for Windows Vista."

The Unwashed Masses (80,000 and Counting)

Of course, the execs I've profiled in this chapter are just the tip of the Microsoft iceberg. With 80,000-plus employees, there's no way to characterize the "typical" or "average" Microsoft employee. And until fairly recently, very few past, current, or future Softies had ways to make their voices heard by more than just their colleagues.

Then came blogs. Individual Microsoft employees started blogging en masse in the mid-part of this decade. There are thousands of Microsoft employee blogs hosted on the company's Microsoft Developer Network, TechNet, and Live Spaces forums, as well as on a variety of third-party platforms. A handful of anonymous Microsoft-employee-run blogs—Mini-Microsoft, MicroStiff, and Microsoft eXtreme Makeover, to name a few—began offering Microsoft employees (and trolls posing as Softies) a place to air their questions, grievances, and more. Almost overnight, it seemed, everything from Microsoft's hated stack-ranking employee-evaluation system, to its pay scale, was under debate on various blogs for anyone to see.

These gripes became characterized, rightly or wrongly, as Microsoft's "morale problem." Couple blogs with the near-instantaneous communication technologies like e-mail, blogs, instant-messaging, Twitter, and so on, and every time a Softie quit or defected to a competitor, word traveled fast, contributing further to the public perception that the once peaceable kingdom of Microsoft was falling apart.

"With 80,000-plus employees, there's no way to characterize the 'typical' or 'average' Microsoft employee."

It's hard to prove which came first: Microsoft-perceived morale problems or increased transparency, which exposed employee dissatisfaction. Would Microsoft's decision earlier this decade to revoke the free towels it provided for those who wanted to use the corporate showers have gotten the same kind of publicity—and fairly rapid resolution (in favor of the towel-loving employees)—if bloggers and commenters didn't expose those issues? If bloggers didn't have public forums where they could advocate for more Google-like employee benefits, would Microsoft be moving employees into more modern office spaces with new fast-food and other retail outlets on campus?

Who (Still) Wants to Work for Microsoft?

Where does the truth lie? Is Microsoft, as so many research/brand surveys claim, still one of the best U.S.-based companies for which anyone could hope to work? Or is Microsoft's heyday as a tough but rewarding work environment a thing of the past? Are all the smart Softies gone—as I've had more than one long-time Microsoft customer/partner tell me in recent years—never to be replaced?

"It's hard to prove which came first: Microsoft-perceived morale problems or increased transparency, which exposed employee dissatisfaction."

While the ABM (Anything But Microsoft) camp of Microsoft competitors and their customers would like to paint Microsoft as a has-been that is having no luck keeping and hiring new talent, Microsoft's track record here tells a different picture. During fiscal 2007, Microsoft hired thousands of new employees in Redmond and abroad. And it attracted some big name hires, like the gaming group's Don Mattrick (from Electronic Arts) and Technical Fellow Don Ferguson (from IBM). That said, as mentioned at the start of this chapter, Microsoft has lost some veterans, too, especially to Google, Facebook, and other hotter, newer upstarts.

> *"Are all the smart Softies gone—as I've had more than one long-time Microsoft customer/partner tell me in recent years?"*

Especially in the past year-plus, Microsoft has been putting extra muscle into recruiting younger employees, especially for the growing raft of consumer jobs opening up at the company. Although Microsoft is no longer the coolest kid on the block, it still carries clout. As one 20-year-old tester told me this year, his goal is still to work for Microsoft someday—something he's wanted to do since he was three.

Bottom line: Microsoft's future leadership story is rather murky right now. But, at least for now, there's still a future Softie born every minute. ...

Microsoft 2.0: Products on the Near-Term Radar Screen

4

> *"When everyone says that something is true, be very skeptical," (Intel's) Mr. Grove advised. Question the obvious.*
>
> *THAT is easier said than done, especially when corporations become so invested in their own "paradigm" that they grow blind to signs that "the times they are a-changin'." How else to explain that Mr. Gates, writing in the first edition of his 1995 treatise on the future of computing, made no mention of the Internet, the very force that began to disrupt (and is still disrupting) his company's core business from virtually the day the book appeared?"*
>
> —G. Pascal Zachary, *"Genius and Misfit Aren't Synonyms, or Are They?"*
> June 3, 2007, New York Times

Since Microsoft time began, Chairman Bill Gates has been the guy at Microsoft charged with providing a high-level roadmap—the one who was authorized to make sweeping generalities about what was next for Microsoft and the computing industry as a whole. Gates didn't hesitate to push products and technologies in which he was a big believer: Tablet PCs, IPTV, speech/natural language input, multi-touch interfaces (like what's built into Microsoft's Surface "PlayTable" computer). Several of Gates's pet projects have met with a less-than-enthusiastic reception by the computing public—in spite of the benediction of Microsoft's founder.

Now that Gates won't be around to determine and articulate what's next for the Redmondians (and his Chief Software Architect replacement Ray Ozzie seems none too interested in fulfilling a similar function), there isn't really any technologist at the top of Microsoft's org chart publicly outlining what's next for the company.

That doesn't mean that it is impossible to predict what's coming, however. And that's what I'll try to do in these next two chapters.

> *"Windows still had 92 percent of the client operating-system market share worldwide."*

Microsoft has five main food groups—Windows client, servers and tools, business systems, online services, and entertainment and devices. I'm not attempting to catalog Microsoft's thousands of products and product SKUs here. Instead, I'll highlight products and technologies that are going to have a serious impact on Microsoft's revenue stream in the coming few years. This chapter covers near-term products that will matter to Microsoft, its customers, partners, and competitors; Chapter 5 focuses on the longer-term product bets the company is making.

Before leaping into the great unknown, however, here's a quick reality check:

- Windows still had 92 percent of the client operating-system market share worldwide, according to 2007 estimates from International Data Corp. Apple's Mac OS X has 4.1 percent, and Linux has a mere 3.8 percent, according to the IDC market researchers. (Next time you hear the very vocal Mac and Linux backers talking about how they're going to be eating Windows' lunch any day now, remember these numbers.)
- Microsoft Office still has 90+ percent of the desktop productivity suite market, according to various analyst calculations I've seen. Yes, there are rivals to Office, including OpenOffice.org, Corel, StarOffice, ThinkFree, and Google. And there are a lot of vocal backers of these products' file formats, online capabilities, and so forth. But these products have barely dented Microsoft's Office, in terms of user acceptance and overall share of the business.

So while Microsoft is out there dabbling in all kinds of new revenue streams—from ERP and CRM software, to Xbox gaming consoles and Zune portable music players—sales of Windows and Office are what makes Redmond run, and will likely keep it running for the next several years.

I'm restating what many may consider obvious because many of Microsoft's most vocal critics seem to have forgotten just how key Windows and Office are to Microsoft's past, present, and future. They want to believe that Microsoft is ready to turn on a dime just because Apple is doing X or Google is doing Y. While that kind of excitement sells virtual (and print) newspapers, it doesn't reflect reality.

Consider this true story: When discussing Windows Vista with a representative of a major U.S. TV news program last year, I had a heck of a time convincing her that the Apple and Linux desktop operating-system share combined was, at the time, less than 5 percent of the worldwide total. She was incredulous, noting that if it were true, they were surely a vociferous 5 percent. That's an understatement.

All this isn't to say that Microsoft's client operating-system and office-suite competition should be dismissed out of hand. Apple has shown a considerable amount of momentum in the past year, with several technology influencers in the press and the development communities becoming some of Apple's biggest fanboys and girls.

In May 2007, market researchers with NPD released new data that found that Apple had become the fifth largest notebook-PC retailer (although the study omitted Dell Computer, which sold through direct channels only). NPD also claimed that Apple's desktops have crossed the 10 percent market share mark and MacBooks are now closing in on 15 percent of the laptop market.[1]

The existence of Apple's BootCamp and Parallels virtualization software, allowing Mac users to run Windows applications on their Apple hardware, has eliminated a major stumbling block for users interested in standardizing on Apple systems in a Windows world. But at the end of the day, it is still a

---

[1] New NPD numbers on Apple PC market share: Market watchers at NPD have been tracking Apple's desktop and laptop market share on a monthly basis. Their June 2007 numbers can be found here: www.computerworld.com/action/ article.do?command=viewArticleBasic&articleId=9025540. More recent consumer market share numbers I have seen are estimating Apple to now own somewhere between 5 and 7 percent of the consumer PC market.

Windows world, and Apple doesn't seem interested in going after Enterprise customers, or mainstream, non-hipster consumers, other than students, from what I've seen.

Is Microsoft finally considering Apple more of a viable threat to Windows than it used to? Definitely — and primarily because of the "halo effect" created by iPod and iPhone users who subsequently gravitate toward other Apple products, specifically Macs. But is Microsoft quaking in its boots because of Apple's market growth, which has occurred almost entirely in the consumer space? I'd still say no. There is no question that Microsoft is looking to Apple for cues about how to do user interface/experience for Windows. But Apple is also watching Microsoft, too, and is keeping tabs on how the Redmondians are tweaking Windows' more visual aspects with each and every release.

> "Is Microsoft finally considering Apple more of a viable threat to Windows than it used to? Definitely."

The same reasoning applies to the Microsoft–Google contest. Every time Google announces that it is launching another Web version of a productivity application to its stable of apps, the doomsdayers proclaim the end of Microsoft Office is nigh. (To me, a more credible challenge to Office than Google Docs & Spreadsheets is StarOffice—distributed by Google as part of the Google Pack. But StarOffice still has a minuscule share of the overall office-suite market, even outside the United States, which is its stronghold.) Microsoft must field a Web-ified version of Office (or at least one that includes Open Document Format file-format support), or be done for, the critics say.

Call me a skeptic. Or a Microsoft shill. Or both. But here's what I think is more likely to happen. ...

Ballmer's List

There's one group that hasn't lost sight of where Microsoft's bread is buttered, and that's Microsoft's management. The Redmond brass is hyperaware that

Windows and Office are Microsoft's core businesses—and are likely to stay the core moneymakers for at least the next three years and possibly longer.

In February, 2007, during a financial-analyst briefing in New York, Ballmer shared with the audience his short list of opportunities, predicting that Microsoft will be able to sustain a half billion dollars or more in new margin growth over the next three years.[2] The speech got next-to-no press coverage. As jaded Microsoft watchers are likely to interject, maybe Ballmer intended to lead Microsoft's competitors astray by providing an overly conservative, less-than-forthcoming list. But given that Ballmer was addressing Wall Street, I'm more inclined to believe his speech spelled out what—at that in 2007—Ballmer believed to be Microsoft's plan of attack through the end of the decade.

(Ballmer gave an update to his Wall Street speech in February 2008, with a slightly shorter and less detailed priority list. Given that the content of the most recent Strategic Update speech was almost identical to the more-detailed one from 2007, I'll use the 2007 one as a guide.)

> *"The Redmond brass is hyperaware that Windows and Office are Microsoft's core businesses."*

Here's how Ballmer set the stage for introducing his priority list:

> *This is a list of nine opportunities that I track, that I think of, that I kind of watch and try to interject myself with from time to time. No one of these is less than a half a billion dollars of new gross margin growth over the course of the next three years, fiscal years '08, '09, '10. That doesn't mean we're going to get at least half a billion per, but each one of them we have clear line of sight to at least half a billion, and in some cases to much, much bigger numbers than that. I have them sort of rank ordered frankly from largest to smallest on this list.*

---

[2] Highlights regarding Microsoft CEO Steve Ballmer's top investment picks for Microsoft for the next three years can be found in Appendix A.

His list of nine:

1. **Windows Client Revenues**—From OEMs (PC makers and system builders). Ballmer put this in perspective:

   [OEM revenue] remains from a revenue perspective ... not a percentage basis ... the largest growth driver for Microsoft revenue, gross margin over the next three years. This doesn't require us having massive invention in emerging markets. This is just PC growth that we have line of sight to with our largest customers where piracy is relatively low in the developed countries.

2. **"Desktop Value" Revenues**—Derived from corporations big enough to have an IT department. This is Office and other desktop-productivity-focused revenues.

3. **Server Revenues**—Windows Server, database, security products. Ballmer said he sees this as an arena where Microsoft has a good opportunity to grow its business vis-à-vis Linux.

4. **"Mature Desktops"**—That is, add-on revenues in corporations where there's already some penetration of Windows and Office. Client-access licenses are a key growth driver here. Ballmer's exact words:

   We actually have an opportunity in the corporate world to go get more people signed up for our desktop software. And when I say desktops, I mean Windows, I mean Office, I mean the Client Access Licenses that support the desktops.

5. **Emerging Market Savings**—Especially due to Genuine Advantage Initiative anti-piracy crackdown campaigns/mechanisms.

6. **Advertising**—Especially via adCenter, Microsoft's online ad system—and the properties fueled by it.

7. **Xbox**—Particularly in dollars derived from Xbox Live, attached hardware, and attached software.

8. **Sales of Office**—To small businesses and consumers.

9. **Windows Mobile**—Operating-system sales to cell-phone and PDA makers.

At the same time, Ballmer also shared with Wall Street analysts another list. This was of six additional opportunities where Microsoft may derive longer-term growth, but where he admittedly had "less visibility."

Ballmer's next six high-growth picks:

1. **Piracy**—From cutting piracy outside major corporations, that is, Genuine Advantage anti-piracy crackdowns among small-business and consumers.
2. **Office Live**—Microsoft's growing stable of small-business service add-ons to Office and SharePoint Server.
3. **Business Services**— Particularly the Microsoft-managed and -hosted versions of Exchange Server and Office Communications Server that Microsoft has sold to a handful of large customers. (Some know this set of services as the "Energizer" pilot, since Energizer Holdings was the original guinea pig for Microsoft's hosted-services trial.)

> *"OEM revenue 'remains from a revenue perspective … not a percentage basis … the largest growth driver for Microsoft revenue, gross margin over the next three years."'*

4. **Zune MP3 Player**—And all the attached hardware, software, and services that will accompany it.
5. **TV**—Particularly IPTV. Microsoft has been sinking money, time, and energy into IPTV since it fielded its original "Tiger" video-on-demand service back in 1994. During the past decade, Microsoft has participated in several less-than-successful IPTV trials all over the world. CEO Ballmer has been quoted as saying he believes IPTV could be what kick-starts Microsoft's stock price—if and when the company ever gets IPTV right.[3]

---

[3] Ballmer on IPTV as a key to Microsoft's future success. In a March 2006 interview with *Fortune* magazine, Microsoft's CEO has some rosy predictions (yet again) for IPTV. When asked what might get Microsoft's stock moving, Ballmer replied: "We've got companies like AT&T and Verizon driving this Internet television stuff very aggressively. If you can get a few bucks a month on a lot of televisions around the world, that's a pretty darn big opportunity."

6. **Healthcare**—Ballmer hinted that Microsoft was planning to go public soon with an offering on the consumer side of healthcare. In October 2007, Microsoft launched HealthVault, a client application plus a Live service that will allow consumers to build and maintain a personal health record. One of the inputs into this health record will be results from Microsoft's health search-engine, also known as HealthVault, which is based on the MedStory search technology Microsoft bought in 2006.

What should a Microsoft customer, partner, or competitor make of Ballmer's list? Read on.

Windows Remains Job No. 1

If you take away nothing else from this chapter, understand this: Windows is going to continue to be Microsoft's top priority for the next few years.

> *"If you take away nothing else from this chapter, understand this: Windows is going to continue to be Microsoft's top priority for the next few years."*

Microsoft historians will recall that the infamous showdown back in the mid-1990s between former Windows chief Jim Allchin and former Internet Explorer (IE) honcho Brad Silverberg was all about whether Windows or the Web should be Microsoft's leading franchise. Allchin won that battle, IE became an integrated Windows feature, and Microsoft spent the next decade jealously guarding its Windows franchise, in the face of various governmental/legal challenges to it.

In spite of the current services emphasis across all Microsoft divisions, including the Windows client one, Windows software isn't going away. For the next few years—maybe longer—Microsoft will continue to make client-based Windows software the centerpiece of its product family. Even if Microsoft ends up fielding a hosted, ad-funded version of Windows, as some insiders say is the current plan of record, Microsoft isn't going to abandon Windows on the desktop/notebook anytime soon.

At the same time, Microsoft is intensifying its campaign to curb software piracy, especially outside the United States. And the primary focus of this campaign is Windows.

"This (anti-piracy campaign) is one of the places I'm most excited about the technology and the opportunity we have," former Director of Windows Client Marketing Mike Sievert told Wall Street analysts in early 2007. "Vista makes piracy harder" and the differences between pirated and "genuine" software more obvious, he said. "With WindowsXP, the pirated version of XP was the exact same as the genuine," he said. But with Vista and its Genuine Advantage lockdowns, the difference is striking, he said.[4]

In early 2007, Microsoft officials stated publicly that they expected Chinese sales of Microsoft products to be up 20 percent in the coming year, owing to a combination of new products plus a crackdown on software piracy. Anti-piracy measures sound like they'll contribute the bulk of the expected revenue increase (although Microsoft's decision to halve the price it's charging in China for Windows Vista hasn't hurt sales any).

> *"Ballmer has been quoted as saying he believes IPTV could be what kick-starts Microsoft's stock price—if and when the company ever gets IPTV right."*

"Only about 30 percent of Lenovo PCs now being sold will ultimately contain pirated Windows systems, down sharply from 90 percent last year," said Timothy Chen, chief executive of Microsoft's Greater China region.[5]

Momentum around the most recently released version of Windows also shows just how key Windows Client will continue to be to Microsoft's future.

In spite of several lukewarm reviews and mixed perceptions in the market, Microsoft maintains that Vista, launched on January 30, 2007, has been selling. By the start of January 2008, Microsoft claimed to have sold more than

---

[4] Sievert on the promise of WGA: The head of Windows Client marketing, Mike Sievert, told Wall Street analysts in March 2007 that cracking down on pirates could yield substantial revenue and market share returns for Microsoft. See more on Sievert's remarks here: http://blogs.zdnet.com/microsoft/?p=351.

[5] Microsoft sees piracy crackdown yielding a 20 percent increase in sales in China: The Reuters story that is the source of this statistic, from April 10, 2007, is here: www.reuters.com/article/ousiv/idUSTP28617820070410?pageNumber=1.

100 million copies of Vista. Millions of devices (everything from peripherals to PCs) were Vista-compatible. Even though the 100 million figure represented the number of copies sold to channel partners, not to end-user customers, it was still impressive.

Microsoft officials were crowing about their success in upselling customers to more expensive premium versions of Vista, on both the business and consumer sides of the equation. Microsoft has been counting on the premium upsell to help buoy Windows revenues for the past few years, but with Vista, the strategy became even more obvious—and seemingly, obviously successful. The Vista Business SKU, for example, has five times the (revenue) "uplift" of Windows Home Server Premium, Microsoft executives told Wall Street last year.

The Near-Term Windows "Next" Wave: Fiji and Service Pack 1

While Vista will be what fuels Microsoft's Windows Client growth through at least 2009 or 2010, the Windows Client team is readying several "next" releases that also will help drive momentum.

> *"Microsoft officials stated publicly that they expected Chinese sales of Microsoft products to be up 20 percent in the coming year, owing to a combination of new products plus a crackdown on software piracy."*

Getting real information on any of these has been a struggle. With Windows Vista, Microsoft's Client team, now under Director of Windows Engineering, Steven Sinofsky, adopted a much more restrictive information-flow policy. Instead of overpromising and underdelivering, Sinofsky wants the Client team to do the opposite. Sinofsky seems to believe that achieving this goal requires Apple-like secrecy.

Starting in late 2006, Microsoft's Windows Client team was under strict orders not to discuss any Windows futures. When asked about Microsoft's plans for Windows Vista Service Pack 1 (SP1), the first expected collection of bug fixes plus a couple of new features, company brass offered evasive answers, with CEO Ballmer himself even claiming that Microsoft had no definitive timetable or plans for such an update. The company line: Vista was so solid that users didn't really need to wait for SP1 to roll it out.

These explanations for SP1's whereabouts were not well-received by a number of Microsoft's corporate customers, who typically wait to deploy a new operating-system release until at least the SP1 version has shipped. Luckily for these customers, one of Microsoft's own executives "slipped up" and noted that SP1 was in the works and likely to ship around the same time as Windows Server 2008.[6]

Around mid-2007, a surprising middleman forced Microsoft's SP1 hand: The U.S. Department of Justice. The DOJ antitrust division received a complaint from Google in late 2006 that claimed that Vista violated the terms of Microsoft's antitrust-compliance agreement. Rather than face more costly and time-consuming litigation—which still might happen, given the fact that the European Commission is continuing to look into antitrust complaints levied by Google and other Microsoft competitors—Microsoft acted proactively and said that it would alter the Instant Search desktop-search functionality in Vista to make it work better with third-party desktop-search products. Microsoft was required to provide details as to how it would roll this functionality out to customers who already purchased Vista. SP1—a first beta of which Microsoft conceded it planned to deliver before year-end 2007—would be the vehicle, company officials acknowledged.

> *"Instead of overpromising and underdelivering, Sinofsky wants the Client team to do the opposite."*

Microsoft didn't end up making users wait until year-end for the first public beta of SP1, after all. Instead, the company delivered it in the early fall. Microsoft released the final version of SP1 in February 2008, and began rolling it out to users in the March/April timeframe.

---

[6] Out of the mouth of babes: In November 2006, Server and Tools Chief Bob Muglia went on the record saying that Microsoft's goal was to ship Windows Server 2008 (Longhorn Server) and Windows Vista Service Pack 1 together. The full story is here: www.eweek.com/article2/ 0,1895,2060137,00.asp.

In addition to desktop-search modifications, here's what else made it in:

- **Performance Tweaks**—Lessening the amount of time it takes to copy files and shut down Vista machines.
- **Improved Transfer Performance**—And decreased CPU utilization via support for SD Advanced DMA.
- **Support for ExFAT**—The new file format for flash memory storage and other consumer devices.
- **Improvements to BitLocker Drive Encryption**—To allow not just encryption of the whole Vista volume, but also locally created data volumes.
- **The Ability to Boot**—Extensible Firmware Interface (EFI) on an x64 machine.
- **Improved Success Rate**—For firewalled MeetingSpace and Remote Assistance connections.

> *"Another near-term deliverable that Microsoft's Client team has tried to cover up is 'Fiji.'"*

Another near-term deliverable that Microsoft's Client team has tried to cover up is "Fiji," an update to the Media Center components that Microsoft built into Windows Vista Ultimate. Several Vista users have been up front that the Media Center components of the Ultimate release weren't all they were cracked up to be. Supposedly, Fiji—plus Windows Vista SP1—will add the missing fit and finish to the Media Center components in Vista.

There's also talk that *Fiji*, known these days by the far-less-sexy *Media Center + 1* moniker, could be the vehicle via which Microsoft delivers some new consumer functionality akin to Apple's iLife add-ons for Mac OS X. Again, Microsoft officials repeatedly have declined to talk about Fiji. But I've heard from various industry sources that Microsoft's been working on technology code-named *Monaco* that could take the form of a music-making program

---

[7] Microsoft's *Monaco*: Monaco is one of those codenames I heard quite a bit about in 2006 and next-to-nothing about ever since. When I first heard talk of the product, it was described to me as an Apple GarageBand competitor. More details on Monaco are here: http://blogs .zdnet.com/microsoft/?p=150.

similar to Apple's GarageBand.[7] (Last I heard, Fiji was looking like a second-half-of-2008 deliverable, at best.[8])

Dates and codenames aside, what will be included in these near-term Windows releases? In spite of the Sinofsky-imposed cone of silence, there've been a few hints, several of which have come from Microsoft Chairman Gates himself.

Windows at the Turn of the Decade: Everything Including the Kitchen Sink

In early January 2007, Gates told a group of bloggers with whom he held a private audience at the Consumer Electronics Show to expect the next version of Windows to feature more speech and digital-ink functionality and to take better advantage of 64-bit processing power.

At the Vista launch in New York in late January of that year, Gates went further in an interview with *Newsweek's* Chief Technology Correspondent Steven Levy. The relevant part of their exchange:

> *Levy: So can you give us an indication of what the next Windows will be like?*
>
> *Gates: Well, it will be more user-centric.*
>
> *Levy: What does that mean?*
>
> *Gates: That means that right now when you move from one PC to another, you've got to install apps on each one, do upgrades on each one. Moving information between them is very painful. We can use Live Services [a way to connect to Microsoft via the Internet] to know what you're interested in. So even if you drop by a [public] kiosk or somebody else's PC, we can bring down your home page, your files, your fonts, your favorites and those things. So that's kind of the user-centric thing that Live Services can enable. ...[9]*

---

[8] Microsoft's *Fiji*: Another Microsoft codename that's seemingly fallen out of favor in recent months is *Fiji*. But Microsoft Most Valuable Professional, Chris Lanier, (who specializes in all things Media-Center-related) blogged in June 2007 that the "Vacation to Fiji" would be held up until the latter half of 2008. See his post here: http://msmvps.com/blogs/chrisl/archive/2007/06/12/959530.aspx.

[9] Steven Levy vs. Bill Gates: Here's the full February 2007 Q&A between Microsoft's Chairman and *Newsweek's* Chief Technical correspondent, in which Gates offered some broad hints about Windows 7: www.msnbc.msn.com/id/16934083/site/newsweek/.

I would have asked one more follow-up: Was Gates hinting that Microsoft will more tightly integrate its currently stand-alone Windows Live services right into the operating system? Was he simply talking about a shared address book or contacts list that users could access from the cloud? Or was he talking more about the possibility of storing user data on a USB flash drive—a project codenamed "StartKey"—which has its roots in the Microsoft–SanDisk announcement in mid-May 2007, via which the pair committed to developing smart USB devices allowing users to carry their complete personal computing environment on thumb drives?

Given that brand-new Windows features often take years from the time when Microsoft brass first describe them to when they actually debut in a new Windows release, I'm wagering it could be a while until we see any of these next-gen Windows features at which Gates hinted. In the post-Gates era, there will likely be fewer feature previews from the Windows Client team. In the new Microsoft world order, features are not to be discussed (even privately) until they are locked and loaded.

> "Was Gates hinting that Microsoft will more tightly integrate its currently stand-alone Windows Live services right into the operating system?"

Regardless of the internally insisted-upon ban on talk about Windows futures, there've been enough slipups and leaked beta invites to provide guidance on other Windows-related products coming in the next decade.

In spite of predictions by some company watchers, Windows Vista is not the last big-bang release of Windows Client that Microsoft is planning. While the company is looking for ways to release more Windows service packs and updates more frequently, that doesn't mean it's doing away with the familiar, fat Windows Client.

In fact, the next full-fledged version, known internally at Microsoft as *Windows 7* (building on Vista's Windows 6.X build-number naming convention), is currently expected to hit in late 2009 or 2010. That timing isn't all that surprising, given that the Client team is attempting to get on the "every-two-year" release cycle to which the Windows Server team already has transitioned.[10]

---

[10] A Microsoft executive with the company's Core Operating System Division (COSD) floated the 2009 date at the beginning of 2007, only to have the marketing team issue a public statement days later in response to "speculation on the next version of Windows." But in mid-2007, Microsoft told its own sales force that Windows 7 would more likely be a 2010 product.

Microsoft officials refused to divulge any details about Windows 7, other than to acknowledge that the release will come in both 32-bit and 64-bit flavors. Microsoft also is expected to deliver more and more Windows components as services, as of Windows 7, with several of those services available to Software Assurance volume-license subscribers only.[11] Windows 7 is expected to be based on a slimmer "MinWin" kernel, likely to incorporate a hypervisor virtualization platform, and expected to include a new "StrongBox" facility that will help isolate drivers and applications from the core operating system. From early reports, it sounds like Windows 7 will be more like Windows Server 2008, in terms of the ways it will allow users to choose which components to install, based on "roles."

There's also a Windows 8 on the Microsoft timeline, as well. When that will hit, how it will be delivered, and what kinds of features it will include are definitely not anywhere near final, at this point.

> *"In spite of predictions by some company watchers, Windows Vista is not the last big-bang release of Windows Client."*

Creating more horizontally and/or vertically tailored versions of Windows, going forward, is another way Microsoft is expected to continue to grow its client operating-system coffers.

Microsoft is working on a product tentatively known as the *Kitchen Client*, which is expected to be the first of what it plans to make a family of customized Windows platforms designed for specific rooms around the home. The Kitchen Client isn't meant to be a whole new Windows SKU; instead, it's likely to debut as an add-on layer for Windows, similar to the way the Microsoft Origami Experience Pack is an add-on "experience" for ultramobile PCs (UMPCs).

Among the features Microsoft is planning to make part of its forthcoming kitchen computing environment are a family calendar, recipe center, entertainment features, and a shared bulletin board, according to those claiming to

---

[11] Windows 7: All we know so far. One of the only substantial pieces of information to leak about Windows 7 (so far) has been its tentative ship date. I tried to put the Windows 7 information gleaned from Microsoft's big sales conference in context here: http://blogs.zdnet.com/microsoft/?p=592.

be in the know. The Kitchen Client will integrate with various Windows Live services.

In fact, at least according to one version of the story I've heard, the Kitchen Client originally was expected to debut in the form of one or more Windows Live services. A team of about 50 Softies was working on a "Family Center Live" project code-named *Ohana*. One former team member described Ohana to me this way:

> It was supposed to be a product that was an integrated experience to connect the family and provide vendors (think Home Depot) ways to communicate with the customer [via Ads]. It would have a calendar (think more like iCal), lists, notes (think stickies), etc., that would work like a family.

> *"Creating more horizontally and/or vertically tailored versions of Windows, going forward, is another way Microsoft is expected to continue to grow its client operating-system coffers."*

It sounds like the original Ohana concept is dead, but the tailored-Windows-experience one is not. I haven't heard a timetable (tentative or otherwise) for the Kitchen Client, but it sounds like it's on its way.

There's a related effort underfoot by the Windows Embedded team at Microsoft to introduce Web services that will complement the devices and appliances built around Windows CE and Windows Vista Embedded. As with the case of Kitchen Client, it looks like the home is the first target for these services (SPOT in your coffee pot, anyone?). The Smart Personal Objects Technology (SPOT) effort is definitely a minor one, but the team is still alive—and is working on an eventual successor to Universal Plug and Play (UPnP)—a kind of web-service-for-devices-type offering.

Microsoft also is working with consumer electronics and other hardware vendors to help them get full versions of Windows to run on increasingly small, lightweight, and portable devices. The first generation of the WindowsXP-based *Origami*, or ultra-mobile PC, systems weren't well-received by the market, to be kind. The second wave of UMPCs, running Windows Vista, might prove to be more attractive.

At the Windows Hardware Engineering Conference in May 2007, Microsoft outlined some of the specs it's expecting the second wave of so-called Vistagamis to sport.[12] Among them:

- Not only seven-inch, but also five-inch displays
  - Lower-power LED-backlighting
  - Screen resolutions of 1024 × 600 (not the 800 × 480 minimum common with the first-wave UMPCs)
  - WiMax and integrated WWAN connectivity (supplementing the existing 802.11 b/g wireless and Bluetooth connected devices)
  - New input options, including thumb/QWERTY keyboards, along with the more-standard touch, stylus, and thumb-based controls on current UMPC models
- 1 GB-plus of RAM
- Three to four hours of 3-cell battery life
- Weight of less than 1.5 pounds

Until the price point for these systems hits the $500 range, however, they're likely to be more niche than mainstream products.

The Bigger Picture: Expanding the Market for Windows

Microsoft also is continuing to tinker with Windows variants for markets in developing countries, as well as investigating how/when/whether to provide business users here and abroad with new delivery and distribution mechanisms.

Windows Starter Edition is an SKU that Microsoft first introduced in pilot form in 2003. When Microsoft fielded its initial Windows Starter Edition releases, built around WindowsXP, the company was responding to the gains that Linux was making in developing nations that were unwilling and/or unable to pay for Windows systems. Microsoft officials, not surprisingly, were reticent to mention software piracy or Linux's growth as the driving forces

---

[12] New UMPC specs outlined. For more on what the Softies said at the Windows Hardware Engineering Conference in 2007 about the recommended guidelines for *Vistagamis*, check out this report from my ZDNet blog: http://blogs.zdnet.com/microsoft/?p=448.

behind Starter Edition. Instead, they touted Microsoft's interest in lessening the digital divide, not the rise of Linux, as the impetus for its push into emerging markets.

> *"As with the case of Kitchen Client, it looks like the home is the first target for these services (SPOT in your coffee pot, anyone?)."*

Whether it's philanthropy or capitalism (or, most likely, a mix of both) fueling Microsoft's growing "Unlimited Potential" campaign matters less than the fact that the company is making it a centerpiece of its Windows Client business. Currently, there are nearly 30 XP Starter Edition releases, each tailored for a specific geographic audience. In October 2006, Microsoft announced it had sold its 1 millionth copy of Starter Edition.

In 2007, Microsoft's Market Expansion Group announced its roll-out plans for Vista versions of Starter Edition. Ultimately, Microsoft expects to release as many as 80 different, geographically customized Vista Starter releases, officials have said.

The Vista versions of Starter will not include the Vista Aero user interface, which makes sense, since Starter is designed to run on low-cost PCs that don't offer souped-up graphics capabilities. Vista Starter releases will allow for multi-user accounts, but won't permit those sessions to run concurrently. Vista Starter will include all the same activation and authentication requirements as full-fledged Windows Vista—plus an additional authentication component designed to ensure that the user of the cheaper Starter edition actually is located in the country/market for which the software was developed.

Microsoft has added a stripped-down version of Office to some of its Windows Starter test versions. While officials won't comment on whether an "Office Starter Edition"-type product is on the books, Microsoft already is fielding a $3 Student Innovation Suite (consisting of Windows plus Office) for users in developing nations.

Starter Edition isn't Microsoft's only Windows play in developing nations. Microsoft is experimenting with new ways to charge for Windows outside the United States, as well. A pay-as-you-go program for Windows, known as *FlexGo*, has been offered in a handful of developing countries since May 2006. Under FlexGo, Microsoft and partners—including AMD, HSBC Bank Brasil,

Infineon Technologies, Intel, Lenovo, Phoenix Technologies, and Transmeta—allow users to buy PC usage time using prepaid cards similar to those sold by cell-phone makers in various countries.

As part of FlexGo "Next," Microsoft plans to shift its emphasis from pay-as-you-go to subscription-based pilots, company officials said at the Windows Hardware Engineering (WinHEC) conference in Los Angeles in May 2007. While pay-as-you-go had "high consumer appeal," according to Microsoft, it didn't have sufficient user volume for the financial institutions providing credit to the user base. Given the explosion in availability of consumer credit, subscriptions are emerging as a more popular option.

> *"Whether it's philanthropy or capitalism (or, most likely, a mix of both) fueling Microsoft's growing 'Unlimited Potential' campaign matters less than the fact that the company is making it a centerpiece of its Windows Client business."*

Under the FlexGo program, users make initial down payments on mid-range PCs and make monthly payments for software and broadband services from their local telcos, much the way customers pay cable providers for TV and Internet access. Microsoft and its partners will allow users to sign up and pay for their subscriptions in a variety of ways, ranging from ATMs and point-of-sale terminals, to the Web.

FlexGo systems require activation and Windows Genuine Advantage authentication. Once subscribed, users will be reminded via notifications and account status screens as to the amount of time they have remaining before their systems will move to "borrowed time," and, ultimately, a locked status for lack of payment. In order to unlock systems that have degraded

> *"Microsoft is experimenting with new ways to charge for Windows outside the United States, as well."*

because of lack of payment, users will need to obtain a code from the FlexGo partners.

During the latter half of this year, Microsoft will be adding new hardware to the list of systems supported under the FlexGo program, including AMD-Infineon ASIC- and Intel-based options.

Somewhere Out There: Windows across Many Cores … and in the Cloud

Deliverables, like some kind of "Windows in the cloud," is not a near-term prospect. Here, I'll simply mention that technological advances in virtualization, multi-core technology, and data-center reliability all will have profound impacts on what Windows looks like and how it works in the not-too-distant future.

> *"Technological advances in virtualization, multi-core technology, and data-center reliability all will have profound impacts on what Windows looks like and how it works in the not-too-distant future."*

Computer scientists already are mulling the kinds of changes that will be required at the operating-system and programming-language levels in order to accommodate client systems with 8-, 16-, and 64-bit processors.

At the 2007 Future in Review conference, Microsoft officials told attendees that the next releases of Windows will have to be "fundamentally different" in order to accommodate future multi-core machines. But that's about all they said.

Microsoft Research and high-performance-computing teams already are laboring over how to make Windows more able to handle many cores and accommodate parallel processing.

Microsoft Research has been working for the past several years on a non-Windows-based microkernel operating system known as *Singularity*. The entire Singularity effort encompasses the Singularity OS, a new programming language (Sing#), and new software verification tools. The Singularity OS revolves around software isolation of processes and is written as 100 percent managed code.

Some industry watchers say it's only a matter of time until Windows management finally decides that Windows has become so complex, large, and unwieldy that Microsoft will decide it's less of a pain to start over with a brand-new operating system than to continue to try to "fix" Windows. If and when it does, Microsoft may not have to face the unsavory prospect of having to cut the backward-compatibility cord. Instead, Microsoft simply could opt to make a virtualized version of some older release of Windows available on top of whatever new operating system replaces Windows, some are speculating.

If and when that happens, might Microsoft decide to make Windows as we know it a free, ad-supported service, as opposed to a fat-client software product? This idea isn't as crazy as it sounds. Back in 2005—which was a year before the Chief Software Architect Ray Ozzie Internet Disruption memo—Microsoft Chairman Gates gave serious consideration to one of the papers he read as part of his regular ThinkWeeks. That paper was about how and if Microsoft should make Windows itself a free, ad-based service.[13]

Another option, and one that Microsoft also seems to be exploring, is using SoftGrid, the application virtualization technology that Microsoft acquired from Softricity in 2006, to allow customers to run Windows applications as managed services. In mid-2007, Microsoft was evaluating what a "Managed SoftGrid" service from Microsoft might look like. Microsoft could opt to take it to market as a managed-desktop client service, a managed thin-client service, or a managed-terminal-service service, among other options.

> *"Might Microsoft decide to make Windows as we know it a free, ad-supported service, as opposed to a fat-client software product?"*

---

[13] More on Microsoft's early thoughts regarding making Windows a service: News.com got a peek at a ThinkWeek paper from 2005 outlining Microsoft's thinking regarding ad-supported apps and system software. From the paper: "An ad-supported version of the operating system could make some sense, the Microsoft researchers argue in their Think-week piece, noting that the product reportedly earns $9 per year per user. It seems possible that we could match that revenue via ads, but there are difficult UI (user interface) issues to solve, since the OS does not have a natural way to display ads that does not annoy users," the Microsoft workers said in the paper. One suggestion is a low-end version of the operating system that comes bundled with other ad-supported programs, such as Works, Outlook Express and Windows Media Player. However, the writers point out that "it's not clear how to prevent these elements from being replaced." News.com's full story is here: http://news.com.com/Microsoft+eyes+making+desktop+apps+free/2100-1014_3-5951569.html.

Bottom Line: Give Windows Users What They Want

When I've asked Windows users what they want from the next versions of Windows, their responses are usually quite humble. The majority aren't asking for voice or ink or improved natural-language query capabilities. They want fewer security prompts, more workable power management, and more supported drivers from the get-go.

> *"'I would like to see an OS (operating system) where the last thing you actually notice is the OS,' Harvie said."*

I thought Windows user Bob Harvie from Houston, Texas, said it best, when I asked readers of my "All About Microsoft" blog on ZDNet for their thoughts on what they wanted next from Windows.

"I would like to see an OS (operating system) where the last thing you actually notice is the OS," Harvie said. "I don't open my refrigerator wondering about the composition of the refrigerant or the material the door handle is made out of. I buy it, it's efficient, it looks okay and it cools my food. Fifteen years on, we part. I am asking for an OS that behaves and looks like a car, or maybe a fridge."

Office: Its Own Worst Enemy

Like Windows, Microsoft Office is a victim of its own success. Microsoft has a more than 90 percent share of the desktop-productivity-suite market. Every time the company introduces a new version of Office, its biggest competitor is the existing version(s) of Office.

A growing number of Microsoft watchers believe that Microsoft is working on a skunkworks project: a Web-ified version of Microsoft Office that will go head-to-head with Google Docs & Spreadsheets, Thinkfree, Zoho, and the growing family of hosted office-suite solutions on the market.

I cannot say with 100 percent certainty that Microsoft hasn't got this kind of project working in a back room somewhere. (After all, it's still widely believed—despite Microsoft's vehement denials to the contrary—that Microsoft had ported Office to Linux back in the late 1990s and was investigating when and whether to field the product. Because Linux on the client has not taken off, Microsoft supposedly decided against rolling out Linux for Office, so the theory goes.)

In 1999, Microsoft actually ran a pilot project via which it tested a hosted version of Microsoft Office 2000, which, at the time was christened *Office Online*. Microsoft's press release, announcing a handful of launch partners—including British Telecommunications PLC, CenterBeam Inc., Digex Inc., Equant, FutureLink Corp., Micron Electronics, and Qwest Communications—explained the new pilot service this way:

> *"A growing number of Microsoft watchers believe that Microsoft is working on a skunkworks project: a Web-ified version of Microsoft Office."*

> *Office Online will deliver the complete Office 2000 suite to a range of clients running Windows and Windows CE operating systems using Windows NT or Windows 2000's Terminal Services. This hosting solution has the ability to deliver the complete Windows experience and application functionality through terminal emulation. Since the release of Office 97, corporations have deployed Office via the Windows Terminal Server over corporate or private networks. With Office Online, customers can now access their Windows-based desktop and Office applications by simply connecting to a Windows Terminal Server running Office 2000 using an Internet connection. Office 2000 has been specially tuned for running in a hosted environment, adjusting dynamically and providing optimal performance for the online user. Office Online will offer familiar, industry-leading Office applications including Microsoft Word, Microsoft Excel, the Microsoft PowerPoint presentation graphics program, Microsoft Access, Microsoft Publisher, the Microsoft FrontPage web site creation and management tool and the Microsoft Outlook messaging and collaboration client.*[14]

---

[14] The original Web-ified version of Office: Office Online 2000. Here's the press release announcing its launch back in 1999: www.microsoft.com/presspass/press/1999/ Nov99/02KPR.mspx.

After a relatively short trial period, Microsoft deemed the product a clunker and scuttled the project. Today, there is still an "Office Online" web site, where Microsoft provides Microsoft Office documentation, downloadable add-ons, clip-art, templates, and the like. But it is quite different from the original Office Online service.

> "A year ago, Microsoft officials admitted that the company was testing quietly a "pay-as-you-go' rental scheme for Office."

So will Microsoft give a Web-based version of Office another try? Not in the near term, I'd wager. That said, in late 2007, Microsoft did take an interim step, with the introduction of Office Live Workspace, a service designed to allow home and small-business users to access their documents online and share their work with others.

But a full Web-based version of Office itself? I know that a lot of respected market watchers believe Microsoft will deliver this kind of solution before the end of the decade. But I don't see why. What would Microsoft have to gain? Few corporate customers are interested in a Web-based productivity suite; they believe their corporate data are too precious and sensitive to entrust to a third-party hoster—even (or especially, take your pick) Microsoft. A hosted version of Office might appeal more to small/mid-size businesses who are more open to running hosted/online versions of their applications. Better to offer this group a hosted version of Microsoft Works—or perhaps a Microsoft managed-desktop client service that encompassed both Windows and Office?

Office Trials ... and Errors

While I don't have reason to believe that Microsoft is conceding that Google Gears + Google Apps means that the existing office-productivity user base is ready to migrate wholesale to the Web, Microsoft has been engaged in a few recent experiments and trials to determine just how Web-centric its Office users want to be.

A year ago, Microsoft officials admitted that the company was testing quietly a "pay-as-you-go" rental scheme for Office, akin to the FlexGo Windows-rental trials in which it also is engaged.

Via its Office Prepaid Trial, which it conducted in South Africa, Mexico, and Romania, Microsoft has been investigating whether users might be willing to pay $15 (U.S.) a month or so to use Microsoft Office 2003. Microsoft relied on system builders to sell users cards that provide them three months' worth of Office 2003 usage for a set fee. As opposed to FlexGo, where an entire PC system (hardware and software) is leased, under the Office Prepaid Trial, only Office (either the Office Small Business or Office Student and Teachers Edition) was rented out.

Under terms of the Office Prepaid Trial, users must return to the system builders who sold them their original PC in order to purchase another three-month incremental of Office-rental time. If a user decides against re-upping, the version of Office 2003 that is on the user's PC goes into reduced functionality mode, providing users with nothing more than the ability to view documents.

In July 2007, the Softies announced that the initial Prepaid Trial pilots were a success and expanded them to include Office 2007 in South Africa and Romania. More markets are likely to be added in the coming months.

Microsoft also is planning to add Office to its FlexGo pilot program the next time that the company refreshes the products that are part of the

> *"Office today is seen by many as a bloated product that includes loads of features that very few people ever use."*

FlexGo bundle. Currently, FlexGo covers Windows and PC hardware only. In the next round of trials, users will be able to lease a single bundle including hardware, Windows, and Office, Microsoft officials have said.

Another way Microsoft could make Office (as well as Windows and just about every other Microsoft product) available via the Web without doing a Web-hosted version is via virtualization.

Microsoft has made no bones about the fact it is working to virtualize every element of the computing stack, from the hardware, to the operating system, to applications. Microsoft already is offering its Software Assurance and Terminal Services customers its SoftGrid technology so that they can run applications virtually.

What if Microsoft were to offer some or all of the applications that comprise Microsoft Office as virtualized apps/services? After all, application virtualization allows users to run multiple versions of the same application on the same machine at the same time—without the worry of having one application overwrite another. The service streams an application to a user's desktop, loading only the pieces s/he needs. App virtualization gives Microsoft a way to deliver everything from connected/disconnected support, identity/policy-based centralized management and monitoring, and anywhere access to Office applications. In January 2008, Microsoft announced that any version of Microsoft Office that is still supported by Microsoft can be virtualized. Microsoft gave its official blessing to using SoftGrid to run multiple versions of Office side-by-side on the same device/system.

Office 14: More of the Same

In the nearer term, however, Microsoft's goals for Office are much more modest.

Just like the Windows team, the Office team is focusing on two simultaneous missions: Introduce new and compelling features that will make existing customers want to upgrade and grow the overall "office productivity" market.

Office today is seen by many as a bloated product that includes loads of features that very few people ever use. So Microsoft can't simply keep cranking out more and more new Office features and modules and hope it will stumble magically on something that will win over laggards still running Office 2003, Office XP, or Office 97 (yes, there are still customers of the 10-year-old release out there). Neither Infopath, Microsoft's electronic forms module, nor OneNote, its note-taking add-on, had users banging down the door. And the new Office Ribbon interface seems to have attracted as many haters as it has converts.

Again, like Windows, the Office ship is a tough one to turn. In the same way that Windows Fiji and Windows 7 aren't expected to diverge in any significant way from the path established by Windows Vista, Office 14 isn't expected to be a wild and crazy departure from Office 12.

(There is no Office 13, by the way. Superstition prevails! Office 12 was Office 2007. Office 14 will likely be christened Office 2009 or Office 2010, depending on when it ultimately arrives. Given that the next version of Windows is a 2010 deliverable, I'd bet Office 14 is, as well.)

Office 14, as of this writing, is expected to be wending its way through the beta process in 2008 and to ship in 2009.

Microsoft is focusing on a handful of "investigation areas" in planning the next version of its Office client, server, and services products, according to a Microsoft slide deck, a copy of which I had a chance to see before Microsoft deleted it from the Web.[15] These areas include individual productivity, communication and collaboration, Enterprise content management, business process and business intelligence, Office as a development platform, and manageability and security.

If Microsoft sticks to its knitting, Office 14 may:

- Enable users to perform more complex tasks more easily (more Ribbon user interfaces for more Office apps would be my guess as to what this means).
- Provide more self- and community-based help options.
- Deliver improved search relevancy.
- Include tighter integration of unified communications, unified identity, and unified policy/compliance/support across all apps and for all devices.
- Focus on "flexible storage solutions for digital asset management."
- "Bring BI (business intelligence) to the business process itself, as opposed to having it as an isolated as-needed activity."
- More tightly integrate declarative programming and improved Business Data Catalogue capabilities into the core Office development platform.
- Provide tools to make global deployments easier, with new "federated, offline and virtualized models."
- Improve SharePoint's offline capabilities. Given that Microsoft has been referring to SharePoint Server as being at the heart of its Web 2.0 strategy—and as being its "social computing platform"— the forthcoming offline improvements aren't too surprising. After all, Google, Zimbra, and all the other Web 2.0 cool kids are playing up their offline capabilities as major selling points.

---

[15] AeroXP.org on Microsoft's Office 14 slide deck: Microsoft (not surprisingly) ended pulling a slide deck outlining its plans for Office 14 from the Web. But before that happened, the enthusiasts at AeroXP.org got a good look at it and wrote up what they saw: www.aeroxp .org/index.php?categoryid=10&p2_articleid=42.

Pretty lofty goals, at this point. But they're clear enough to make it evident that Office 14 will be more like Office 2007 than it will any of its current or future competitors.

More Office Customization on Tap: Roles and OBAs

Even though it's seemingly loath to take a major detour with Office, Microsoft isn't completely beyond hedging its Office bets.

In addition to simply adding even more features to the next versions of Office, the Microsoft Business Division staff also is exploring ways it can attract and keep users by (1) customizing Office for certain job functions or "roles"; and (2) making Office the de facto front end for a variety of server-based, line-of-business applications from both Microsoft and its competitors.

Several years ago, I remember Jeff Raikes, the president of Microsoft's Business Division, asking me whether I wouldn't prefer to use "Office for Journalists" rather than plain-vanilla Office. At the time, I wondered whether Microsoft was intending to develop customized versions of Office for tens, if not hundreds, of verticals—Office for Lawyers, Office for Bankers, Office for Insurance Clerks, Office for Plumbers. … Sounded crazy to me, but maybe it would fly. …

> *"Even though it's seemingly loath to take a major detour with Office, Microsoft isn't completely beyond hedging its Office bets."*

Whether or not that was Microsoft's intention at the time, it's not the strategy the Office team is pursuing at present. Instead, like several other Microsoft business units, the Office team is tailoring its product around a predetermined set of roles.

In the business application space, Microsoft is working to make its four different ERP offerings all look more like Office. On top of that, Microsoft has used the concept of "personas" to design role-based interfaces, tailored for more than 60 different ERP job functions. Sammy, a manager of shipping and receiving (and one of the Dynamics personas) would see one view of Dynamics NAV, based on his job functions. Production Planner Eduardo, another persona in Microsoft's role taxonomy, would see a different view and have different permissions and applets included as part of his

Office/Dynamics desktop. Over time, Microsoft is intending to make these Office-like role-based interfaces more dynamic, by allowing them to access Web services, such as Excel Services, a component of Microsoft's SharePoint Server.

In March 2007, Microsoft announced a new "ERP light" client, known as Microsoft Dynamics Client for Microsoft Office and SharePoint, that takes the whole idea of Office as the front end for Microsoft Dynamics a step further. The new Dynamics client for Office/SharePoint is one of a number of OBAs, or Office Business Applications, that is being developed by Microsoft and other software vendors.

Microsoft has been working to hone its definition of OBA for the past couple of years. Microsoft Architecture Strategist Mike Walker posted a succinct definition on his blog last year:

> *OBAs are a new breed of composite applications that bring together the front-office and back-office. They do so by unlocking the value assets in the enterprise. These consist of line-of-business systems built by developers and Commercial Off The Shelf (COTS) solutions. OBAs surface this valuable functionality through familiar interfaces making them more accessible and actionable to information workers.*[16]

In a nutshell, OBAs are all getting more developers to build applications that use Office and SharePoint Server as front ends for lots of different back-end systems. The first OBA was Duet, an Office front-end/SAP back-end combo developed in conjunction by Microsoft and its ERP rival SAP. The OBA concept emanated from the idea that most business users spend the bulk of their days inside Outlook or Excel. So why not make their look-and-feel experience look and feel like the applications to which they are most accustomed?

In cases in which third-party software vendors are unlikely to do their own OBA front ends for their line-of-business apps, Microsoft is looking for "creative" ways to convince them and their customers to do so. In April 2007, for instance, Microsoft announced a contest to encourage developers to find ways

---

[16] Mike Walker on OBAs: Microsoft Architecture Strategist Mike Walker offers a lot of great information understandable by laypeople, not just other architects, about Microsoft's Office Business Applications products and technologies. His blog can be found here: http://blogs.msdn.com/mikewalker/.

to integrate Office 2007 front ends with Oracle server applications. The winner of the so-called O2 OBA Challenge would receive $25,000 to implement the resulting mash-up.

> "In a nutshell, OBAs are all getting more developers to build applications that use Office and SharePoint Server as front ends for lots of different back-end systems."

Microsoft also is working actively with third-party software vendors, resellers, and integrators to encourage them to build both Office and SharePoint front ends to existing business software.

OBAs are a new way for Microsoft to convince customers they need to upgrade to the latest and greatest version of Office. Instead of positioning Office as a "mere" desktop productivity suite, Microsoft is working to make the Office applications must-have, tightly integrated elements of line-of-business applications. Watch for Microsoft to push Office as an interface, not just a bunch of desktop apps, to keep market share up in the coming few years.

Growing the Office Market: Unified Communications

In the same way that Microsoft is looking to grow its Windows market share in the face of near-complete U.S. market saturation by expanding the overall market for Windows, the company is pursuing a similar strategy on the Office front. In Office's case, this expansion means convincing customers that they need Office/Exchange/SharePoint for more than just run-of-the-mill desktop productivity purposes. Microsoft wants customers to think of its products as cornerstones for making their daily communications more productive.

Enter the concept of "unified communications." Microsoft wants its VOIP, Web conferencing, instant-messaging, unified contact lists, always-on "presence" functionality, integrated inboxes, and other related technologies to be the way that businesses and consumers stay in constant touch. (Forget whether you want to be always available and findable. In Microsoft's view, disconnecting completely is not an encouraged option.)

In an early 2007 interview with News.com, Microsoft Business Division President Raikes said the amount of R&D investment Microsoft was sinking into unified communications and VOIP "is the largest R&D investment beyond what we do in the core of Office" in his business unit.[17]

Microsoft is putting most of its unified-communications eggs in the Exchange Server and Office Communications Server (OCS) baskets, as it moves to take on Cisco and other PBX/telco vendors. OCS is Microsoft's combined instant-messaging/VOIP/ audio-video conferencing server, and the successor to Microsoft's Live Communications Server product. Exchange is Microsoft's e-mail server. OCS 2007 doesn't require Exchange Server to work, but Microsoft officials emphasize the unified-messaging synergies of the two communications products.

> *"In Office's case, this expansion means convincing customers that they need Office/Exchange/ SharePoint for more than just run-of-the-mill desktop productivity purposes."*

SharePoint as Microsoft's Next Killer OS?

Microsoft learned some valuable lessons, thanks to the U.S. Department of Justice and the handful of states who sued the Redmond software maker for antitrust violations in the late 1990s. One of those lessons was that Microsoft's strategy of boldly integrating previously stand-alone products into its operating systems was likely to get Microsoft in hot water. (That hasn't stopped Microsoft from continuing this practice, as Microsoft's 2007 brush with Google over Microsoft's decision to integrate desktop search "middleware" into Windows Vista showed clearly.)

Instead of being quite so blatant, Microsoft has taken a quieter back route to achieving the same ends via two related strategies: (1) baking SharePoint reliance into more and more of its products and (2) requiring users to buy pricey client-access licenses (CALs) in order to use Microsoft's servers.

---

[17] On the importance of unified communications, Jeff Raikes, the head of Microsoft's Business Division, told News.com in March 2006: "Well, basically, one way to quantify it is that the amount of R&D investment that we're putting in with unified communications and voice over IP is the largest R&D investment beyond what we do in the core of Office." The full Q&A with Raikes is here: http://news.com.com/Microsoft+turns+to+telephony/2008-1035_3-6164871.html.

> "On the server side of the house, Microsoft slowly but surely has been tying more and more of its products to SharePoint."

On the server side of the house, Microsoft slowly but surely has been tying more and more of its products to SharePoint—which is either one of Microsoft's best products ever or one of the worst things the company has ever introduced. Having talked to several Microsoft customers and partners about SharePoint, I can definitely say it's a product that elicits strong opinions.

There are two different Microsoft technologies that fall under the SharePoint label. SharePoint Server is a bundle of back-end server applications akin to the Microsoft Office front-end desktop suite. Among the members of the SharePoint Server suite are an Enterprise content-management server, a portal server, a forms server, a search server, a collaboration server, and a business-intelligence server. Windows SharePoint Services is a collaboration platform that Microsoft bakes into Windows client and server. From Microsoft's SharePoint FAQ Web page:

> In addition to its collaborative features, Windows SharePoint Services also exposes platform services and a common framework for document storage and management, as well as search, workflow, rights management, administration, and deployment features.[18]

Microsoft is gunning to make SharePoint Server and Services an inextricable piece of its customers' product fabric. In March 2007, at its annual Convergence conference for its Dynamics ERP and CRM customers and partners, CEO Ballmer stated plainly Microsoft's goals for SharePoint: "SharePoint is the definitive OS (operating system) or platform for the middle tier," Ballmer told an attendee who asked him about Microsoft's increasing sales, marketing, and development emphasis on SharePoint.[19]

---

[18] MS SharePoint FAQ page: Microsoft's centralized SharePoint information hub is located here: http://office.microsoft.com/en-us/sharepointserver/HA101655351033.aspx.

[19] SharePoint as Microsoft's next killer OS: CEO Steve Ballmer told attendees of Microsoft's annual Convergence conference in 2007 that the idea that SharePoint could be Redmond's next big operating system was not far off the mark. Read the context of Ballmer's remarks here: http://blogs.zdnet.com/microsoft/?p=327.

Microsoft's Dynamics ERP and CRM salesforce (both its own and its partners) are pushing SharePoint as part of every Dynamics sale—for example, Microsoft's Dynamics Client for Office, unveiled at the Convergence 2007 conference in March. In addition to functioning as a new user interface layer, the Dynamics Client for Office also is a new Client Access License (CAL) for Dynamics ERP users.

Microsoft buried this fact in its initial Dynamics Client press release. According to a line toward the end of the announcement: "AMR Research estimates that 85 percent of the employees in organizations that have deployed an ERP system are not licensed to use the data and information managed by these systems."

> *"CALs are the bane of many a Microsoft business customer's existence."*

To help right these wrongs, Dynamics Client for Office includes an Enterprise license for Microsoft Office SharePoint Server 2007 and access rights to all of the information and processes managed by a Microsoft Dynamics ERP system.

CALs, CALs, Everywhere

The hidden CAL clause in the Dynamics Client for Office is crafty, but not atypical. If you delve into the fine print for many of Microsoft's server applications, a CAL is not a nicety; it's a requirement.

And it's a requirement that Microsoft continues to hone to its advantage. Exchange Server 2007, for example, instituted a new Exchange Enterprise CAL. Microsoft decided to cut Outlook from the Exchange CAL, a decision that has met with considerable outcry from business users. Microsoft officials did plan to offer an exception for customers who sign up for Microsoft's Software Assurance volume-licensing plan. They'll still be able to get Outlook included as part of Exchange Server 2007.

CALs are the bane of many a Microsoft business customer's existence. There are CALs for Windows Server, Project Server, Systems Management Server, SharePoint Server, and many other Microsoft server products. Different CALs are licensed by the processor, by the seat, by the device, and by the mailbox.

In 2007, Microsoft also introduced a bundle called the *Enterprise CAL Suite*, consisting of a Core CAL Suite (including CALs for Windows, Exchange, SharePoint, and Systems Management Server), plus CALs for

Office Communications Server, SharePoint Enterprise, Exchange Enterprise, Windows Rights Management Services, Operations Management Client, and Forefront Security Suite.

Microsoft is likely to use CALs increasingly as a licensing carrot and stick over the next few years, as well.

Currently, when customers purchase Microsoft software via volume licenses, they can purchase a simple license to run the software, or a license to run the software plus Software Assurance, Microsoft's maintenance license. Software Assurance (SA) covers users for three years' worth of upgrades. To entice more customers to sign up for SA, Microsoft has been adding SA-only benefits to the program. One example is the Enterprise SKU of Windows Vista. The only way customers can obtain this version of Vista—which is identical to Windows Vista Business, with the addition of certain key features, like BitLocker Encryption, a Desktop Optimization Pack, and additional Virtual PC licensing rights, among other incentives—is by purchasing SA.

Users can purchase SA for Windows, Office, and a growing number of Microsoft products, including many CALs themselves.

That sums up where I think Microsoft will be going in the next few years in regard to its two biggest moneymakers: Windows and Office.

Now, in the next chapter, on to the currently less profitable, but potentially lucrative other product streams upon which the Softies are betting going into the next decade.

Microsoft 2.0: Big-Bet Products

5

Gates is probably getting out of technology at the right time. Funnily enough, it's not really a business for nerds anymore. Gates was at the center of the personal-computer revolution and the Internet revolution, but now the big innovations are about exactly the things he's bad at. The iPod was an aesthetic revolution. MySpace was a social revolution. YouTube was an entertainment revolution. This is not what Gates does. Technology doesn't need him anymore.

—*"Bill Gates Goes Back to School,"*
Time *Magazine, June 7, 2007*

Predicting what Microsoft is likely to do in the next two to three years is challenging. But forecasting what Microsoft will introduce and/or kill in the coming decade is Russian roulette.

Partially, this is because the tech market is evolving rapidly, with technologies like multi-core desktop computing and application and operating-system virtualization, changing the landscape seemingly overnight. It's also up for debate whether Microsoft knows what it's planning to do, not just from year to year, but even month to month. Strategies change; people quit and join the Redmondian ranks.

Think about it: Who would have predicted a few years ago that Microsoft would field an iPod competitor? Or that it would hire the creator of IronPython and introduce a new release of that dynamic language under the Microsoft brand? Moving Microsoft may be like turning a Navy carrier, but eventually the big ship can and does pivot.

> *"Moving Microsoft may be like turning a Navy carrier, but eventually the big ship can and does pivot."*

Using as a guide the speech mentioned in the last chapter from February 2007—via which Microsoft CEO Steve Ballmer spelled out for Wall Street analysts his near- and longer-term bets for Microsoft—it's possible to make some guesstimates about Microsoft's longer-term product strategy. That's my starting point for this chapter. I'm also mixing in bits and pieces from papers that Microsoft execs have submitted to Chairman Bill Gates as part of his "ThinkWeek" process, as well as hints from various sources claiming familiarity with Microsoft's roadmaps.

One point to keep in mind—besides the fluid nature of any kind of longer-term strategy predictions in the tech business—is the importance that Microsoft execs have placed and continue to place on diversifying the company's product mix. At the annual Microsoft July 2007 Financial Analyst Meeting, the Microsoft brass, from Ballmer on down, emphasized that Microsoft would continue to pour money into new businesses that might lose money for years, all in the name of diversification.

> *"In short, Microsoft's corporate position is that tech innovation, in the future, will happen more and more on the consumer side first."*

Microsoft's lack of experience in new markets like gaming is no deterrent, officials have said repeatedly. In spite of the company's geeky roots in the developer-tool and operating-system markets, Microsoft will focus just as much, if not more, on new products focused on consumers in the longer term. Chief Software Architect Ray Ozzie made that part of Microsoft's plan quite clear during the July 2007 Financial Analyst Meeting. Ozzie told Wall Street analysts:

> One of the things that I'm extremely happy about, about
> Microsoft, is the breadth. The fact that we have Robbie [Bach's
> Entertainment and Devices] business all the way at the front edge
> lets us build things and work them into an enterprise in a way

that matches the way that it's working in the entire ecosystem. And I think IBM in general, or any IT company that lacks that consumer component, is going to be disadvantaged from the perspective of IT.

We have situations where enterprises really benefit from the fact that the people who come in from the outside already know how to use the tools and technologies. They buy the interesting phones before IT has embraced them and certified them. And this can be challenging for IT, but business also benefits from those dynamics that are going on, on the outside.[1]

In short, Microsoft's corporate position is that tech innovation, in the future, will happen more and more on the consumer side first. I believe, as noted in the Introduction of this book, that a more accurate statement would be that an increasing number of user-interface innovations are being driven by the consumer, rather than the business, side of the technological world. But I'm not running Microsoft. So expect to see Microsoft invest increasingly in and take its cues from the consumer world, rather than the business one, in the longer term.

With those caveats out of the way, here are some of the up-and-comers likely to have an impact on Microsoft's bottom line in the next decade.

The "Other" Windows: Windows Mobile

Microsoft has no choice but to play in the mobile operating-system market. An estimated 1 billion cell phones shipped worldwide in 2007.[2] And in spite of all Microsoft Chairman Bill Gates's talk and interest in Tablet PCs and UMPCs, cell phones look to be the predominant mobile form factor in the next decade—and not just in the United States, but worldwide.

---

[1] More on why Microsoft's betting big on consumer: Straight from the Chief Software Architect's mouth. Here's the full transcript of Ray Ozzie's remarks from the Financial Analyst Meeting in July 2007: www.microsoft.com/msft/speech/FY07/QAFAM2007_2.mspx.

[2] Yankee Group estimates 1 billion cell phones shipped worldwide in 2007. Comparatively, according to a survey by the Consumer Electronics Association, 76 percent of U.S. households owned at least one cell phone, 37 percent had at least one notebook or laptop computer, and 62 percent a digital camera. These stats are all in this CNN article from last May: http://edition.cnn.com/2007/BUSINESS/05/28/gadgets.labels/.

> "If current trends are any indication, Microsoft will attempt to deliver a new version of Windows Mobile every 18 to 24 months."

According to Microsoft's own data, the mobile devices business is the smallest, dollarwise, but one of the fastest-growing revenue sources for the company. Microsoft is continuing to roll out new Windows Mobile releases at a regular clip—with the next being Windows Mobile 7.

At the heart of Windows Mobile 7, like all Windows Mobile releases, is the Windows CE kernel. The Mobile team builds each Windows Mobile release around this kernel. The Mobile team subsequently delivers to carriers new Windows Mobile versions, atop which they, in turn, build their various smartphone products. The carriers typically introduce their new Windows Mobile phones about six to nine months after they receive the code from the Softies.

Windows Mobile 7 (at one time code-named *Photon*) is rumored to include improvements in Outlook Mobile, as well as OS-based enhancements supporting WiFi, WiMax, VOIP/GSM, CDMA, and other emerging cell technologies. Touch and gesture recognition will be part of the Windows Mobile 7 interface, although it may not be available for all models of phones.[3] Windows Mobile 7 is expected to be the first release of the Windows Mobile platform that doesn't come in separate Pocket PC and smartphone flavors: It will be one merged release.

If current trends are any indication, Microsoft will attempt to deliver a new version of Windows Mobile every 18 to 24 months. Currently, Microsoft is expected to release Windows Mobile 7 in 2009 and Windows Mobile 8 around 2011, if the company sticks to its shipping pattern.

In addition to being a small but quickly growing business in its own right, Windows Mobile also is increasingly important to Microsoft as a venue to

---

[3] "Inside Microsoft" blogger Nathan Weinberg got his hands on an interesting Microsoft document in early January that discussed some of the planned changes coming to Windows Mobile 7 and Windows Mobile 8. Windows Mobile 7 will use touch gestures, similar to how the iPhone operates, according to Weinberg's information. "You will be able to flick through lists, pan, swipe sideways, draw on the screen," he said. Read his full post here: http://microsoft.blognewschannel.com/archives/2008/01/06/exclusive-windows-mobile-7-to-focus-on-touch-and-motion-gestures/.

promote and grow its Search business. The Windows Live team is focused heavily on making sure that the Live experience on mobile devices is as good as, if not better than, what it is on client PCs. The Live Search for Windows Mobile Version 2 release—with new requested functionality such as movie show times, restaurant ratings, and better GPS navigation—that Microsoft announced in summer 2007 was delivered to rave reviews.

Windows Mobile is not Windows in miniature. There are a set of very different dynamics in this space.

As opposed to the case in client operating systems, Microsoft is not the dominant operating-system vendor in the mobile world. The Symbian OS, which powers phones from Nokia, Samsung, Motorola, and LG phones, among others, owns nearly three-quarters of the market, according to

> *"Windows Mobile, in 2006, had cornered only 5 to 6 percent of the market."*

recent estimates from Canalys. Linux powers another 15 percent or so of the existing phones. Windows Mobile, in 2006, had cornered only 5 to 6 percent of the market.[4] In the fourth quarter of 2007, sales of Windows Mobile phones from 50 different vendors combined were outpaced by sales of the iPhone from Apple alone, Canalys said.[5] Microsoft's acquisition in February 2008 of Danger Inc., the inventor of the Sidekick and a provider of consumer mobile services, could give Microsoft an entry into a piece of the mobile market (premium phones aimed at consumers, not businesses) that it so far has done little to tap. But the company definitely has an uphill battle on its hands in this up-and-coming space.

Microsoft has been dabbling with new ways of extending the mobile platform so as to make it a more viable primary client—especially in countries where PCs are still too expensive for most individuals to own. Over the past couple of years, Microsoft Research officials showed off prototype systems,

[4] Cell phone market share data: The Q3 2006 data cited in this chapter are sliced and diced over at Seeking Alpha: http://ce.seekingalpha.com/article/40578.

[5] Data for the fourth quarter of 2007 was even more telling, regarding Microsoft's lackluster position in the mobile space. According to Canalys, Apple moved into the No. 3 position worldwide in mobile phones. And in the U.S., in the fourth quarter of last year, Apple captured 28% market share vs. the 21% for all Windows Mobile providers combined. The full Canalys study results are here: http://www.canalys.com/pr/2008/r2008021.htm

which allowed users to connect their mobile phones to their TVs to create a home-made, low-cost system with a mobile phone as its primary CPU.[6] Some have suggested that such a configuration might be the way Microsoft and its partners make an end run around the One Laptop Per Child systems backed by Nicholas Negroponte & Co.

> *"Microsoft's Windows Live and MSN online strategies have been works in progress (to put it diplomatically) for the past couple of years."*

In any case, Microsoft execs are starting to talk up mobile phones as real alternatives to Tablets, UMPCs, and laptops. As Microsoft Chief Research & Strategy Officer, Craig Mundie, told attendees of the 2007 Windows Hardware Engineering Conference, the lines as to what constitutes a mobile system are truly beginning to blur—and will only get more fuzzy as time goes on.

I think one of things that you see is the beginning of another trend, a trend where, whether it's up from the phone or down from the laptop, the idea of having a more and more potent computing experience in a mobile environment, Mundie said, *the distinction being mobile is something that you actually use while you're moving as opposed to a computing facility you can move someplace else and then use, and I think the lines may blur among these things, but we're very focused on what it's going to take in order to be able to create this mobile computing environment.[7]*

Windows Live and MSN: Keys to the Past or Future?

Microsoft's Windows Live and MSN online strategies have been works in progress (to put it diplomatically) for the past couple of years.

---

[6] Could a Smartphone rigged up to a TV be Microsoft's One Laptop per Child alternative? Maybe. See Chief Research and Strategy Officer Craig Mundie's views on the topic from his Windows Hardware Engineering Conference 2007 keynote: www.microsoft.com/Presspass/exec/craig/05-15-2007WinHECMundie.mspx.

[7] Chief Research and Strategy Officer Mundie's blurring-the-lines quote came from the same WinHEC keynote address: www.microsoft.com/Presspass/exec/craig/05-15-2007WinHECMundie.mspx.

Some consider the Windows Live family of services to be little more than warmed-over versions of MSN services, like Hotmail and Messenger. While there are several Windows Live versions of the tried and true family of MSN products, Windows Live is more than just a new name on old bottles.

I would beg to differ. If you understand what Microsoft's doing (or at least trying to do) with Windows Live, you understand how its Software Plus Services (S+S) strategy will unfold over the next few years.

One obvious caveat: It's still up-in-the-air, at this point, how Microsoft's acquisition of Yahoo and its various consumer services and content—if consumated—is going to be merged into Microsoft's online-systems business. CEO Steve Ballmer has gone on record saying he believes the Yahoo brand is a strong one which Microsoft has no plans to abandon. But it's still fuzzy exactly which Windows Live/MSN services content will survive and which will be superseded by Yahoo's equivalent offerings. The only certainty: It will take Microsoft years to fully digest Yahoo and get its combined services house in order.

It's unlikely that even something as disruptive as the Yahoo acquisition is going to derail or even change the course of Microsoft's S+S strategy, however. And Windows Live services, as well as Yahoo's own instant-messaging, e-mail, photo-sharing, bookmarking and other consumers' services, are and will be Microsoft's S+S guinea pigs.

> *"In Microsoft's taxonomy, there have been three kinds of services."*

In a nutshell, S+S is Microsoft's strategy to extend its stable of software products with services counterparts. In some cases, these services will be brand-new add-ons to a software product; in other cases, they will be a Web-based version of an existing client- or server-based software product (like Microsoft's Dynamics CRM Live, e.g.).

In Microsoft's taxonomy, there have been three kinds of services: Foundation/shared services, like Microsoft's storage service (in all of its different guises); attached services, like disaster-recovery and anti-spam services, such as those provided by Windows Defender; and finished services, like the various Windows Live Hotmail, Windows Live Messenger, Windows Live Expo, Windows Live Photo Gallery, and the like.

An adjunct to the foundation services is the Live services that are part of what Microsoft has described as its Live development platform/APIs (application programming interfaces). Microsoft officially debuted the Windows Live platform at Mix '07 in Las Vegas in April. Officials also announced in April a simpler and more standardized set of unique user-based pricing and licensing terms for its Windows Live APIs. Their hope—to entice not only other teams inside Microsoft, but third-party developers, as well, to build on top of Microsoft's core set of APIs when developing new software services.

> *"Every time Google announced a new service, Microsoft made sure it was right there with a tit-for-tat alternative."*

It was actually well in advance of Mix '07 that the Live team first had discussed its plans for a development platform. The team has been endeavoring to create and make available a set of common infrastructure APIs that it would share across most, if not all, of its Live services (both Windows Live and other Live properties). These infrastructure APIs include identity, relationship, storage, communications, payments and/or points, advertising, and domain APIs. The Live team also has been working on a set of what it has called "application services APIs," which include instant-messaging/VOIP, search, Spaces (blogging), mapping, mail/calendar, and classifieds APIs.

Whoever Has the Most Services ... Wins (?)

Like services archrivals Google and Yahoo, Microsoft came out of the services gate fast—almost recklessly so. Throughout 2006, it looked like the Windows Live team had been given carte blanche to roll out as many new beta services as it could, as rapidly as possible.

> *"By April 2007, Microsoft had pruned this list somewhat and had started dropping the 'Windows' piece of the 'Windows Live' brand for certain services."*

Seemingly, it didn't matter if new Live services had a clear raison d'être or overlapped with existing offerings. The only thing that was for sure was that every time Google announced a new service, Microsoft made sure it was right there with a tit-for-tat alternative.

Several of these new services barely worked. Others worked OK in beta but were disastrous in their final forms. And getting users moved over from the beta to final versions was not always a smooth process.

By summer 2006, there were more than 40 different "Windows Live" branded sites and services for which Microsoft was monitoring tester feedback.

Here's the list of Windows Live/Live properties Microsoft publicly acknowledged supporting as of July 2006:

- Windows Live Academic Search
- Windows Live Book Search
- Windows Live Call
- Windows Live Call for Free
- Windows Live Custom Domains
- Windows Live Dev
- Windows Live Expo
- Windows Live Favorites
- Windows Live Feeds
- Windows Live Gallery
- Windows Live ID
- Windows Live Ideas
- Windows Live Image Search
- Windows Live Local
- Windows Live Mail
- Windows Live Mail Desktop
- Windows Live Messenger
- Windows Live Mobile
- Windows Live Mobile Mail
- Windows Live Mobile Search
- Windows Live Near Me Search
- Windows Live News Search
- Windows Live Newsbot
- Windows Live OneCare
- Windows Live Product Search
- Windows Live Publishing Portal
- Windows Live QnA
- Windows Live Safety Center
- Windows Live Search
- Windows Live Search Answers
- Windows Live Search Center
- Windows Live Search Help
- Windows Live Search Macros
- Windows Live Search Translation
- Windows Live Shopping

- Windows Live Spaces
- Windows Live Toolbar and Desktop Search
- Windows Live Web Search
- Windows Live Web Search SDK
- Windows Live WiFi Suite
- Windows Live.com

By April 2007, Microsoft had pruned this list somewhat and had started dropping the "Windows" piece of the "Windows Live" brand for certain services. Here's the April 2007 list of beta and final services/sites for which the Windows Live team was collecting tester feedback:

- Live Maps
- Live QnA
- Live Search
- Live.com
- Windows Live Account
- Windows Live Alerts
- Windows Live Call
- Windows Live Call for Free
- Windows Live Custom Domains
- Windows Live Dev
- Windows Live Expo
- Windows Live Favorites
- Windows Live Gallery
- Windows Live Hotmail
- Windows Live ID
- Windows Live Ideas
- Windows Live Mail desktop
- Windows Live Mail for mobile
- Windows Live Messenger
- Windows Live Messenger for mobile
- Windows Live Mobile
- Windows Live OneCare
- Windows Live OneCare Family Safety
- Windows Live OneCare Safety Scanner
- Windows Live Product Upload
- Windows Live Publishing Portal

- Windows Live Shopping
- Windows Live Spaces
- Windows Live Toolbar and Desktop Search
- Windows Live Web Search
- Windows Live Writer

Note that neither of these lists includes services that are now branded as MSN, some of which were formerly branded as "Windows Live," such as Windows Live WiFi. And there are a bunch of Window Live services, some acknowledged by Microsoft and some not, that aren't on these lists at all. Windows Live TV (originally codenamed *Nemo* and, later, *Orbit*) isn't on here, nor is Windows Live SkyDrive, Microsoft's cloud-storage service, listed.

By June 2007, Windows Live officials were admitting publicly that the plan was to hone the list of Windows Live properties even further and group together at least a handful of these services into a core suite. Microsoft decided to deliver a common installer and updater that would work across a core group of its Windows Live services. More precisely, the Windows Live core suite became the "Windows Live" software—any of the Windows Live entities that installed on users' PCs. The services-only Windows Live offerings—things like Live Search, Windows Live Messenger, and the like—would not be considered part of the suite.[8]

Going forward, the Windows Live team seems to be focused on requiring both a software and a services component for each of its offerings. Windows Live Photo Gallery is the software; Windows Live SkyDrive (and/or Windows Live Spaces) is its service complement. Windows Live Calendar Desktop is the software; its complementary service is Windows Live Calendar. Windows Live Mail desktop is the software; Windows Live Hotmail is the related service.

Will the Real Windows Live Core Please Stand Up?

Just to clarify (while again noting that nothing's been really clear when it comes to Microsoft's Live strategy), the term *Windows Live Core* is a bit ambiguous. There seem to be two projects to which the Softies refer as *Windows Live Core* (one of which is more like a Windows Live core with a lowercase "c").

---

[8] Thanks to LiveSide.Net's (www.liveside.net) Chris Overd for explaining the distinction between Live software and Live services.

There's the aforementioned suite of core Windows Live services, which will share a common digital identity, installer, and updater.

> *"Just to clarify (while again noting that nothing's been really clear when it comes to Microsoft's Live strategy), the term Windows Live Core is a bit ambiguous."*

But there's also another Windows Live Core that the Softies describe internally as "a mesh of all devices, data, apps and contacts." Microsoft watchers, including yours truly, have made some educated guesses that Windows Live Core, at least on the back-end, is little more than a fancy name for the Windows Live infrastructure, to which some have referred as Microsoft's *Cloud OS* or *Cloud DB*. Microsoft has assigned some of its heaviest hitters to the Cloud OS team, including the father of VMS and Windows NT, Dave Cutler; Windows kernel architect, Amitabh Srivastava; database expert, James Hamilton; .NET Developer Platform leader, David Treadwell; and networking/datacenter pioneer, Abolade Gbadegesin.

This back-end Windows Live Core infrastructure is likely to mesh (pun intended) with a data replication project under way at Microsoft that is code-named *Harmonica*. (Microsoft switched codenames in 2007, from *Harmonica* to *Ibiza*, but the underlying idea remains the same.[9])

Ibiza is now known as the *Microsoft Sync Framework*—which is designed to allow developers to add synchronization, roaming, and offline access to apps, services, and devices. (Ibiza is not to be confused with another Microsoft synchronization service, FeedSync. FeedSync is the technology championed by Microsoft Chief Software Architect, Ray Ozzie, that was formerly known as RSS Simple Sharing Extensions. The Microsoft Sync Framework includes support for FeedSync.[10])

---

[9] *Harmonica* and *Ibiza*: Check out my ZDNet "All About Microsoft" codename glossary for more on these two technologies. More on "Harmonica": http://blogs.zdnet.com/microsoft/?p=649. and for more on Ibiza: http://blogs.zdnet.com/microsoft/?p=651.

[10] For more on the similarities and synergies between Microsoft Sync Framework and FeedSync, check out this blog post from my ZDNet blog here: http://blogs.zdnet.com/microsoft/?p=1029.

There are supposedly at least two different databases figuring into the Microsoft synchronization infrastructure. One of these is known as the *Cloud Database* (*CloudDB*); the other as *Blue/Cloud*. CloudDB is a file-system-based storage system, sources say; Blue is a hosted version of SQL Server under development by the SQL Server team, they claim. Last I heard, Microsoft was hoping to roll out Blue to a very limited set of customers/partners, starting in 2008.[11]

One other codename worth keeping an eye on in this space is *Volta*.[12] Volta is "a Microsoft Live Labs project dedicated to extending the .NET programming model to incorporate the Cloud." Exactly how you extend .NET to work across the Cloud—beyond embedding a subset of the Common Language Runtime environment in Silverlight (Microsoft's Flash killer)—seems a bit squishy, at this point. But in the next few years, Volta will likely move from the incubation to the commercialization stage, and Microsoft will have more of a story for developers wanting to tap into all these Cloud-based services and resources.

Back here on earth, from a user perspective, Live Core will manifest in the form of a persistent "PC experience" that will look the same on a mobile device, a Web browser, and/or a desktop client machine. A user's core set of Favorites, data, and settings will remain consistent regardless of the computing environment.

Microsoft CEO Steve Ballmer explained the user concept quite succinctly during a keynote in the spring of 2007. He said that Microsoft is thinking in terms of "what would a PC look like if it were PC Live" in devising its

> *"Volta is a Microsoft Live Labs project dedicated to extending the .NET programming model to incorporate the Cloud."*

---

[11] More information about how Microsoft's Cloud/Blue Cloud databases fit into the company's grand cloud-computing scheme can be found at http://blogs.zdnet.com/microsoft/?p=394.

[12] What, exactly is Microsoft's Volta? Non-techies, go here: http://blogs.zdnet.com/microsoft/?p=433. Techies might prefer this Channel 9 Web cast with Volta's main man, Erik Meijer: http://channel9.msdn.com/ShowPost.aspx?PostID=324060#324060.

Windows Live, Office Live, Live Search, CRM Live, and ERP Live product sets.[13]

Service Packs: Product or Service?

Windows Live services ultimately may end up being more than "just" service complements to software products. They also could become the way that Microsoft moves away from traditional Service Packs and enables Windows customers to obtain more rapid, digestible fixes and updates to products in the not-too-distant future.

> *"Windows Live services ultimately may end up being more than 'just' service complements to software products."*

Up until the release of Windows Vista, Microsoft had followed a predictable schedule of releasing a new Windows variant and, several months or years later, providing users with one or more Service Pack (SP) follow-ons. SPs tend to consist primarily of bug fixes but may also include new features. (For a while, Microsoft attempted to ban completely new features from SPs, but that practice seems to have become a thing of the past.)

Starting with Windows Vista, Microsoft brass began to make noise about SPs becoming passé. Because Microsoft regularly releases fixes and patches via Windows Update, why should users wait for a big-bang SP, they asked aloud. In spite of Microsoft's intentions, several corporate customers balked at any move by Redmond to do away with SPs. Larger customers prefer SPs to updates delivered over the Web, they've said. Several companies block Windows Update/Automatic Update downloads for security and application-compatibility reasons. And many prefer to install updates in one fell SP swoop every year or so, instead of having to deal with a constant barrage of Web-based updates.

---

[13] Ballmer's full statement, from an April 2007 Townhall event with IT professionals on the Redmond campus: "Microsoft will be taking its "experiences" and applications and "projecting them into the SaaS world," Ballmer said. He said Microsoft is thinking in terms of "what would a PC look like if it were PC Live" in devising its Windows Live, Office Live, Live Search, CRM Live and ERP Live product sets." My full blog post on Ballmer's remarks is here: http://blogs.zdnet.com/microsoft/?p=398

In spite of these legitimate objections, Microsoft is continuing to push to make more of its fixes and updates Web-based deliverables. And not just for Windows. Microsoft is moving to do the same for Office and more and more of its other products, as well.

One of the key reasons that Microsoft is interested in pushing updates via the Web is agility. When it comes to security fixes, it's fairly obvious why Microsoft is relying on the Web to get patches into users' hands and machines on a monthly—or sometimes more frequent—basis. Delays mean potentially exploitable software. But speed also is behind Microsoft's desire to push non-security-specific updates and patches via the Web too. Microsoft CEO Ballmer has vowed that Microsoft will never again take five years to release a new version of Windows. One way to get more frequent updates out the door more quickly is via the Web.

Windows Vista is a case in point. Microsoft released the Vista code to manufacturing in November 2006. At that point, there were relatively few third-party drivers that were ready to roll. But in the months since it dropped the final Windows code, Microsoft's own internal divisions, as well as outside software developers, pushed hundreds of drivers out to customers via Windows Update/Automatic Update.

> *"Going forward, Microsoft is likely to rely additionally on Windows Live services to get new features and fixes into customers' hands more quickly."*

Going forward, Microsoft is likely to rely additionally on Windows Live services to get new features and fixes into customers' hands more quickly. Take, for instance, Windows Vista's Photo Gallery feature. Photo Gallery—a Vista subsystem allowing users to store, edit, and manipulate their photos and movies—is baked into Vista. But Microsoft announced in mid-2007 that it planned to field a new Windows Live Service known as Windows Live Photo Gallery, which would supersede the Photo Gallery that is integrated into Vista. Windows Live Photo Gallery adds Web storage and photo-sharing to Photo Gallery's feature list. Vista users who sign up for the final version of Windows Live Photo Gallery will be upgraded automatically to the Live Photo Gallery bits. Instead of having to wait for a whole new release of Windows to get the improved photo-handling functionality, Microsoft is getting it out to customers more quickly, via a Live service update.

Even in the case of users who purchase Windows preloaded on new PCs, Microsoft still could look to Windows Live as a way to get the latest updates and fixes to them more quickly. Microsoft's Live team has been working to sign deals with PC vendors via which they will preload links to various Windows Live services on new machines. In March 2007, Lenovo and Microsoft announced an agreement via which Lenovo will preload Windows Live Toolbar and access to Web search via Live.com on ThinkPad notebooks, ThinkCentre desktops, and Lenovo-branded PCs.

Microsoft's OEM sales team is driving hard to secure more deals with other Microsoft PC partners like the Lenovo one. Microsoft can get the most recent set of features and fixes for a Windows release into users' hands by getting PC makers to include links to the latest Windows Live releases on new systems. When users start up for the first time, they'll be able to download the most up-to-date features and functions via Windows Live.

What about MSN?

For a while in late 2005/early 2006, it looked like Microsoft was going to scrap MSN as a brand, and possibly also as a portal. Windows Live was the hot commodity.

But in the eleventh hour, MSN got a reprieve. And, at least for the next few years, it seems that Microsoft has no intentions of doing away with MSN. Whether this will continue to hold true if and when Microsoft adds another major consumer portal—Yahoo.com—to its holdings, is somewhat less clear. But I'd think that two consumer portals would mean twice the amount of monetizable content. So I'd expect Microsoft to try to keep both MSN.com and Yahoo.com alive for as long as practically possible.

> *"In the eleventh hour, MSN got a reprieve."*

Given that MSN.com was attracting 465 million unique users a month (at that time), Microsoft ultimately decided it shouldn't abandon users who preferred an entertainment portal as their gateway to the online world. If Microsoft could convince these MSN users to try one or more Windows Live services, they'll be hooked, they reasoned. At the same time, Microsoft decided it would position MSN as "the best partner for media companies." Instead of competing with these potential partners, Microsoft would give them a venue for ads, content, and more.

"We want to become the distribution point and aggregation point for our partners," said former Microsoft Online Services Chief Steve Berkowitz.

Berkowitz used a mall analogy in explaining Microsoft's thinking in the online services space. "Our business model is we will own the real estate for the mall … and we get a fee on the way in and the way out," Berkowitz said.[14]

In the fall of 2006, Microsoft surprised many by branding its so-called YouTube killer as "Soapbox on MSN Video," instead of "Windows Live Video." At the Consumer Electronics Show in January 2007, I'd swear I saw a banner for "Windows Live Money." If it was, in fact, in the works, that branding change never happened. Instead, there still was, at least at the time I submitted this manuscript, a full panoply of services that are branded as MSN—everything from MSN Dating and Personals (with Match.com) to MSN City Guides. According to one Microsoft internal estimate I saw in mid-2007, there were more than 400 MSN web sites, including the granddaddy of them all, MSN.com, hosted in three primary Microsoft global data centers.

> *"MSN.com and the MSN-branded services run on the same data-center servers and use the same back-end infrastructure as Windows Live and the growing family of Microsoft-hosted services."*

MSN.com and the MSN-branded services run in the same data-center servers and use the same back-end infrastructure as Windows Live and the growing family of Microsoft-hosted services. They are all using a common core publishing platform (codenamed *Bedrock*), feed-management system (codenamed *Shuttle*), SQL Server back-end, diagnostics/monitoring system (code-named *Fuse*), and distributed services/caching technologies. While we're on a codename roll, the complete back-end infrastructure for Microsoft's data centers running its various Live services is codenamed *Autopilot*.

Search: A Destination or a Convenience?

MSN also has evolved into a key component of Microsoft's services push for another reason. MSN is the perfect place for Microsoft to integrate Live

---

[14] Microsoft Online Services honcho Steve Berkowitz keynoted the Lehman Brothers Technology Conference on December 6, 2006. A full transcript of his remarks is here: www.microsoft.com/Presspass/exec/craig/05-15-2007WinHECMundie.mspx.

Search. Just think if all of the 400-million-plus unique users of MSN.com started using Live Search as their default search engine. ... Microsoft's distant third place in the Search market share might gain more than a few points. And whether Microsoft ends up folding Live Search into Yahoo Search or maintaining two search engines for the foreseeable future, it will now be able to profit from a second search-centric portal (Yahoo.com)

This point wasn't lost on Berkowitz and other Microsoft execs. At a Lehman Brothers technology conference in December 2006, Microsoft first broached the idea of "convenience" search versus "destination" search.

> *"The over-riding mission is to get searchers to search more with Microsoft."*

Google and Yahoo have had a lock on destination search—that is, searches that are done by going specifically to a search page. But "convenience" search—which relies on the proclivity of users to use whatever search facility is embedded on a web site or within another service—is where Microsoft has more than a fighting chance to grow.

Microsoft has made it plain that it intended to embed Live Search (the entity once known as Windows Live Search, and before that, MSN Search) into all of its services. The default search engine on MSN.com? Live.com? On Xbox Live? Office Live? Within Windows Live Hotmail, Windows Live Messenger, Windows Live Expo, Windows Live Spaces? You guessed it—Live Search.

Microsoft embedded an offshoot of Live Search—its desktop search technology that it calls *Instant Search*, into Windows Vista. Instant Search is not, despite Google's legal department's claims to the contrary, a clone of MSN Desktop Search. In order to head off another potential antitrust suit, Microsoft agreed in mid-2007, following a legal complaint lodged by Google, to alter the Windows Vista code so that desktop-search engines other than Instant Search would perform well on Vista. Microsoft altered the Vista desktop-search components as part of its Vista Service Pack 1 update. (Microsoft's proactive move seemingly ended up failing to appease Google, which convinced the European Commission to launch a probe in early 2008 over Microsoft's search-bundling practices. Whether the probe will morph into a full-blown antitrust suit remains to be seen.)

Microsoft's Live Search team set some ambitious goals for itself under boss, Satya Nadella, who took over the group in mid-2007. Starting with a major update in the fall of 2007, the Search team is planning to deliver two fairly major Search releases (a spring and a fall release) each year. In the interim, the team is now charged with rolling out incremental Search functionality updates.

Under Nadella, the Search team is laser-focused on improving search relevance—not just by tweaking the search algorithm, but also by tuning the data platform and mining capabilities. But the over-riding mission is to get searchers to search more with Microsoft. Microsoft plans to promote its search engine more on MSN.com via categories like "Popular Searches" and "A List Searches." Microsoft was expected to rebrand its www.live.com destination site to improve search visibility as well. ("Live It!"—or even "Yahoo Search It!"— sure don't have anywhere near the verb power of "Google It!")

The Redmondians also have been experimenting with ways to give users financial incentives to improve its search share. Starting in March 2007, Microsoft began offering enterprise customers an incentive program to get them to use Live Search. Under the "Microsoft Service Credits for Web Search" program, Microsoft agreed to pay companies something between $2 and $10 per computer, annually, plus a $25,000 "enrollment credit" for agreeing to get its users to try Live Search for a year. Microsoft initially planned to sign up 30 North American, European, and Japanese users to participate in the trial program, officials said. If the trial pans out, Microsoft was considering adding more participants in its "pay for search" program.

Microsoft also kicked off in 2007 a rewards-based promotional strategy under the Club Live Search banner. By offering prizes for points earned through playing search-based games, Microsoft managed to grow its destination-search share in a noticeable (though by no means massive) way.

And on the "let's make a deal" front, Microsoft's sales team seems to be

> *"On the 'let's make a deal' front, Microsoft's sales team seems to be learning what it takes to steal business away from its competitors."*

learning what it takes to steal business away from its competitors. In mid-2006, it won Facebook's ad business. In mid-2007, it signed a three-year ad-platform deal with Digg. Once the company truly begins assimilating its $6 billion aQuantive purchase, Microsoft's ad/search story is likely to get a lot more cohesive and convincing. And with Yahoo, Microsoft obviously will have more search firepower (when and if it it digests its takeover target) on a variety of fronts.

But back to plain-old Live Search. In addition to integrating Live Search into existing Microsoft services, Microsoft also is expected to make it the cornerstone of its adCenter technology. adCenter is Microsoft's online advertising platform. (Yahoo has its own online ad platform, known as Panama, which has not been as successful; most Microsoft watchers are expecting Panama to be one of the first Yahoo assets Microsoft will ax.)

As the Softies have noted repeatedly, the worldwide advertising market is two-and-a-half to three times as big as the software marketplace.[15] Early on, Microsoft Chief Software Architect, Ray Ozzie, saw the advertising handwriting on the wall and articulated the increasingly important role it would play in Microsoft's future strategy in his infamous October 2005 "Internet Services Disruption" memo. Ozzie wrote:

> Online advertising has emerged as a significant new means by which to directly and indirectly fund the creation and delivery of software and services. In some cases, it may be possible for one to obtain more revenue through the advertising model than through a traditional licensing model. Only in its earliest stages, no one yet knows the limits of what categories of hardware, software and services, in what markets, will ultimately be funded through this model. And no one yet knows how much of the world's online advertising revenues should or will flow to large software and service providers, medium sized or tail providers, or even users themselves.[16]

---

[15] Size matters: The software biz vs. the ad biz. Online Services head, Steve Berkowitz, told attendees of the Lehman Brothers Technology conference in 2006: "So, when we look at the advertising marketplace, I think it's really interesting to look at the size of the advertising marketplace. We can talk numbers, $500 billion, $580 billion, $600 billion. I mean, numbers keep flying around, and the whole point of it is, it's a huge marketplace. It's two-and-a-half to three times as big as the software marketplace in total. It actually has tremendous, tremendous potential. I mean, you look at the breakout of the advertising marketplace, you look at print being $176 billion; you look at directories, you know, it's $87 billion; you look at direct mail, it's $79 billion; and then you look at online being $27 billion; TV being another $151 billion; and radio being another $34 billion." The full Berkowitz transcript can be found at www.microsoft.com/Presspass/exec/craig/05-15-2007WinHECMundie.mspx.

[16] Ozzie's Internet Services Disruption memo from October 2006, revisited. See excerpts from Ozzie's Live blueprint in Appendix A.

In the summer of 2007, Microsoft announced its plans for one of its first major ad-funded offerings: An ad-funded version of Microsoft Works, which is Microsoft's productivity suite for consumers and small businesses. Microsoft officials said they planned to field trials of an ad-funded Works. The new version will be called Microsoft Works SE 9 and will be distributed by

> *"As important as it is to Microsoft's future, Windows Live is just the tip of the Microsoft 'Live' iceberg."*

a select group of participating PC makers through the middle of 2008. Microsoft will decide whether to continue offering the ad-funded version based on customer feedback.

Meanwhile, Microsoft is mulling lots more ad-funded product possibilities, including an ad-funded version of its Office Accounting Express product; various Office Live subscription-based add-ons to Office; and Microsoft downloads and "shareware" and more, officials have said.

In the longer term, Microsoft Research has been pioneering new ways that Microsoft might also make strides in search personalization and sharing. At Microsoft's March 2007 TechFest research showcase, Lili

> *"Microsoft is mulling lots more ad-funded product possibilities."*

Cheng, a Microsoft researcher who helped Microsoft develop the desktop search feature that is built into Windows Vista, demonstrated a new "search-based authoring" tool known as *Mix*. Mix is an interface focused on helping users aggregate, publish, and share search results. With Mix, users can assemble "dynamic documents" that include search information garnered from desktops, intranets, and the Web.

The Rest of the Live Family

As important as it is to Microsoft's future, Windows Live is just the tip of the Microsoft "Live" iceberg. Per Chief Software Architect Ozzie's directive, just about every product group at Microsoft is looking to add one or more "Live" services component to just about every one of its products.

Among some of the known existing and planned offerings in the Microsoft Live product pipeline:

- **Office Live**—SharePoint and other small-business services designed to complement Office on the client. Microsoft released the final version of the first iteration of its Office Live bundles in November 2006. In late 2007, Microsoft added an Office Live Workspace offering to its Office Live stable. That service adds an online editing and sharing capability to Office and other desktop productivity suites.
- **CRM Live**—A Microsoft-hosted version of its Dynamics CRM product available in 2008.
- **ERP Live**—Still to be determined, but looking more like add-on services designed to complement Microsoft's Dynamics ERP products than hosted ERP. (There's a chance it could mean both.)
- **Xbox Live**—A subscription-based set of online gaming services for Xbox users that Microsoft has offered since 2002.
- **Games for Windows LIVE**—A service designed to allow Windows-based gamers to play against Xbox gamers. This is the service formerly known as Live Anywhere.
- **Silverlight Streaming**—Not technically one of the "Live" branded services, but the same concept: an online service complement to Microsoft's Silverlight alternative to Flash. Microsoft released an alpha of this free hosting service for developers creating rich-media content using Microsoft Expression Studio tools and third-party offerings in April 2007.

As is the case with Windows Live, it hasn't been all smooth sailing for Microsoft's other fledgling Live offerings—starting with confusion around the branding.

> *"It hasn't been all smooth sailing for Microsoft's other fledgling Live offerings—starting with confusion around the branding."*

Office Live, for example—although allegedly one of the pet projects of outgoing Microsoft Business Division President, Jeff Raikes—has suffered from a variety of woes, starting with its name. To many, *Office Live* implied a Web-ified version of Office. That's not what Office Live is, however. Office

Live, in its first iteration, is a bunch of workgroup and web services designed to complement Office running on a client PC.

When Microsoft rolled out the first three Office Live SKUs in November 2006, it did a bit of a bait and switch. Originally, Microsoft said it planned to deliver three different versions of Office Live: Basic, Collaboration, and Essentials. But when it rolled out the final version of its first Office Live line-up, the SKUs were Basic, Premium, and Essentials. Those who had been testing Collaboration were moved automatically to the pricier Premium SKU. In February 2008, citing customer confusion, Microsoft merged all three SKUs into one and made Office Live Small Business a free product, supplemented by various paid, add-on subscription services, like Store Manager, an e-commerce service.

Microsoft is looking not only at building out brand-new services, but also at extending Office Live—and other Microsoft products—with other kinds of existing Microsoft and third-party services. For example, in October 2006, Microsoft introduced Office Accounting Express 2007, the low end of its accounting software line. More interesting than the core accounting software were the add-ons to it available on a subscription basis, including:

> *"Microsoft is looking not only at building out brand-new services, but also at extending Office Live—and other Microsoft products— with other kinds of existing Microsoft and third-party services."*

- **ADP Payroll**—$169 per year. Electronic filing available for an additional $60 per year. ADP Total Payroll Service: "Customized price as specific pricing depends on the number of employees, frequency of payroll and additional services requested."
- **Credit Card Processing via Chase Paymentech**—$9.95 per month.
- **PayPal Payment Services**—CCP Plan for $9.95 per month, plus $20 per month in bank-processing charges. PayPal Payments Pro credit-card processing is available for a monthly fee of $20.
- **Marketplace Services**—Up to 80 free listings/downloads per month for Basic; up to 200 listings/downloads per month for $9.95.
- **Equifax Credit-Profile Service**—Pay per use. Business credit reports on your own business, from $4.95 and up. Credit report with score: from $39.95 and up.

It's not hard to see the writing on the wall here. Subscription service add-ons will become a big focus for Microsoft. Some of these services will come from Microsoft; probably just as many will come from third-party providers, who offer Microsoft royalty payments of some kind for the right to latch their services onto Microsoft's core offerings.

> *"Subscription service add-ons will become a big focus for Microsoft."*

Like it does for the rest of the Live family, Microsoft has some big hopes for Office Live. And if at first it doesn't quite succeed, Redmond's ready to try and try again until it does.

During his July 2007 Worldwide Partner keynote, Chief Operating Officer Kevin Turner told conference attendees that Microsoft believes in two to three years Office Live will be one of the most important product families for the company as a whole. In Turner's words:

> We fully believe and expect in two or three years Office Live will be one of the most deployed, most utilized of all the products that we have in the Microsoft portfolio. Certainly it won't be as big as Windows in a couple of years, but we do believe it will reach our top three or four largest deployed applications that we have around the world. There's millions and millions of small businesses that we can reach, and we've got a big opportunity to drive it with Office Live, and there's a huge opportunity for you as partners to participate in it.[17]

That's a pretty tall order for a set of technologies that currently looks like this:

- **For consumers:** Office Live Workspace — a service that will allow Office users to collaborate and share documents online.
- **For small businesses:** Office Live Small Business.

---

[17] Office Live's unlimited potential: Microsoft Chief Operating Officer, Kevin Turner, shares the company's big dreams for Office Live at the Worldwide Partner Conference in 2007. The transcript of his remarks is here: www.microsoft.com/Presspass/exec/turner/07102007WPCKevinTurner.mspx.

- **For enterprise users:** Office Online — the growing family of Microsoft-hosted services for larger users, including Office Exchange Online, Office SharePoint Online and Office Communications Online.

Live: The Next Generation

In spite of these ambitious goals, Microsoft isn't just throwing a bunch of Live services out there to see what sticks—as it was doing just a couple of years ago. Those early days of seemingly reckless Live service rollouts seem to be dwindling. But that doesn't mean the company has decided against fielding any new Live services.

Officials with the Windows Live team have been loath to discuss unannounced services. But it's still possible to read the tea leaves and make some

> *"Microsoft targets several different vertical markets. But healthcare stands above them all."*

predictions about some of the likely directions in which Microsoft will take its services platform in the coming months/years. Here are a few of my expectations.

Going Vertical: Windows Live Healthcare

Microsoft targets several different vertical markets. But healthcare stands above them all, in terms of Microsoft's commitments. As of mid-2007, Microsoft employed more than 600 healthcare-related employees. These weren't just salespeople; there were also developers in the ranks. In late 2007, those employees introduced Microsoft's first Software+Service healthcare offering, HealthVault. HealthVault comprises a client application that complements the Live service that together will allow consumers to build and maintain a personal health record. One of the inputs into this health record will be results from Microsoft's health search engine, also known as HealthVault, which is based on the MedStory search technology Microsoft bought in 2006.

Microsoft is expected to roll out more Windows-Live-type healthcare services, including some still unannounced business/enterprise services aimed at hospitals who want secure access to that same information. The business service could be linked to the Azyxxi healthcare product Microsoft bought in 2006 that is designed to provide a single view of all of a given patient's health records, however and wherever they are stored. (In February 2008, Microsoft rebranded the impossible-to-spell-or-pronounce Azyxxi as "Amalga.")

Will Microsoft develop similar insurance, banking, retail, and other verticalized Windows Live services, going forward? As of 2007, there were no indications these were in the works. But if healthcare ends up taking off—and/or if Google gets into any of these vertical service arenas—I wouldn't be surprised to see Microsoft follow suit.

Building Out Full Suites: Windows Live Safety Platform

Beneath the Windows Live family, Microsoft is loosely bundling families of services into suites. In mid-2007, officials said they were working on a suite of core Live services (Messenger, Mail, Spaces, etc.) that would share a common installer. But there seem to also be other suites of related services in the making, as well.

The "Windows Live Safety Platform" is an example of this phenomenon. Microsoft was looking to bundle anti-spam, anti-phishing, its Family Safety Settings parental controls, and URL and IP reputation services into a suite of inter-related Windows Live services. Anticipate more of these kinds of groupings as Microsoft continues to sort out its Live branding in the coming months/years.

Turning Packaged Software into Services: Hosted Microsoft Works

In some cases, Microsoft isn't simply adding a service component to its software. Consider Microsoft Works, Microsoft's low-end productivity suite for small/home office users. In 2006, Microsoft officials hinted that the company was considering turning Works into a hosted service.[18] My guess: If it ever does, a Works service could debut as a member of its Office Live family. For now, however, Microsoft is focusing primarily on testing Works' viability as an advertising-supported product, not a service.

Where Do Managed Services Fit In?

There's a whole other set of services that Microsoft is rolling out that make use of the Live infrastructure but aren't (so far, at least) branded as "Live."

---

[18] Is there a Hosted Works in the making? See *BusinessWeek*'s "Microsoft Brings the Works Online" from September 14, 2006: www.businessweek.com/technology/content/sep2006/tc20060914_764614.htm?chan=top+news_top+news+index_businessweek+exclusives.

Like many of its competitors, Microsoft is developing a full complement of managed services, which are hosted by Microsoft in its own data centers. These Enterprise services are centrally managed like Windows Live, Office Live, and other Microsoft Live offerings.

Microsoft began piloting the first of these services in 2005 with Energizer Holdings. Microsoft provided managed-desktop services, as well as managed Exchange, SharePoint, and Live Communications services, for Energizer Holdings to test the waters. By mid-2007, Microsoft had signed up four paying Enterprise customers (including Energizer) for these and other forthcoming Microsoft managed services. Microsoft's core set of managed services is now on the company's price list, and Microsoft is actively courting customers for these services, officials have said.

> *"Microsoft has said that it expects these and additional forthcoming Microsoft managed services to appeal only to its larger customers."*

Microsoft is considering delivering a managed-service implementation for nearly every one of its software products, officials have said. A managed business-intelligence bundle, consisting of SQL Server, Performance Point (Microsoft's business-scorecard product), and SharePoint Server, is in the pipeline. A Forefront Online managed security service is in the wings, sources have said.

Company officials are toying with other ideas, such as a managed SoftGrid application-virtualization service—which could take the form of a hosted application-distribution service, a desktop-management service, or some other related offering. Another possible managed service that could debut sooner rather than later: A managed thin-client service based on Terminal Services or another of Microsoft's virtual-machine products.

> *"Like many of its competitors, Microsoft is developing a full complement of managed services, which are hosted by Microsoft in its own data centers."*

Microsoft initially said that it expected these and additional forthcoming Microsoft managed services to appeal only to its larger customers—those with 5,000 seats and above. To date, the company has been relying on resellers, integrators, and hosting specialists to offer hosted versions of Exchange, Communications Server, and other existing products to primarily small/mid-size businesses and consumers. It is becoming increasingly apparent, however, that Microsoft is on a collision course (yet again) with its partners. At the 2007 Worldwide Partner Conference, company officials repeatedly emphasized that partners need to be providing more than "just" hosting of Microsoft products. The message was loud and clear: Get out of our way or get steamrolled.[19] And in early March, Microsoft admitted as much, committing to deliver directly to customers of all sizes Microsoft-hosted versions of Exchange, SharePoint and Office Communications Server in the coming months.

Consumed by Consumer Offerings: Xbox, Zune, and IPTV

Even though this book is entitled *Microsoft 2.0*, Microsoft's more entertainment-focused products get relatively short shrift here. Why? Although they are all going to be key investment areas for Microsoft in the coming decade, I'm still not convinced the Xbox, Zune, IPTV, and other related technologies are going to have as much impact on Microsoft's bottom line for years to come, as its enterprise products.

Will Microsoft be known primarily as a gaming company, rather than a software vendor, in the next decade? I'm doubtful. A consumer-electronics powerhouse? Again, I'm not persuaded.

Undeniably, however, Microsoft is spending lots of energy, time, and money to hedge its bets with these up-and-coming businesses. The Redmondians are looking to create a virtuous circle of "Connected Entertainment" that encompasses not just Microsoft's traditional development tools, operating systems,

---

[19] Microsoft walks the fine services line with its partners. CEO Ballmer does a good job playing down potential channel conflict, which is likely as Microsoft steps up its services push. Best quote: "While we will start offering much more transparently and vigorously these managed communication and collaboration services, based upon the work that we've done with Energizer, we will want you to resell those services, we will also want to support partners who choose to host their own communication and collaboration services using Exchange, OCS, Active Directory, SharePoint, et cetera. So, this is a case where we'll have a service that we want you to participate in, and we'll want to support you in offering your own direct services." The full transcript of Ballmer's Worldwide Partner Conference 2007 keynote is here: www.microsoft.com/Presspass/exec/steve/2007/WPC2007.mspx.

and business software—but that also embraces its entertainment offerings. Example: Microsoft's Massive In-game technology will fuel not just Xbox games, but also PC-based games and even Microsoft's Surface multi-touch table. Another: Microsoft's "Pika" Media Center technology, which allows Media Center content to be streamed to TVs.

Microsoft has done a real about-face in terms of its thinking about the importance of consumer devices over the past few years. Earlier this decade, Chief Software Architect Gates proclaimed repeatedly that the PC, not the gaming console, would be the centerpiece of users' home-entertainment hubs. But these days, Microsoft officials are singing a different tune. The Xbox team seemingly has convinced the rest of the company that an Xbox and/or a TV—not a PC—is the "box" around which users converge in their living rooms.

> *"I'm still not convinced the Xbox, Zune, IPTV, and other related technologies are going to have as much impact on Microsoft's bottom line as its traditional products."*

A similar reversal of strategy occurred around digital rights management (DRM). Until 2007, Microsoft insisted that Windows Media's Plays for Sure was its one and only consumer DRM solution. In January of that year, CEO Steve Ballmer admitted that Microsoft had decided the Zune DRM was really the only way the company could go head-to-head with Apple and others in the entertainment business. Again, the PC was no longer the automatic winner in another Microsoft contest.

In spite of the momentum it has inside the company, the entertainment component of Microsoft's Entertainment and Devices division suffers from various problems around design, branding, and "coolness" that are less of an issue for the geekier product families in Redmond. The first Zunes sported bigger screens than iPods but still were seen by the consumer masses as heavy, unhip clunkers. The Xbox 360 made substantial headway against Sony and was seen as a real gaming platform—until Nintendo introduced the Wii. Around the same time, Microsoft had to concede that a substantial number of Xbox users were encountering the dreaded "Three Rings of Death" console failure that Microsoft finally agreed to fix in mid-2007, to the tune of more than a billion dollars.

Gates's obsession with consumer technologies in general, and IPTV in particular, seems to have been passed on to CEO Ballmer and others at the company. Microsoft has not been seen as a credible player here, and the market has been incredibly slow to take off, in spite of constantly rosy analyst predictions about IPTV's potential. But that combination of factors hasn't stopped Microsoft from pouring billions into IPTV—a fact about which Microsoft's brass doesn't seem apologetic.

> *"Gates's obsession with consumer technologies in general, and IPTV in particular, seems to have been passed on to CEO Ballmer and others at the company."*

"TV is a really important part of Microsoft's vision for connected entertainment," General Manger of Microsoft TV, Christine Heckart, told attendees of a Pacific Crest Technology Conference in August 2007: "There are 1.6 billion TVs in the world. Software is the next evolution of the TV, and we see TV as really going all on demand except for maybe sports and breaking news. And we really see software being the transformative next step in the evolution of TV. … So, it's a super important part of connected entertainment."[20]

The bottom line: At it looks now, Microsoft is going to continue to pour money into its entertainment products and keep at them until they finally get them right. After all, Ballmer has said he isn't afraid of taking on investments that take five, seven, or even 10 years to begin yielding profits. Microsoft is planning hefty Xbox investments over the next few years and is planning more Xbox outreach to non-classic gamers, as well as potential customers in markets where the company has been less successful, especially Japan and continental Europe. It is continuing to spend time and money building new music and entertainment services for Zunes and mobile phones. And Microsoft, citing consumer demand, is looking into getting the Surface multitouch technology into one or more consumer form factors a lot faster than the company originally planned.

---

[20] Microsoft is still backing IPTV to the hilt. The full transcript of General Manager Christine Heckart's talk at the Pacific Crest Technology Conference in August 2007 is here: www.microsoft.com/msft/download/transcripts/fy07/ChristineHeckart080707.doc.

As noted at the start of this chapter, Microsoft execs believe that many of the most important computing technologies and trends are debuting on the consumer side of the business these days. Microsoft needs to play here if it wants to be ahead of the commercialization curve, according to arguments from CEO Ballmer, Chief Software Architect Ozzie, Entertainment and Devices President Robbie Bach, and other Microsoft officials. (Obviously, not every company would or does

> *"At it looks now, Microsoft is going to continue to pour money into its entertainment products and keep at them until they finally get them right."*

agree with the "innovation comes from the consumer world" argument: Just ask IBM, SAP, Oracle, and Salesforce.com.)

Skepticism aside, there are some real, applied lessons that the Xbox Live team is teaching the rest of Microsoft. I blogged about these lessons on my ZDNet "All About Microsoft" last year. I think the list is worth repeating, since other divisions at Microsoft are studying what the Xbox team has done right and are attempting to apply those learnings to future iterations of their own products and services.

Ten Lessons from the Xbox Live Team

The Xbox Live team has been at the forefront of Microsoft's efforts to reach out to its user community and learn how to profit (not just monetarily) from it.[21]

Almost every November since Microsoft launched its Xbox Live online-gaming service in 2002, Microsoft has updated the service component of its gaming offering in some way. The more than 10 million paying customers the Xbox Live service had attracted as of early 2008 show that Microsoft's onto something here.

---

[21] "Ten Lessons the Xbox Team Can Teach the Rest of Microsoft": My original and full post on my ZDNet "All About Microsoft" blog on this topic can be found here: `http://blogs.zdnet.com/microsoft/?p=421`.

"Everything needs to be live now because customers are demanding it," JJ Richards, General Manager of Microsoft's Xbox Live unit, told me in mid-2007. "You want to go to where your community is and build around it," Richards noted. "And once you are connected, your ship cycle is totally different. You can roll out new stuff every six months. This changes your staging and prioritization of features."

> *"The more than 10 million paying customers the Xbox Live service had attracted as of early 2008 show that Microsoft's onto something here."*

Here are other lessons the Xbox Live is sharing with various Microsoft product teams:

1. **Tiers need to be clear and simple**—In Xbox Live, there is gold and there is silver. Fewer, simpler SKUs are better.
2. **The dashboard is the UI**—Users want access to lots of data, all in one place. They don't want to have to hunt for it.
3. **An online marketplace sells content**—Making Microsoft and third-party wares available as a one-stop shop helps move more add-on hardware, software, and services.
4. **Arcade**—Not everyone is a shooter-game pro. Users come with different skill sets and interests. Some prefer "Geometry Wars" to "Gears of War."
5. **Achievements are a way to stay in touch**—The more ways you can encourage community members to keep in contact with one another, the better.
6. **Ubiquitous voice and text are de rigeur**—In the Web 2.0 world, everyone's a multi-tasker. All services and apps should bake in messaging, mail, and other unified-communications technologies.
7. **Roaming accounts are key**—Users want their audio and video content, contact lists, address books, favorites, and other settings available on any device, anywhere at any time.
8. **Build communities within your community**—Gamerzones in the Xbox world allow similar types of users to more easily connect.

9. **Points are the new online currency**—The easier you make it for users to buy, the more they'll buy.

10. **Gamerscore = reputation**—Other divisions at Microsoft have been wrestling with how to rank community participants by "reputation" to help users gauge which content/commentary to trust.

There's lots more in the next couple of chapters about the business models, including info on some of the newer, less tried and true ones on which Microsoft's next-gen businesses are betting.

Microsoft 2.0: Tried and True Business Models

6

It takes Microsoft only 10 hours to exceed the quarterly profits of Red Hat. ... Microsoft's daily net income is about $52 million. That's $52 million in pure profit every 24 hours. ... So the next time you're ready to bury Microsoft, look at the company's balance sheet first.

> —*Joe Panettieri from a January 28, 2008, blog post entitled "Seven Stunning Facts about Microsoft's Profits"*

What is Microsoft's current business model? According to the company's web site:

At Microsoft, we employ a low-cost, high-volume business model that supports local economic development. From the beginning, we have built our business by creating inexpensive software that millions of customers can use without extensive training, services, and support. This approach enables local economies to harness technology sooner and compete globally. Our easy-to-use software also makes it possible for nontechnical workers to start employing a wide range of technology productively without specialized training.[1]

Sounds relatively straightforward. And until fairly recently, it has been. It was plain how Microsoft made—and planned to continue to make—its money: Sell large volumes of software at a relatively low cost. This was Chairman Bill Gates's legacy and it is what made Microsoft the $50 billion software powerhouse it is today.

---

[1] Microsoft summarizes its business model quite succinctly on its Global Citizenship page on the Microsoft.com site. The full text, originally posted by the company in October 2005, can be found here: www.microsoft.com/about/corporatecitizenship/citizenship/knowledge/businessmodel.mspx.

> *"It was plain how Microsoft made—and planned to continue to make—its money: Sell large volumes of software at a relatively low cost."*

Under Gates, Microsoft generated the bulk of its revenues from software preloaded on PCs and servers by its so-called Original Equipment Manufacturer (OEM) partners, coupled with volume-license deals with large Enterprise customers. It also sold quite a bit of software through retail chains. The company had—and still has—a relatively small direct sales force. The majority of its sales were racked up by partners—resellers, integrators, software vendors, networking experts, consultants, and the like.

By the time Chief Software Architect, Ray Ozzie, penned his "Internet Services Disruption" memo in October 2005, it was clear that nearly every source of Microsoft's revenues was in the process of undergoing some radical changes. If Microsoft intended to continue to be a player in its existing and new markets, its business model was going to need a near-total overhaul, Ozzie argued.

Yet in fiscal 2007, the majority—approximately 40 percent, according to some estimates—of Microsoft's revenue still came from multi-year licensing contracts with companies of all sizes. Regular (non-annuity) licensing deals accounted for another 15 percent of Microsoft's revenues. About 30 percent of sales were attributable to OEM preloads on new client and server systems. And the remaining 15 percent of sales were garnered from shrink-wrapped/retail channel sales, royalty payments, consulting fees, and a few other sundry sources.[2]

Here are some more granular data points from Microsoft's August 2007 10K:

- No sales to any individual customer accounted for more than 10 percent of Microsoft's FY 2007 revenues.

---

[2] Percentages attributable to OEM, volume licensing, and the like are available in gory detail as part of Microsoft's annual 10K filing. The filing can be obtained online here: www.microsoft.com/msft/download/FY07/Final%2010K%202007.doc. Additional dissection of Microsoft's licensing numbers can be found here: www.microsoft-watch.com/content/vista/if_not_vista_enterprise_then_what.html.

- Sales to Dell and its subsidiaries accounted for approximately 11 percent and 10 percent of FY 2006 and 2005 revenues, respectively. "These sales were made primarily through our OEM and volume licensing channels and cover a broad array of products including Windows PC operating systems, Microsoft Office, and server products."
- OEM preinstall remains huge in the Windows client channel, representing 80 percent of total Windows client revenue in FY 2007.
- Volume license deals are more important in the Server and Tools piece of Microsoft's business. About 45 percent of server revenue came from multi-year licensing agreements in FY 2007; another 30 percent came from "fully packaged product and transactional volume licensing programs." Only 10 percent came from OEM preloads. The rest: consulting and product support.
- Office revenues comprise 90 percent of total Microsoft Business Division revenues. MBD includes Office, CRM, and ERP products from Microsoft. About 25 percent of total MBD revenue is from sales directly to consumers.

Bottom line: Two years after Ozzie issued his "business-models-are-a-changin' " wake-up call, Microsoft still continued to earn its revenues the way it had for years—by selling software preloaded on new machines and via volume-licensing arrangements. Because Microsoft is a tough ship to turn, this pattern will most likely continue for the next two years, at least—in spite of CEO Steve Ballmer & Co.'s obsession with all things Google-competitive.

> *"Two years after Ozzie issued his 'business-models-are-a-changin' wake-up call, Microsoft still continued to earn its revenues the way it had for years."*

There's no doubt that Microsoft is battening down the hatches for major shifts—post Gates—in its business models and revenue streams. Microsoft officials have said publicly that they expect Windows and Office revenues to account for a gradually smaller percentage of overall sales, starting around 2009 or so. In fact, by the turn of the decade, Microsoft expects as much as

25 percent of its sales to be attributable to online advertising, officials have said.[3]

This chapter and the next will examine the current and future revenue sources from which Microsoft will make its billions over the coming years. This chapter will dig into the current and near-term business models and revenue sources; Chapter 7 will focus on the "untried but unavoidable" business models Microsoft is likely to adopt as the tech market turns.

As I did in the previous two chapters, I'll start by stating a few caveats.

> *"There's a very real risk that Microsoft may end up spreading itself too thin by diversifying into too many markets outside its core areas of expertise."*

While it's fashionable in some corners to project that Microsoft is going to have the rug pulled out from under it in the next two to 10 years, with Apple, Google, and/or Red Hat emerging victorious, I just don't see this happening. The era of Windows as an impenetrable fortress is waning, but it's still got a few good years of cash-generation in it.

There are unstoppable forces—the rise in popularity of hosted services, the growing importance of the cell phone as a computing platform, the inroads that open-source software has made on the closed-source world—that are pushing Microsoft to leave its lucrative comfort zone. Contrary to what many company observers believe, Microsoft employees (from Ballmer on down) know this and are reacting to it at varying degrees of speed. Because it's going to take more than a couple of years to topple a company that's spread its tentacles so deeply into corporate and consumer markets over the past 30 years, Microsoft has some—but not an unlimited amount of—time to react and readjust.

Yes, tech change is happening at a faster and faster pace. Yes, a number of the hottest new companies are spearheaded by 20- and 30-somethings who

---

[3] Can Microsoft really generate a quarter of its revenues from online advertising by the turn of the decade? In October 2007, CEO Steve Ballmer made the rounds with that bold prediction. *International Herald Tribune* had coverage here: www.iht.com/articles/2007/10/02/technology/msft.php.

consider a 50-plus-year-old CEO like Steve Ballmer (and a 40-something tech journalist like yours truly) to be dinosaurs.

There's a very real risk that Microsoft may end up spreading itself too thin by diversifying into too many markets outside its core areas of expertise. I've argued a few times that Microsoft should stick to its geekier enterprise knitting and leave consumer markets like gaming and digital media players to companies with more know-how in those spaces. But one also could argue that if Microsoft fails to establish itself as an advertising powerhouse, it still has a shot at being a productivity-tool leader or one of the

> *"By last year, as noted in Microsoft's 10K annual report, issued in August 2007, Microsoft was doing a lot more than just selling software through its traditional channels."*

top three gaming vendors. Yes, Microsoft's grand diversification plan means that the Redmondians might go off on a foolish spending spree and lose multiple millions or billions on a business that the company ends up dumping. But it also means Microsoft has a chance of stumbling into a business that could end up catapulting it into a whole new, still unmonopolized territory.

Microsoft really needs to find a way to keep Windows and Office relevant as the notion of Web-ified, virtualized software and services takes off in the coming decade. Microsoft needs to keep trying new avenues to find its way in the gaming, advertising, and mobile markets. It needs money and time—and those are things that only cash cows like Windows and Office can provide. Consequently, to me, Microsoft's current and future business models in the Windows and Office space remain crucial ones on which to keep tabs.

Microsoft's Myriad Monetary Streams

At Microsoft's July 2007 Financial Analyst Meeting, CEO Steve Ballmer addressed Microsoft's challenging goal of evolving simultaneously a host of different business models. Ballmer told Wall Street analysts and press in attendance that:

> [M]ost of the companies who have software as a competence
> have one business model. IBM has a business model. Cisco has a

business model. SAP has a business model. Google has a business model. Apple has a business model. We are going to have multiple competencies, and multiple business models living all in the same body, and it almost means they need to be modeled and thought about separately. And certainly as we think about them, we are dead-set and serious about being world class in each and every one of these ... dimensions.[4]

Microsoft has been laying the groundwork for these changes for the past couple of years. By last year, as noted in Microsoft's 10K annual report, issued in August 2007,[5] Microsoft was doing a lot more than just selling software through its traditional channels. It was manufacturing and selling hardware (keyboards, mice, gaming consoles, and gaming peripherals, with the soon-to-be-introduced Surface multi-touch table in the wings, too). It was developing and distributing video games. It was adding to its stable of personal services with several new Windows Live and Xbox Live services and starting to build out a family of business-focused services via Office Live, Dynamics CRM Live, and more. And the company was starting to stick its toe into the managed-services waters, as well.

In spite of this panoply of business models, Microsoft's primary distribution channels in 2007 remained much the same as they had been to date:

- OEMs and customized system builders
- Distributors and resellers (large-account resellers, value-added resellers, distributors, and retail outlets)
- Volume license agreements (Open, Select, Enterprise Agreements) forged directly between Microsoft and its customers and/or between customers and resellers
- Online

---

[4] At its annual meeting for Wall Street analysts and press, CEO Steve Ballmer spent a good part of his remarks discussing why Microsoft is diversifying beyond Windows and Office, and, as a result, will have multiple business models across different units. The full transcript of his remarks is here: www.microsoft.com/msft/speech/FY07/BallmerFAM2007.mspx.

[5] Microsoft's aforementioned annual 10K is a great source of data on all things business-model-related. Again, it can be found on the Microsoft Financial web site here: www.microsoft.com/msft/download/FY07/Final%2010K%202007.doc.

While the players are pretty much the same in each of these categories as they've been for a while, the market forces and issues between Microsoft and its sales channels have changed considerably.

OEMs: Keep Your Friends Close and Your Enemies Closer

Microsoft and its system-vendor partners always have had a symbiotic relationship. PC and server vendors have needed operating systems to power their hardware. Microsoft makes operating systems.

But symbiotic doesn't necessarily mean smooth. On the way toward building its Windows monopoly, Microsoft has made sure that preloading Windows was a deal that few, if any, of the biggest so-called Original Equipment Manufacturers (OEMs) could refuse. Around the time it launched Windows 95 in 1995, Microsoft instituted a Windows licensing arrangement with its PC-maker partners that still, to this day, largely remains intact. Originally known as the Market Development Agreement (MDA), this program dictated how and for how much Microsoft would license Windows to OEMs.

> *"Microsoft has made sure that preloading Windows was a deal that few, if any, of the biggest so-called Original Equipment Manufacturers (OEMs) could refuse."*

OEMs were given a choice: Promote and sell the heck out of Windows 95, and you'd get it for about $60 to $70 or so per copy. Failure to pull out all the sales and marketing stops would result in a higher price per copy.

As I reported in a story on how the MDA worked back in 1998:

> *The Windows 95 MDAs listed a dozen or so criteria through which OEMs could lower their per-machine fees. Those agreeing to preload the operating system on at least half of their PCs each month got a knock-off. Those agreeing to display the Windows 95 logo prominently on their advertisements got another benefit.*[6]

---

[6] I did a lot of research around the time of the U.S. Department of Justice antitrust trial against Microsoft into the company's Market Development Agreement (MDA) program, as it was at the very crux of the DOJ/state's case against Microsoft. I reported a summary of my findings in the first cover story of Ziff Davis's now-defunct *Smart Reseller* magazine. The original Web version of that story "Who Is Microsoft's Secret Power Broker?" is gone, but a rehosted version can be read here: http://practical-tech.com/business/who-is-microsofts-secret-power-broker.

Tier 1 vendors—those who moved the greatest number of Windows copies, got the best treatment and best price. There were only a handful of vendors who made it into Tier 1, including Compaq Computer Corp. and Gateway 2000 Inc. (as Hewlett-Packard Co. and Gateway were known a few years back). Tier 2 was the next dozen to 15 vendors who received a slightly less favorable rate per copy, even if they agreed to do their darndest to sell and promote Windows. Tier 3 OEMs got an even less favorable rate. And "white box" system vendors: They got whatever Microsoft could charge.

> "Microsoft officials have said publicly that they view preloads as a relatively untapped method for Microsoft to increase Office market share in a heavily saturated market."

As Microsoft historians know, the U.S. Department of Justice antitrust case against Microsoft resulted, in part, in Microsoft being forced to level the MDA playing field. These days, its Top 20 OEMs all are charged the same price per copy for Windows. And system builders and OEM are now all part of the same "channel sector," resulting—at least in theory—in better business terms for custom system builders.

In spite of these changes, the same core group of OEMs remain Microsoft's staunchest allies and have the most bargaining power with the Redmondians. Microsoft's OEM partners include all the biggest names: Acer, Dell, Fujitsu, Fujitsu Siemens, Gateway, Hewlett-Packard, Lenovo, NEC, Samsung, Sony, and Toshiba.

It's been a tumultuous few years for Microsoft's OEM division. In late 2007, Corporate Vice President J. Scott Di Valerio resigned his post to go work for Lenovo. In February 2008, Microsoft appointed the latest OEM-business hopeful, company veteran Steve Guggenheimer, to oversee its sales, marketing, and pre-sales engineering efforts involving PC makers, device makers, multinational and regional OEMs, and embedded system manufacturers.

The newest battlefront for Microsoft and its PC-maker partners is services. Since 2005, Microsoft's OEM unit has been negotiating with OEMs over which Windows Live services they'll preload and/or provide links for on new PCs. PC makers have been using Microsoft's rivalry with Google and Yahoo as a bargaining chip. In 2005, Dell, for example, signed a much-ballyhooed agreement with Google, which involved Dell preloading Google desktop search on certain Dell desktops and laptops.

Another arena where Microsoft and OEMs are continuing to barter is in the area of Office preloads. Microsoft officials have said publicly that they view preloads as a relatively untapped method for Microsoft to increase Office market share in a heavily saturated market. While some Microsoft PC partners already do offer Office preloaded on new systems, the vast majority do not.

That's where Microsoft's "Office-Ready PC Program" comes into play. In conjunction with its consumer launch of Office 2007 in January 2007,[7] Microsoft launched this new program. Among the elements of the new program:

- OEMs and system builders can preinstall and sell Microsoft Office Home and Student 2007 (which was previously sold only at retail).
- OEMs may offer customers a free 60-day trial of Office on new PCs and subsequently sell the customers the Office license after the initial PC purchase. With over 50 percent of small businesses purchasing Microsoft Office separately within 60 days of a new PC purchase, this represents "a significant new sales opportunity for system builders that were previously only able to sell Microsoft Office at the time of a new PC sale," according to Microsoft's web site touting its Office-Ready PC Program.

Expanding the Market for Windows…

Preloading its software on new PCs is only one of the ways Microsoft is counting on continuing to line its coffers with Windows earnings. Over the past couple of years, Microsoft also has shown its hand, in terms of its plans to grow its Windows share, in spite of the fact that it already has saturated the market for client PC operating systems.

When you own in excess of 90 percent of the client OS market, as Microsoft does, you need to make sure that you (1) maintain your existing

---

[7] For more details on how Microsoft changed its business model to permit more retail and PC-vendor preloads of Office 2007, check out the company's PR release, "Microsoft Office: Ready for Business," here: www.microsoft.com/presspass/press/2006/jul06/ 07-11InnovationDay1UmbrellaPR.mspx. A full explanation of the terms of the program for OEMs and system builders can be found here: http://oem.microsoft.com/downloads/ northamerica/2007Office/2007officepartnersellsheet.pdf.

user base each and every time they upgrade (i.e., don't give users reasons or incentives to become "switchers"); (2) make sure you are wringing every penny out of your current user base; and (3) find new and untapped pockets into which to expand.

> *"Microsoft also has shown its hand, in terms of its plans to grow its Windows share, in spite of the fact that it already has saturated the market for client PC operating systems."*

With the launch of Windows Vista, Microsoft began, in earnest, to pursue the second and third of these goals. Goal No. 1—ensuring your users want (and are willing to pay for) each and every new version of Windows—has proven more elusive. Many Microsoft watchers believe that Vista's less-than-smooth launch and first year resulted in Microsoft creating a bigger potential switcher market than ever before. If it wasn't Vista's initial dearth of drivers or annoying User Account Control prompts, it was its even more restric-tive digital-rights-management (DRM) policies and seemingly insatiable CPU and GPU demands ticking off customers, left and right. User discontent came to a head in the fall of 2007, when Microsoft ended up bowing to customer/partner demand and extending the life of WindowsXP by five months; as a result, PC makers were allowed to continue to sell WindowsXP preloaded on new machines, at customers' requests, through June 2008 (rather than January 2007, as Microsoft originally had stipulated).

In terms of convincing customers to pay for more costly, more feature-rich versions of Windows, Microsoft has found more success. In its first year of Vista sales, Microsoft, as it had planned, sold considerably more Vista Home Premium and Vista Ultimate consumer SKUs than it did Vista Home Basic. On the business side, the company convinced users of the value of Vista Business and thus sold more of it than Home Premium. Microsoft also met with suc-cess with its Vista Enterprise SKU, which it made available only to Software Assurance volume licensees.

While it's obvious that Microsoft wants to sell pricier versions of Windows because it can charge its OEM partners and customers more for them, it might not be apparent just how much incentive Microsoft has to upsell customers.

But on a couple of occasions in 2007, company officials acknowledged publicly that Vista Business provides Microsoft with "five times the uplift of Windows Home Premium." Microsoft's message that Windows Vista "shines great" on pricier hardware becomes more understandable when this dollar amount is taken into consideration.[8]

There's only so much milk you can coax from a cash cow, however. That's why Microsoft isn't relying solely on upselling to continue to maintain Windows revenues. The Redmondians also are trying to seed Windows in markets that aren't already saturated. Enter Microsoft's Unlimited Potential program.

> *"Microsoft isn't relying solely on upselling to continue to maintain Windows revenues."*

Microsoft has set an ambitious goal for itself—to get Windows PCs into the hands of 2 billion people by 2015. (It was already at the 800 million mark in early 2007, company officials said.[9]) One of the main ways it is counting on making good on this is via its Unlimited Potential program.

Via Unlimited Potential, Microsoft is looking to seed Windows in emerging markets (like India, Russia, and China), as well as in the poorest nations. A stripped-down, localized, less pricey Windows Starter Edition SKU is Microsoft's main vehicle for entering these markets. In some cases, however, Microsoft hasn't been adverse to simply cutting prices for Windows and Office to gain more of a toehold in the markets in specific countries. (China comes

---

[8] Mike Sievert, former General Manager of Windows Client Marketing, has bragged more than once about how much money Microsoft (and, to a lesser extent, its OEM partners) can make by upselling customers to more expensive versions of Windows. In March 2007, during a conference call with analysts, he talked up the claim that premium SKUs of Windows Vista could bring in five times the profits of more basic versions of the product. Read more on his remarks here: http://blogs.zdnet.com/microsoft/?p=351.

[9] Microsoft has been steadily upping its predictions of how quickly it will hit the "2 billion Windows users" mark. At the Consumer Electronics Show in January 2007, company officials said that Microsoft had reached the "800 million Windows users worldwide" mark. Back in 2004, Microsoft officials predicted that the company would hit the 1 billion user mark by 2010. But by mid-2007, the company's execs were citing the 2-billion-by-2015 estimate on a regular basis, as documented here: http://news.zdnet.com/2008-9595_22-6212609.html.

to mind here, where Microsoft agreed to halve the price of Vista and to drop the price of a bundle of Office Home and Student and XP Starter Edition to $3 a copy.)

Microsoft has waffled, in terms of whether to position Unlimited Potential as more of a philanthropic/citizenship effort—one that fosters local innovation, creates sustainable social/economic growth, and transforms education—or a business-centric initiative. Regardless of the PR tact, between 2003 and April 2007, Microsoft sold 2 million copies of Windows XP Starter Edition and Windows Vista Starter, the company claimed. Microsoft had introduced the products in a total of 139 countries and 24 languages. But the company's goals are even more ambitious. Starter is one small piece of the growing Microsoft empire among lesser-developed nations. From the company's "Global Citizenship" site:

> *A few years ago, we set a goal that, by the end of this decade, we would help bring the benefits of technology to 250 million underserved people worldwide. We recognize that we cannot do this alone. That's why our two flagship digital inclusion programs, Partners in Learning and Unlimited Potential–Community Technology Skills Program, build on the strength of partnerships with governments, schools, nongovernmental organizations, and community organizations. Working together, we are bringing valuable technology skills to teachers, students, and others—more than 135 million people so far, putting us more than halfway to our goal.*[10]

Another way Microsoft is looking to extend its presence in markets where it hasn't got near-monopoly status already is via FlexGo. The company also is tweaking its subscription-based FlexGo hardware–software-services bundle plan and is rolling out updated versions in Brazil, India, Mexico, and Russia. (I'll share more on this and other Microsoft subscription projects in the next chapter.)

---

[10] During the past year-plus, Microsoft has been pushing its Unlimited Potential/Starter messaging harder than ever. (It's hard to say how much of that push has come from Third World philanthropist Bill Gates himself.) The passage quoted here comes from a note signed by Gates and CEO Ballmer on the Microsoft Global Citizenship site and can be found at www.microsoft.com/about/corporatecitizenship/citizenship/default.mspx.

But the bottom line is that every copy of Windows and Office that Microsoft can get any cash for (any at all) is better than nothing. And currently, in many markets, including in the United States, Microsoft is making zilch from Windows, as a result of piracy.

...And Restricting the Market for Windows

Speaking of piracy, no chapter on Microsoft's current and near-term business models would be complete without a mention of Windows Genuine Advantage (WGA). Microsoft is counting on software piracy crackdowns to help it grow its Windows market share in the coming few years.

Data vary on how much money Microsoft is losing as a result of software piracy. But even Microsoft haters agree that the number is a big one. Microsoft, for its part, continually trots out Business Software Association numbers, showing how commercial software vendors are annually losing

> *"Microsoft attributed to WGA the biggest counterfeit software bust ever last year."*

countless millions because of software piracy. Microsoft attributed to WGA the biggest counterfeit software bust ever last year, when the Chinese government and the FBI announced a sting operation netting more than $500 million worth of counterfeit products.

In 2007, Microsoft took its software piracy message a step further, emphasizing that piracy puts its customers at risk, security-wise. Forget how that malicious software got into user shops; all Microsoft cares is that it is eradicated, all in the name of safeguarding its precious customers. According to a Yankee Group study on WGA/OGA—commissioned and paid for by Microsoft—which was released to the public on January 22, 2007,[11] more than 50 percent of consumers and small business admit they've discovered "some instances of counterfeit or pirated software in their organizations at some time."

All sarcasm aside, there are pluses and minuses (and seemingly more of the latter) attributable to Microsoft's WGA and Office Genuine Advantage (OGA) initiatives. Since 2004, when Microsoft launched a pilot of its WGA program,

---

[11] The text of that January 2007 Yankee Group study, which termed WGA a "win–win" for Microsoft and its partners, is here: http://download.microsoft.com/download/3/6/3/ 363e4976-3abd-4eab-b2e2-a643342bc869/Yankee_Group_Piracy_Research_Whitepaper.pdf.

more than 500 million users validated their software using Microsoft's authentication and anti-piracy mechanisms. A startling 20-plus percent of users found their software to be "non-Genuine" (including the less-than-1 percent, or 5 million, who were identified erroneously as pirates, according to Microsoft's stats). And tens of thousands of counterfeit reports have been filed as a result, the Softies have said.

Currently WGA consists of two components—validation and authentication. Every copy of Windows, Windows Server, and Office currently must be validated within a set grace period or it will cease functioning. Validation is online registration. Authentication is the second closely related step in the Microsoft Genuine one–two punch. Authentication means proving that software is not counterfeit. Until earlier this year, if Windows Vista failed to pass Microsoft's anti-piracy gamut, the Aero users interface, Windows Defender anti-spyware, and ReadyBoost memory-expanding technologies were disabled. After an hour, functionality was further crippled and the product went into "Reduced Functionality" mode. As part of Vista Service Pack 1, however, Microsoft did away with the very unpopular Reduced Functionality Mode punishments. Instead, going forward, Vista will nag users repeatedly until their copy of Windows passes the "Genuine" test. The slightly kinder and gentler Vista warnings aren't expected to hurt Microsoft's new anti-piracy revenue stream—which was adding about 5 percent to the company's OEM Windows growth as of the end of 2007.[12]

It isn't just individual copies of Microsoft software that need to be validated and authenticated. Businesses running Vista Business, Vista Enterprise, and Windows Server 2008 are required to track their product-license keys via one of two WGA methods: Multiple Activation Keys (MAK), which are aimed at smaller companies and/or isolated machines; and Key-Management Service (KMS), designed for companies with 25 or more machines.

"All Microsoft products will eventually use the Software Protection Platform," according to Cori Hartje, director of Microsoft's Genuine Software Initiative. Even products like Flight Simulator X, which went gold in mid-September 2006, included WGA elements. Expect future versions of SQL

---

[12] More information on Microsoft's decision to kill its Vista "kill switch"—as well as on how much money its WGA anti-piracy program was contributing to its bottom line—is available in this December 2007 *Information Week* article: www.informationweek.com/news/showArticle.jhtml?articleID=204700436.

Server and Exchange Server to be among the next products to require Volume Activation 2.0, Hartje said in an interview I did with her in October 2006.[13]

Resellers by Any Other Name

OEMs and hardware partners are just one element (albeit, a large and powerful one) in Microsoft's ecosystem. Another is the nearly 400,000-strong group of value-added resellers (VARs), solution providers, integrators, distributors, and other middlemen who act as Microsoft's primary direct sales force.

Microsoft does have hundreds, if not thousands, of sales reps on the Redmond payroll. But Microsoft's channel of resellers is far larger and is responsible for a far larger revenue source than Microsoft sales and Microsoft Consulting Services (MCS).

There are entire magazines and web sites dedicated to covering Microsoft's "channel" of resellers, so I won't attempt to provide anything other than a very high-level overview of how Microsoft makes money from its resellers. Structurally, as explained in Microsoft's 10K annual report, these are the entities that comprise the Microsoft channel:

> *"OEMs and hardware partners are just one element (albeit, a large and powerful one) in Microsoft's ecosystem."*

- **LARs (Large-Account Resellers)**—Resellers that sell licenses (usually Enterprise Agreements) of Microsoft products exclusively to top-tier accounts.
- **Direct-Market Resellers**—Resellers moving Microsoft products directly to customers primarily via the Web.
- **VARs (Value-Added Resellers)**—Resellers that sell licenses of Microsoft products to all sizes of customers. Microsoft and many of its resellers increasingly are eschewing the VAR moniker, seemingly because it connotes a low level of "value added." The preferred term for Microsoft VARs, as of late, has become *Solution Providers*.

---

[13] The full text of the interview I did in October 2006 with Cori Hartje, director of Microsoft's Genuine Software Initiative, is available on my ZDNet, "All About Microsoft" blog here: http://blogs.zdnet.com/microsoft/?p=29.

- **Distributors**—Suppliers to the LARs and VARs. Examples: Ingram Micro, Tech Data, CDW, Dell, Insight Enterprises, Software House International, and Software Spectrum.
- **Other "Reseller" Partners**—System integrators, network providers, hosting specialists, all of whom provide specialized consulting, networking, and other services for various Microsoft products to customers of all sizes.
- **Retailers**—Circuit City, Best Buy, CompUSA, and the like. Not a huge distribution point for anything other than consumer-focused software and hardware (keyboards, joysticks, mice) for the Softies, but still part of the overall "channel."
- **ISVs (Independent Software Vendors)**—While they seldom "resell" Microsoft software as part of their applications, ISVs also are part of Microsoft's partner ecosystem. In some cases, ISVs pay Microsoft royalties for elements of its software stack that developers opt to include in their final products. An interesting stat: Microsoft believes that there are 75,000 ISVs worldwide, with the top 2 percent, or 1,700 ISVs, in the pool of those generating more than $10 million annually in software revenue, generating 80 percent of the revenue. Obviously, these big boys are Microsoft's primary focus, from a partner standpoint, but the Redmondians want to leave no potential ISV partner by the wayside.[14]

Regardless of the size and type of reseller, customers buy software and/or services from them. The resellers pay Microsoft for the software they resell. A virtuous circle ensues … at least that's how it's supposed to work. But, unsurprisingly, the circle seldom remains unbroken. In reality, problems like lock-in from an ever-growing Microsoft software stack and channel conflict (Microsoft competing with its own channel partners) have led and continue to lead to channel unrest.

Locked In and Locked Out: Two Faces of the Same Channel Coin

The concept of a software stack in and of itself isn't problematic—and isn't unique to the Windows world, as evidenced by other successful stacks like

---

[14] All of these ISV stats come from a post by Dan Lohmeyer on the Microsoft ISV blog at http:// blogs.msdn.com/msftisvs/archive/2007/08/22/how-does-microsoft-work-with-isvs.aspx.

Java and LAMP (Linux, Apache, MySQL, Perl/PHP). Vendors build a platform, and resellers of the .NET/Windows platform—be they software developers, system integrators, or any other kinds of middlemen—can develop offerings that sit on top of it. Thanks to the supporting platform, channel partners don't need to waste time worrying about the code plumbing. Instead, they can concentrate on building their customized applications and services.

This model keeps all the players happy as long as the underlying stack doesn't become a prison with increasingly higher and higher walls.[15] But some channel partners, especially developers and resellers in the business-software space, fear this is what's happening with the Microsoft stack. To cut to the chase: Even though growing the stack might make financial and business sense for Microsoft, it won't work if Microsoft's largest sales force (aka, its channel partners) don't buy in.

Microsoft's stack started out as .NET and Windows. Then the company added SQL Server, Office, SharePoint Services, and SharePoint Server to its suggested development platform. Next, elements of Microsoft's ERP and CRM wares became part of the platform.

Back in 2003, when Microsoft began growing its software stack in earnest, company officials made no bones

> *"The concept of a software stack in and of itself isn't problematic—and isn't unique to the Windows world."*

about Microsoft's plans for the project. At the lowest level, Microsoft reached out to ISVs who simply wanted their products to run on top of Windows. At the next level, Microsoft attempted to convince software vendors to make use of the functionality that is built into Windows, the .Net Framework and SQL Server. Ultimately, Microsoft wanted to convince ISVs who committed to all of the base software to go all the way and build into their products dependencies on class libraries and tools that build on top of the .Net Framework.)

Cut to the present: Microsoft is continuing to pursue a similar strategy—and not just in terms of software, but also services. Take, for example, Titan, Microsoft's CRM platform. Titan—also known as Microsoft CRM 4.0—is

---

[15] For more on how Microsoft outlined its concept of the software stack upon which it was encouraging its partners to build, check out this write-up I did in 2003 regarding Microsoft's view of what constituted the software stack: www.microsoft-watch.com/content/operating_systems/microsoft_looks_to_recruit_isvs.html.

more than just an application; it's also the platform underlying Microsoft's CRM application. In other words, Titan, as a platform, includes data management and modeling, workflow, presentation management, and online–offline synchronization. Microsoft's idea is to allow third-party developers and resellers to build non-CRM specific applications on top of the core Titan development platform.

> *"There are two problems with Microsoft's increasingly voracious platform appetite: lock in and squeeze out."*

There are two problems with Microsoft's increasingly voracious platform appetite: lock in and squeeze out. Channel partners who go along with Microsoft's suggested course of action by embedding more and more Microsoft components into their applications and services are locking themselves, not to mention their customers, into the Microsoft platform. What happens when a customer decides to use MySQL, not SQL Server, as the database beneath its home-grown real-estate app? If the app was designed around SQL Server from the get-go, ripping it out and replacing it may not just be difficult—it could be impossible.

A related and increasingly common problem that resellers are encountering is the squeeze play. The bigger the piece of pie owned by Microsoft grows, the smaller is the remaining portion for its channel partners. In the Titan example, Microsoft is encouraging its partners to leave workflow, data management, and synchronization in Microsoft's capable hands. But workflow, data management, and synchronization are all places where partners traditionally have charged customers for "value added" development, deployment, and maintenance.

Make Way for the Microsoft Managed-Services Steamroller

Microsoft's all-consuming appetite for a bigger and bigger bite of the stack looks like it will get worse, not better.

If Microsoft's software-development and reseller partners don't keep moving up the stack, they'll be flattened by Microsoft. This dynamic is happening at an even more rapid clip in the services realm. Microsoft is expanding, via its growing managed-services business, into a territory it previously relegated to its system integrator and network-service provider partners.

Microsoft tested the managed-services waters a few years back by running a managed-desktop-services pilot program for customer Energizer Holdings. In 2005, Microsoft began providing Energizer with desktop management services, handling everything from software distribution, to upgrades, to antivirus/anti-spyware and other security services, for thousands of Energizer users.

By summer 2006, Microsoft quietly had begun selling Microsoft-managed and -hosted Exchange and SharePoint to Energizer and three other large corporate customers. Microsoft managed services were officially on the price list, and Microsoft Consulting Services and its direct sales force were out hawking them to any interested customers. In the fall of 2007, Microsoft branded these managed services as "Office Online."

> *"If Microsoft's software-development and reseller partners don't keep moving up the stack, they'll be flattened by Microsoft."*

Elements of that managed-service line-up include: Office Exchange Online (Microsoft-hosted Exchange), Office SharePoint Online (Microsoft-hosted SharePoint), and Office Communications Online (Microsoft-hosted Office Communications Server), with more additions (such as the anticipated Forefront Online managed security service) to come.

At Microsoft's annual partner conference in July 2007, Microsoft's message to partners was that they needed to make way for the Redmond services steamroller. Allison Watson, corporate vice president, Worldwide Partner Group, explained in a sugar-coated way via a canned Q&A on Microsoft's web site:

> With software plus services, Microsoft will be pointing its partners in a new direction. At the (partner) conference, we will outline a framework for how partners can participate and make money with this new opportunity, framing the monetization approach for how partners participate financially within the new software plus services model. As more products become available in the software plus services area, we will continue [to] define the partner revenue possibilities for each. ...
>
> In the future, there will be a range of opportunities for partners to meet a range of needs. There will still be opportunities to resell, refer, add value through professional services, package with customized capabilities, and make money through annuities and

subscriptions—all of this will remain true. However, there will also be abundant new opportunities for innovative, value-added services and customization as these hosted products roll out. We are also attracting exciting new partners who recognize the business opportunities represented by the breadth of our platform and the potential of the software plus services model.[16]

In a white paper it published in July 2007,[17] Microsoft explained how partners could still make money in a Software + Services world. Microsoft downplayed, as it has been doing for much of the past decade, the idea of simply reselling Microsoft software products. Instead, smart partners should be adding value on top of Microsoft's hosted offerings—like Dynamics CRM Live, Microsoft-hosted Exchange, and the like. While Microsoft didn't rule out the possibility of its channel partners continuing to provide hosted versions of Exchange, SQL Server, and other Microsoft products to customers themselves (claiming that Microsoft only planned to sell managed services directly to the largest corporate customers), the handwriting was on the wall. Microsoft is on its way to becoming more of a services vendor in its own right.

In early March, Microsoft made its intentions plain: It fielded a beta of Microsoft-hosted SharePoint and Exchange (via which Microsoft hosts your service and your data) to companies of any size. Microsoft is adding a "provisioning layer" to Exchange and SharePoint to make them multi-tenant-ready. And it is adding a new, per-user license subscription as a new pricing option for the forthcoming release of its Microsoft Online wares. Microsoft is going to allow customers who have purchased licenses for Microsoft's Exchange and SharePoint Server software (not the Microsoft-hosted versions of these products) to trade-in license credits for Microsoft Online managed service versions of these products; or a mix of on-premise and Microsoft-hosted versions.

Volume Licensing, a Carrot and a Stick at a Time

Selling customers of all sizes volume licenses for its products is the way Microsoft earns the bulk of its money. As mentioned at the start of this

---

[16] The full text of Partner chief Allison Watson's canned Q&A regarding Microsoft's partner positioning is available on Microsoft's press site here: www.microsoft.com/presspass/features/2007/jul07/07-10partnerop.mspx.

[17] Microsoft's white paper outlining how partners can still fit into the ever-shrinking Microsoft universe is here: https://partner.microsoft.com/40044198.

chapter, 40 percent of the company's fiscal 2007 revenues came from multi-year licensing deals and another 15 percent from non-annuity-based volume-licensing sales.

There have been volumes written on Microsoft's volume-licensing strategy. Microsoft's volume-licensing choices are complex—so much so that there are consultants who make (very) profitable livings solely by advising customers how to negotiate volume deals with the Redmondians. Volume licensing was and still is so convoluted that Microsoft released a note to the

> *"Selling customers of all sizes volume licenses for its products is the way Microsoft earns the bulk of its money."*

press in the fall of 2007, crowing about how it cut the length of the average licensing contract by half, and reduced the number of required sign-off signatures from tens to just one.[18]

At the highest level, there are three kinds of Microsoft volume licenses, as Microsoft explained in its 10K annual report last year. Customers may license Microsoft products via these licenses either by contracting directly with Microsoft or by going through resellers. The three:

- Open licenses are primarily for small- to mid-size companies. Typical Open customers have between five and 250 licenses for one or more Microsoft products.
- Select licenses are for mid- to large-size companies with more than 250 licenses for one or more Microsoft products.
- Enterprise Agreement (EA) licenses are also for mid- to large-size companies.

Open, Select, and EA customers all currently have a choice of acquiring perpetual licenses and/or Software Assurance licenses. (It's not clear whether Microsoft will continue to allow its volume licensees to license its products in perpetuity, given Microsoft's desire to move more of its customers to an annuity model.)

---

[18] How many Microsofties does it take to reduce the number of customer signatures on a volume-licensing contract? I'm not sure I want to know. But Microsoft was proud enough of its efforts to reduce volume-licensing complexity that it touted the achievement to the press in the fall of 2007: http://blogs.zdnet.com/microsoft/?p=698.

Software Assurance (SA)—which Microsoft introduced in 2001 as part of its Software Licensing 6.0 program—provides users with the ability to obtain upgrades of certain software products over a set period (usually three years). Users can spread their costs out over the three years and are guaranteed free upgrades to certain new product releases that Microsoft introduces during the course of the period for which their SA agreements are in place. Microsoft increasingly is adding "benefits" that are available to SA customers only to entice more to sign up for SA.

While customers have had mixed feelings about SA, Microsoft, under-standably, loves the program and is seeking ways to more firmly entrench SA among customers of all sizes. Microsoft's over-riding volume-licensing goal is to increase the rate of "SA attach" to volume-licensing contracts.

> *"Microsoft also has been dangling the offer of 'extended lifecycle hotfix support' over customers' heads since July 2005 as yet another way to convince them to move to SA."*

Under SA, Microsoft does not guar-antee users that they will obtain new software during the period they are covered. So it's a gamble on customers' parts whether they'll get the latest ver-sion of BizTalk Server or Office as an automatic upgrade under SA, or if the new release will fall outside of their window, requiring them to re-up SA in order to obtain the desired release.

Until the past year or so, the incen-tives that Microsoft offered (beyond spread payments and the possibility of automatic upgrades) weren't all that interesting to most customers. One- to 10-day "Desktop Deployment Planning Service" engagements by Microsoft Consulting or a Microsoft reseller? A one-day "Information Work Discovery Workshop"? Self-paced interactive desktop courses? Zzzzzz.

In late 2006, Microsoft began adding more tangible and enticing offers to SA, in the hopes that it would convince customers of the worth of the annuity licensing model. Depending on your perspective, these new benefits were either carrots or sticks—carrots if you felt they made/kept SA useful to you and your company; sticks if you felt like you were coerced into signing up for SA in order to obtain certain products or SKUs of products available to SA licensees only.

For instance, Windows Vista Enterprise, a new Vista offering that is a step up from Vista Business, is available to SA licensees only. Enterprise is aimed at mid- to larger-size companies and includes full-volume encryption and support for Virtual PC Express, allowing users to run legacy apps in a virtual machine. Microsoft's Desktop Optimization Pack (MDOP), which includes various management and deployment tools—plus SoftGrid application virtualization support—is also a SA benefit only.

Another example: Windows Fundamentals for Legacy PCs (the Windows SKU formerly code-named *Eiger*). Windows Fundamentals, available only to SA customers, is a Windows release based on WindowsXP Embedded Service Pack 2. It's a "bridge solution" that allows customers running older versions of Windows to get new security and manageability without having to upgrade (for a while) to XP or Vista.

Microsoft also has been dangling the offer of "extended lifecycle hotfix support" over customers' heads since July 2005 as yet another way to convince them to move to SA. Extended hotfix support allows users of products that are no longer covered by Microsoft under regular support to obtain continued hotfix support for a reduced rate. SA includes the annual fees for this service as part of the standard SA benefit and also waives the requirement that customers sign up within 90 days of when a product transitions to "Extended Support." Products covered by extended hotfix support include Windows Client and Server, Office Professional, Microsoft Exchange Server, and Microsoft SQL Server, among others.

Microsoft has made some vague statements regarding its SA plans in the future. In 2010, when it is slated to ship Windows 7, Microsoft is expected by many company watchers to make more of the supplementary Windows consumer and business services available to SA licensees only. Analysts with Gartner Inc. went so far as to predict that Microsoft might attempt to make Software Assurance completely mandatory by 2009.[19]

While I doubt that Microsoft—or its customers—is ready to go to such extreme measures (at least within the next few years), there is no doubt that

---

[19] While Gartner Group is one of the most respected of the market research firms in technology—and a favorite of Microsoft and several Microsoft customers—a number of Gartner's predictions on Windows have been off-base over the past couple of years. So I take Gartner's claims regarding Microsoft's Software Assurance becoming mandatory by 2009 with a hefty serving of salt. Microsoft has denied Gartner's contention, as noted here: www.zdnetasia.com/news/software/0,39044164,39374825,00.htm.

Microsoft is going to turn the SA screws more tightly to get more of its customer base to move to the annuity model. The annuity model undeniably gives Microsoft a more predictable and more profitable revenue stream.

Online Services: Past Is Prologue

Microsoft's revenue model is poised to be turned on its head in the next few years. And online services is the biggest reason why.

Until recently, "online revenues" for Microsoft meant the money the company earned from providing users with Internet access to consumers. To a much lesser extent, it also included sales of "premium services," like Microsoft Money, Encarta, Bill Pay, and Radio Plus. In 2002, Microsoft also started to garner some modest online revenues from its Xbox Live gaming service, services it sells through the Microsoft Small Business Center portal, and services and content it sells on a subscription basis through the Microsoft Developer Network.

In the next two to three years, Microsoft is planning that its online services revenues will be a significant contributor to its bottom line. Microsoft started in 2006 to provide advertisers a platform for online advertising built around Web search. Microsoft is selling advertisers placement on some very well-trafficked web sites and services—everything from MSN, to Xbox Live, to Windows Live, and Office Live.

> *"Until recently, 'online revenues' for Microsoft meant the money the company earned from providing users with Internet access to consumers."*

In 2007, Microsoft added contextual advertising to the services it offered. It also purchased for $6 billion aQuantive, the former Avenue A/Razorfish advertising agency and tools provider. aQuantive gives Microsoft an ad network, its own Atlas platform, with its own algorithms and advertisers; and the self-described "world's largest digital media ad agency." And in 2008, capping off its online-services buying spree, Microsoft made its much-publicized bid to acquire No. 2 search vendor Yahoo.

Microsoft officials have said that the search and online advertising worlds have converged already. That's why the Redmondians have been snapping up advertising-related companies (and losing bids to acquire a few others, like

DoubleClick, which Google jumped in and moved to purchase in 2007) like crazy. Platforms & Services President, Kevin Johnson, laid out Microsoft's online-advertising game plan quite succinctly:

> adCenter enabled the buy-sell capability for paid keywords. We attracted advertisers. We exceeded the RPS (revenue per search) that we were getting on Overture in this last year. And we are now expanding adCenter into content ads. In the first quarter of this fiscal year, we're rolling out content ads across our own network, and by the end of the fiscal year, we will have this available for third-party publishers.[20]

Advertising already is becoming more of a central component to many of Microsoft's businesses, including gaming, mobile, and video/music delivery. Especially on the gaming side of the house, Microsoft is dabbling with "experiential marketing," whereby content is integrated inextricably with advertising—for example, the Xbox 360 program Microsoft did with Burger King, via which Microsoft helped create $3.99 games that integrated advertising with content. Burger King sold 3.2 million of these games in six weeks—enough to have an impact on their financial results.[21]

> *"Over the next few years, Microsoft officials believe that they can grow the company to be 'one of the top two' in the online-advertising space."*

For Microsoft's online services business, 2007 was a "foundational" year, in terms of putting its new online-ad-focused platform in place. But that isn't

---

[20] Kevin Johnson, the head of Microsoft's Platforms & Services unit, spent his 45 minutes addressing Wall Street analysts and press at the annual Financial Analyst Meeting (FAM) in 2007 talking about Microsoft's aspirations in advertising (and saying almost nothing about its plans for its bread-and-butter "platforms"). The full text of Johnson's FAM remarks is here: www.microsoft.com/msft/speech/FY07/JohnsonFAM2007.mspx.

[21] Collateral explaining the Microsoft–Burger King collaboration around gaming/advertising is here: http://advertising.microsoft.com/xbox-burger-king.

deterring Microsoft from some big Yahoo-colored dreams. Over the next few years, Microsoft officials believe that they can grow the company to be "one of the top two" in the online-advertising space.[22]

Whether Microsoft can achieve such lofty goals with advertising and a number of its other, newer diversification projects, seems iffy. But if the company fails to build serious market share in the advertising, mobile, online services, and entertainment markets, it won't be for lack of trying. In Chapter 7, I'll share more about how Microsoft thinks it can lessen its dependence on its sacred Windows and Office cash cows in the coming years.

---

[22] Another quote of note from Services & Platforms President Johnson from FAM. Full text is here: www.microsoft.com/msft/speech/FY07/JohnsonFAM2007.mspx.

Microsoft 2.0: Untried but Unavoidable Business Models

7

Will Microsoft be the platform that people want to escape to, or will they be the platform that people want to escape from? Currently they are the platform that people want to escape from, because they are the platform that restricts freedom rather than gives it.

If Microsoft wants to be where the action is, they need to get back to giving people the freedom (and the tools) to do whatever they want.

—"Microsoft 2.0, Now with Less Bubba,"
Mini-Microsoft, October 3, 2007 post

Microsoft has made and still is making—as of this writing—billions of dollars via its existing business models. This year, the company is still counting on being able to turn substantial profits primarily from OEM preloads, volume license deals, and partner bundles. But soon, even the most futuristically conservative Microsoft backers agree that the world will be turned on its head in all of the markets in which Microsoft is fielding products. Software is giving way to services. Social networking is becoming de rigueur for consumers and businesses. And users are becoming increasingly unwilling to be penned in by vendors who won't make their products truly interoperable with offerings from others.

Make no mistake: For at least the next three to five years, regardless of what its competitors do, Microsoft is not going to trade in software for services completely. Such a move would be disastrous for the company from a financial perspective. Regardless of how convincing the Web 2.0-crazed venture capitalists, Google lovers, and other cheerleaders are, don't believe any prognostications that claim Microsoft is ready to roll out an entirely Web-based version of its full Office suite any day now. And even though it shelled out billions to take over Yahoo, Microsoft still isn't going to dump suddenly all of its software businesses and attempt to monetize services only.

Instead, Microsoft will continue beating the Software + Services (S+S) drum, claiming that it makes more sense for customers to use a combination of local and cloud-based offerings.

> *"In this Redmondian rose-colored world, users wield 'the power to choose what's right' for them in terms of business models and deployment strategies."*

Microsoft is positioning S+S as just one point along a "services continuum."[1] In this Redmondian rose-colored world, users wield "the power to choose what's right" for them in terms of business models and deployment strategies. For some users, according to Microsoft, "ownership"/perpetual licensing makes the most sense. For others, a flat-fee subscription is the preferred option. And for others, a metered subscription model is the best fit. Some customers will prefer to keep their software/services "on-premise" in their own data centers. Others will opt for Internet cloud storage. And while some customers will insist that their own corporate IT departments are the only ones administering their software/services/data, others will be fine with relegating this task to an application service provider or hoster.

Sounds good, but isn't S+S just SaaS (Software as a Service) in a Microsoft-logo'd polo shirt? No, argues Microsoft Technology Evangelism Manager Dan Kasun, as well as several other industry watchers. Kasun blogged about the distinction:

> *The benefits to S+S come in the capability to be more modular in implementation—which allows easier integration with complex business processes and a better opportunity to provide functional, productive user interfaces. That is, you can implement S+S in a way that molds to your business and users—rather than forcing*

---

[1] There's a nice, succinct explanation of Microsoft's concept of the Software + Services (S+S) continuum on the Microsoft .Net Interop blog here: `http://blogs.msdn.com/dotnetinterop/archive/2007/05/16/project-astoria-s-s-and-interop.aspx`.

your business and users to conform to your service platform (as is often seen in SAAS models).

In addition, S+S provides a great environment for aggregate business models where several organizations provide disparate services and several other organizations provide the software that provides user interfaces and aggregation of the services. As an ISV or other participant is this ecosystem, you can focus on delivering the best-of-breed functionality based on your competencies, rather than trying to deliver absolutely everything your clients will need.[2]

But even if S+S ends up being seen and believed to be superior to SaaS, Microsoft faces a substantial challenge in moving to the myriad new business models that are taking hold across the industry, while making sure not to completely kill off demand for its existing products as sold through existing channels. Like any company moving to a new modus operandi, Microsoft also needs to strike a balance of moving neither too fast nor too slow.

> *"Microsoft must avoid several obstacles as it moves from the old way of doing business to the new."*

Former Microsoft Chief Operating Officer Bob Herbold outlined in his 2007 book *Seduced by Success* the "nine traps every successful organization must avoid."[3] Although he doesn't call out Microsoft by name in his guidance, it's apparent that he was looking right at the Redmondians in compiling his talking points. Microsoft must avoid several obstacles as it moves from the old way of doing business to the new, including (as Herbold so aptly defined):

- **Neglect**—Sticking with yesterday's business model

---

[2] Microsoft Technology Evangelism Manager, Dan Kasun, also has a readable blog post that takes a stab at a definition of S+S: http://blogs.msdn.com/dankasun/archive/2007/09/24/so-what-is-this-s-s-thing.aspx.

[3] From Robert Herbold, *Seduced by Success* (McGraw-Hill, April 2007). Herbold's list of pitfalls that companies would do well to avoid can be found here: www.leighbureau.com/speaker.asp?id=230.

- **Pride**—Letting products and services become second rate
- **Boredom**—Clinging to your once successful branding
- **Complexity**—Letting processes run the business
- **Bloat**—Losing agility
- **Mediocrity**—Allowing sub-par performance to persist
- **Lethargy**—Nurturing a retirement home culture
- **Timidity**—Permitting turf battles and infighting
- **Vagueness**—Schizophrenic communication

Definitely a tall order—almost on a par with combating torpor, greed, and jealousy. Add in the fact that Microsoft is moving to not just one or two new business models, but a whole slew of them, and all simultaneously, and you have a good view of why CEO Steve Ballmer has his work cut out for him as the next decade begins.

There are a few more points to ponder before delving into Microsoft's next-gen business models. Many Microsoft watchers see Microsoft as:

1. Failing to acknowledge that business models/markets are changing.
2. Being reluctant to move to new business models.
3. Hoping all these newfangled ways of doing business just disappear.

All of these are fallacies.

Microsoft knows quite well that the tech market is mutating, and ever more rapidly. If you doubt that, go back and look at Chief Software Architect Ray Ozzie's 2005 "Internet Services Disruption" memo. Sure, Ozzie was outlining a battle plan that was new to many Softies at the time. But Microsoft's top brass has known for the past few years that a change is gonna come. Although it has gotten next-to-no credit for adapting to new market forces, Microsoft actually has changed its business models on several fronts since Ozzie's memo hit in October 2005.

That said, complete change isn't going to happen overnight. Most of Microsoft's business units (with the exceptions of Home and Entertainment and Developer Division) typically take multiple years to shift gears. Look at how long it is taking Microsoft to figure out what to do with Microsoft Works, its low-end productivity suite. More than two years ago, Microsoft officials were talking about possibly turning Works into a service.[4] In mid-2007, Microsoft went public with its plans to field a year-long test of not a Works service, but an ad-funded version of Works. Microsoft won't decide whether or not to field a commercially available ad-funded Works product until 2009, at the earliest.

Oftentimes, industry watchers equate "new and innovative business model" with anything that Google/Apple/open-source vendors are doing. Microsoft officials have admitted (usually begrudgingly) that they have and continue to look to business models pioneered by its competitors for inspiration. But Microsoft is not Google, Apple, or Red Hat. It's a company that encompasses products that compete with all three of these companies—

> *"Most of Microsoft's business units (with the exceptions of Home and Entertainment and Developer Division) typically take years to shift gears."*

plus offerings from IBM, Oracle, Salesforce.com, Facebook, Intuit, Adobe, Nintendo, and more. Microsoft needs to figure out strategies to compete with gaming vendors, search-engine developers, online-advertising bigwigs, line-of-business application companies, and the like. It's not a one-business-model-fits-all world—at least not for Microsoft.

Compare that reality to Google, as explained by a story in an August 2007 issue of *The Economist* on Google's business model:

> *Google's success still comes from one main source: the small text ads placed next to its search results and on other web pages. The advertisers pay only when consumers click on those ads. "All that money comes 50 cents at a time," says Hal Varian, Google's chief economist.[5]*

---

[4] "Microsoft Brings the Works Online," *BusinessWeek's* take on how Microsoft planned to turn Microsoft Works into a Web-based product, was published in September 2006 (www.businessweek.com/technology/content/sep2006/tc20060914_764614.htm?chan=top+news_top+news+index_businessweek+exclusives). In 2008, Microsoft still has yet to make this move. Instead, all the company has done with Works is field a pilot of a free, ad-based version, while continuing to sell a paid version. But many Microsoft watchers still believe that Microsoft's intention remains to deliver a Web-based version of Works at some point.

[5] From "Inside the Googleplex," *The Economist*, August 30, 2007. www.economist.com/opinion/displaystory.cfm?story_id=9719610.

If only Microsoft could be so laser-focused. But it can't and it isn't. Instead, Microsoft is experimenting with lots of different business models as it moves into the post-Gates era. On the short list (in no particular order):

- Software rental
- Try before you buy
- Online marketplaces
- Ad-funded/Search
- Royalty/IP licensing
- Shared source/Open source
- Attracting amateurs/hobbyists
- Closed hardware ecosystems
- Virtualization

Microsoft's Yahoo acquisition—if and when it is consumated—will definitely and obviously impact Microsoft's ad-funded/search strategy, and to a lesser extent, its "try before you buy," online marketplaces and possibly its open-source models. But it won't derail Microsoft's existing business plans, especially in the other areas on this business-model short-list, I'd argue.

In this chapter, I'll delve into all of these business models that I've labeled as unavoidable and mostly untried—by Microsoft, that is. As seemingly disparate as they are, all of them are likely to have an influence on Microsoft's bottom line in the next few years.

Office (and Windows) for Rent...Cheap?

There are some who would argue that Microsoft already rents all of its software to users. If you look at the fine print in Microsoft's licensing agreements, you could make a case to that effect, given that Microsoft grants users permission to use Windows, Office, and other Microsoft products for only so long as their licenses last. And isn't Software Assurance—Microsoft's volume-licensing program that provides users with upgrades and members-only benefits over a three-year period—basically a "rental" program, as well?

But Microsoft is looking to take the rental concept a lot further, as it moves into the Software + Services space. Services can be monetized in a variety of ways, including paid monthly/yearly subscriptions. A number of Microsoft's competitors have been at the forefront of offering a subscription/services model. Salesforce.com has built its entire business around this model.

Microsoft, while a relative newcomer to the paid-subscription space, does have a few offerings already in its stable. Xbox Live, Microsoft's paid gaming service for Xbox console users, arguably is its most successful. As of January 2008, Microsoft said it had signed up 10 million Xbox Live licensees.

Office Live—in spite of Microsoft's decision earlier this year to cease charging a monthly fee for the base service itself—is still one of the areas where Microsoft is doing the most experimentation in the paid subscription space.

> *"Microsoft is looking to take the rental concept a lot further, as it moves into the Software + Services space."*

Until February 2008, Office Live Basics, Microsoft's entry-level Office service, was its only freebie. Office Live Essentials, Microsoft's mid-level small-business services offering, sold for $19.95 a month. The higher-end Office Live Premium was $39.95 a month. In February, Microsoft, citing customer confusion, collapsed these three different Office Live Small Business SKUs into a single, free Office Live Small Business product. Instead of making money off the base Office Live Small Business services, Microsoft decided to charge for supplementary add-ons, like its Store Manager e-commerce service (now $39.95 per month). If and when users no longer subscribe to the free and/or paid services, they lose access to all of these services—and the data they've parked in them.

(A related offering, Office Live Groove—a team-collaboration product that Microsoft has done little to evangelize—sells for $79.95 per month.)

Windows Live OneCare is another example of an existing paid Microsoft subscription service. OneCare, an antivirus/antispyware/back-up service, costs $49.95 a month for coverage of up to three PCs. The hook? When and if you stop paying, your backed-up data are no longer available to you, and your PC is no longer spyware/phishing-protected.

Paid service subscriptions aren't the only rental model Microsoft is implementing. Outside the United States, the company is testing other kinds of rental programs.

FlexGo, the initial trial of which Microsoft rolled out in May 2006 in conjunction with a group of hardware, telecommunications, retail, and financial services providers, is one such program. Microsoft has been testing the program in Brazil, India, Mexico, and Russia. FlexGo, as Microsoft initially envisioned it, offered customers a choice of a pay-as-you-go option or a simple monthly subscription model. After a year, it became apparent that financial institutions were not so interested in the pay-as-you-go option. Microsoft is planning to move to a subscription-only model in the next round of tests, which were set to commence in early 2008.[6] As part of the new FlexGo trials, users will also have a new option: to lease as a single bundle, Windows and Office, along with their PC hardware.

> "Microsoft also has been testing an Office rental program in a handful of countries outside the United States."

Under FlexGo, users make initial down payments for on mid-range PCs and make monthly payments for the systems, plus broadband services, from their local telcos, much the way customers pay cable providers for TV and Internet access. Microsoft and its partners will allow users to sign up and pay for their subscriptions in a variety of ways, ranging from ATMs and point-of-sale terminals to the Web. Starting this year, users will be able to rent any of the 32-bit Vista SKUs under the program.

FlexGo systems require activation and Windows Genuine Advantage authentication. Once subscribed, users will be reminded via notifications and account status screens, as to the amount of time they have remaining before their systems will move to "borrowed time," and, ultimately, a locked status for lack of payment. In order to unlock systems that have degraded because of lack of payment, users will need to obtain a code from the FlexGo partners.

Microsoft also has been testing an Office rental program in a handful of countries outside the United States. The initial pilot of the "Office Prepaid Trial" allowed select users in South Africa, Mexico, and Romania to pay a monthly rental fee of about $10 for Office 2003. Unlike the case with FlexGo, via which users lease hardware and software together, the Office Prepaid Trial offers Office only. Under terms of the trial, users must return to the system builders who sold them their original PC every time they want to buy three more months of Office-rental time. Users who don't re-up will see their copies of Office go into reduced functionality mode, allowing them to do nothing more than view their documents.

---

[6] For more on Microsoft's evolving thinking about its FlexGo subscription model, check out this blog post I did in May 2007: http://blogs.zdnet.com/microsoft/?p=445.

At the end of 2007, Microsoft expanded its Office rental trials in South Africa and Romania to include Office 2007. In South Africa, Microsoft is testing the option of renting Office 2007 for 199 rand (approximately $30) for a three-month period.

Will Microsoft eventually move to a monthly-rental model for software here in the United States? I've asked the Redmondians a few times in recent years and received the same reply: There are no immediate plans to do so. But no one has ruled out completely the possibility that Microsoft could introduce rental models for Windows, Office, and other products at some point in the future.

As noted in Chapter 6, Microsoft also has contemplated whether it might make more money by turning Windows into an ad-funded service.[7] Microsoft also is actively mulling how and if it can introduce a "pay-as-you-go" scheme for Windows, as evidenced by a patent for which the company applied back in 2005.[8] A core kernel operating system—perhaps something like the MinWin stripped-down Windows kernel[9] that has been developed by Microsoft's Core Operating System team and will be at the heart of Windows 7—would be supplemented by various add-on services, under the system outlined in the modular OS patent.

Providing software and services via subscriptions requires a lot of infrastructure on the back-end if it is to work properly. The Microsoft data centers in the cloud need to provide seemingly unlimited scalability, availability, and

---

[7] Read more about the Microsoft ThinkWeek paper from 2005 that examined the practicalities of turning Windows into an ad-funded service here: http://news.com.com/ Microsoft+eyes+making+desktop+apps+free/2100-1014_3-5951569.html?tag=nefd.top. Even though it's been three years since that paper was published, I'd wager that many of the concepts in it are still under active consideration.

[8] Further evidence that Microsoft is serious about subscription trials of all kinds comes in the form of the company's "Pay-As-You-Go" patent application. More on yet another Microsoft attempt at modularization can be found here: www.istartedsomething.com/20061215/ pay-as-you-go-os-patent/.

[9] Microsoft has been working on componentizing Windows for years. By making the operating system more modular, the company has been working toward slimming down and reducing the complexity of the Windows core. But in late 2007, the Softies acknowledged that they had managed to develop a working "MinWin" core that might be at the heart of Windows 7 when it ships around 2010. I have more details on what little we know so far about MinWin here: http://blogs.zdnet.com/microsoft/?p=842.

reliability. And the supporting mechanisms—the billing systems, authorization/authentication systems, commerce systems, provisioning mechanisms, monitoring capabilities, patching, and so forth—aren't niceties. They're necessities.

> "*Microsoft is growing its data-center infrastructure like crazy.*"

Microsoft is using its cloud infrastructure to provide the backbone for all of its services properties—everything from its Xbox Live gaming service to its Microsoft Office Communications Server Online managed collaboration service. (Even the company's forthcoming HealthVault healthcare service will use the same cloud-computing fabric, with ultra-private patient information stored on separate, extra-secure servers in Microsoft's existing data centers.)

The backbone powering all of these services consists of four layers:[10]

- **Global Foundation Services**—The physical infrastructure that powers the cloud, including data centers, racks of disks, networks, and the people building and monitoring this infrastructure.
- **Cloud Infrastructure Services**—The computing, networking, and storage software layer—the "utility computing fabric." This is where storage, files systems, databases, and searchable storage all come into play.
- **Live Platform Services**—Identity and directory; device management and security; adCenter ad platform; communications and rendezvous and presence. (*Rendezvous*, in this context, means arranging a meeting via a contractual service.)
- **Applications and Solutions**—The services that will run on top of the infrastructure—things like connected entertainment, document sharing and collaboration, hosted and Microsoft managed services, and the like.

---

[10] At its Financial Analyst Meeting in late July 2007, the Softies outlined for the first time publicly and officially the four cloud-computing pillars. Platforms & Services chief Kevin Johnson's explanation of them is here: www.microsoft.com/msft/speech/FY07/JohnsonFAM2007.mspx.

For security reasons, Microsoft won't release stats on exactly how many data centers it has, where they are located, and/or how many servers they house. But like Google, Yahoo, and other online powerhouses, Microsoft is growing its data-center infrastructure like crazy. The company has been researching the concept of portable data centers housed in mobile shipping containers in the name of scalability and portability.[11]

The Live teams—Windows Live, Office Live, CRM Live, and so on—are in the midst of trying to coordinate better its resources, product development, and product marketing across these layers, as well as across groups. As of this writing, the centralized Windows Live team was beginning its planning process for what it's calling *Wave 3*, which is the set of products/technologies/ services due in the next year-plus. (There are Waves 4 and 5 on the drawing board already, too.)

With Wave 3, the Live team is working to hide further the seams between MSN, Live Search, and the other Windows Live services. Wave 3 services will be more mobile-centric, more presence-imbued, and more open to third-party social networks (starting with Windows Live Spaces and Facebook, not surprisingly).

Don't Buy before You Try

The implementation of try-before-you-buy programs doesn't seem like an especially revolutionary or noteworthy strategy. But Chief Software Architect, Ray Ozzie, saw these trial offers as important enough to call out specifically in his "Internet Services Disruption" memo back in 2005. Ozzie opined:

> *It's now expected that anything discovered can be sampled and experienced through self-service exploration and download. This is true not just for consumer products: Even enterprise products now more often than not enter an organization through the inter- net-based research and trial of a business unit that understands a product's value.*

---

[11] Microsoft database expert, James Hamilton, has been doing a lot of research around how mobile storage containers can be used to house portable, scalable data centers. A white paper detailing some of his thinking around modular, commodity data-center design can be found here: `http://research.microsoft.com/~jamesrh/TalksAndPapers/JamesRH_ ModularDataCenterDesign.ppt`. Microsoft is just one of several tech vendors contemplating using storage containers in this way.

*Limited trial use, ad-monetized or free reduced-function use,
subscription-based use, on-line activation, digital license management, automatic update, and other such concepts are now entering
the vocabulary of any developer building products that wish to
successfully utilize the web as a channel. Products must now
embrace a "discover, learn, try, buy, recommend" cycle—sometimes with one of those phases being free, another ad-supported,
and yet another being subscription-based.*[12]

Ozzie has been proven right a few times since penning that memo.
Example No. 1: Office. Office 2007 has been selling like hotcakes since
Microsoft released the product to manufacturing in late 2006. Microsoft and
various company watchers have attributed a substantial part of the strong
sales to Microsoft's try-before-you-buy programs, introduced around the time
of the Office 2007 launch in late January 2007.

A September 2007 report by News.com explained:

*"Microsoft is now the second largest retailer of its own productiv-
ity suite," said NPD analyst Chris Swenson. It's not that people
are going to Microsoft.com and clicking buy. Rather, they are opt-
ing to buy a product code from Microsoft after using trial versions
of the software.*[13]

Direct sales are a new, additional source of Office income for Microsoft.
And while many people consider free trials loaded on new PCs as "crapware,"
meriting immediate removal, others are willing to give free trials a whirl.
Given that Microsoft is stepping up its campaign to convince PC makers to
preload Office on new machines, it's not so farfetched an idea that free trials
are gaining influence on Microsoft's business-software front.

---

[12] This and more excerpts from Chief Software Architect's October 2005 Internet Services
Disruption blueprint can be found in the memos in Appendix A.

[13] NPD analyst, Chris Swenson, unearthed some interesting new sales trends with Office
2007. Specifically, Microsoft is selling a lot more copies via retailers and PC makers than it
had with previously released versions. In fact, in comparing the first six months of sales of
Office 2007 with the same period for Office 2003, Microsoft sold twice as many copies of
its new suite through retail. More on NPD's numbers can be found here: www.news.com/
Running-the-numbers-on-Vista/2100-1016_3-6207375.html.

Another example: Concurrent with its launch, Microsoft made Expression Encoder (the tool formerly known as Expression Media Encoder) available as a free trial downloadable. The trial required users to have a valid Windows Live ID for authentication.

> *"Ozzie has been proven right a few times since penning that memo."*

The fully functioning version was set to expire in 60 days. Another: Microsoft Forefront security products are available in free-trial-download form. This includes everything from Forefront Client Security, to Forefront Security for Exchange Server, to Forefront Security for SharePoint Server.

Microsoft is using a slightly modified tack to encourage users to try Vista before they buy it. The Try Windows Vista (`www.windowsvistatestdrive.com`) site allows users to test both Vista consumer and business features in a simulated environment. The site is powered by Microsoft Virtual Labs and is aimed at small- to mid-size customers. All users need to do is have a browser to see and experience Vista features, ranging from automatic backup scheduling to BitLocker drive encryption. The actual Vista bits (even a subset of them) are never actually installed on the user's PC. A link at the bottom of the site allows users to move from "test" to "buy" with relative ease.

As is the case with Office, Microsoft is looking to free trial versions of its various other software products as an incremental revenue source, not a replacement source. Every additional copy of a product you can end up selling means that one less potentially pirated—or ignored—release is out in the wild.

Online Marketplaces: Electronic Software Distribution Comes of Age

Microsoft has been experimenting with online marketplaces for years but only recently has gotten serious about figuring out what makes them tick. These marketplaces are evolving into a key component of Microsoft's "Find, Try, Buy" strategy.

The success of the Xbox Live Marketplace—Microsoft's online exchange, launched in 2005, for buying/selling any kinds of Xbox games, trailers, and the like—has whetted the Redmondians' appetite for other kinds of online stores/malls. It also has resulted in Microsoft better understanding the concept of micro-transactions, or "points," and how they play in the online-commerce environment.

Showing just how serious it is about building on the points system, Microsoft Chairman Bill Gates himself applied for a patent in March 2006 for a points system—specifically "a mechanism is provided to confirm transactions even without monitoring them, e.g., by issuing perishable, non-redeemable points to a merchant based upon an advertising budget." The patent went on to explain that

> [T]he points can then be issued as redeemable points to a customer, e.g., based upon [when] the customer makes a purchase from the merchant. Points transferred to the customer can verify that a transaction occurred, and can be redeemed for products/services, including a convenient "micro-payment" mechanism.[14]

Microsoft has hinted that it has some ambitious expansion plans for its marketplaces. On the Xbox Live Marketplace, Microsoft has contemplated allowing users to redeem points for real-world objects, like hardware accessories, not just downloadable software and services. Microsoft officials also have committed to providing user-generated gaming content, at some point, on Xbox Live. Microsoft has said it will allow users to charge for this content, via micro-payments.

In the more immediate term, Microsoft is working to build out its partner ecosystem behind its various marketplaces. On the Office Live site, Microsoft is showcasing customized Office Live applications and mash-ups from the company and third-party developers. (The Office Marketplace site also provides a link enabling users to take Office 2007 for a virtual test drive without

---

[14] From the 2006 Microsoft points-related patent: "The claimed subject matter can provide a mechanism that facilitates a new advertising and/or referral architecture in the Internet advertising space, e.g., for advertising on search engine web pages and/or on content web pages. A mechanism is provided to confirm transactions even without monitoring them e.g., by issuing perishable, non-redeemable points to a merchant based upon an advertising budget. The points can then be issued as redeemable points to a customer, e.g., based upon the customer makes a purchase from the merchant. Points transferred to the customer can verify that a transaction occurred, and can be redeemed for products/services, including a convenient 'micro-payment' mechanism." The full patent application is here:
`http://appft1.uspto.gov/netacgi/nph-Parser?Sect1=PTO2&Sect2=HITOFF&u=%2Fnetahtml%`
`2FPTO%2Fsearch-adv.html&r=1&p=1&f=G&l=50&d=PG01&S1=20070179848.PGNR.&OS=dn/`
`20070179848&RS=DN/20070179848.`

having to install any Office bits on their machines, or download a test version with which to dabble.)

The Windows Marketplace is more fully developed and more similar to the Xbox Live Marketplace. Tabs on the site include Top Sellers, Experience Vista, Game Downloads, Security Downloads, and IE (Internet Explorer) add-ons. All kinds of different categories of software are featured on the site, ranging from mobile to music and video. Users can add desired purchases to their "wish lists," which are aggregated on the site. There are hundreds of thousands of paid and free products available on the Windows Marketplace.

Microsoft added in 2005 a software download facility, known as Digital Locker. Digital Locker is designed to allow users to authenticate securely (using Windows Live ID), enter credit card information, and download software onto one or more machines. Both Microsoft and third-party-developed products are available for electronic distribution using Digital Locker.

> *"Microsoft has been experimenting with online marketplaces for years but only recently has gotten serious about figuring out what makes them tick."*

Electronic software distribution (ESD) isn't a new idea. Microsoft has tried it a few times, as far back as in the Windows 95 time frame. So what keeps the Redmondians from giving up on the ESD channel? Xbox Live has shown the Softies that there is a way to build up the attach rate for add-on software products—even those costing just a few dollars—via software downloads. Microsoft is hoping to parlay the Xbox Live experience to similar successes in other software arenas.

In Search of the Best Way to Grow Search

There's no way to sugarcoat it: Google schooled Microsoft when it came to the lucrative potential of search. Microsoft is a quick study, but it has a long way to go to catch up in this space. Instead of letting its distant No. 3 ranking (behind Google and Yahoo) discourage the company from competing, Microsoft has continued to plug away at building its search share in order to strengthen its ability to earn money through search. Microsoft decided to fast-track its search share by attempting to acquire Yahoo—a transaction that had yet to be realized by the time this book went to press.

> *"Microsoft, like other players in the space, knows quite well that search can be parlayed directly into advertising revenues."*

Microsoft execs have spent the past couple of years attempting to grok the dynamics of the search market. Microsoft, like other players in the space, knows quite well that search can be parlayed directly into advertising revenues. The way this works, as explained by Microsoft Platforms & Services boss Kevin Johnson, is[15]

1. First, you need an online audience. To get audience, you need a combination of usage and depth of usage. (For Microsoft, this audience comes from MSN, Windows Live, Office Live, Xbox Live, etc.)
2. Audience aggregation creates inventory.
3. Inventory attracts advertisers and ad agencies.
4. These advertisers and ad agencies need an online ad platform to connect to the aforementioned audience.
5. The ad platform is about driving yield for publishers and return on investment for advertisers. It also is about driving workflow efficiencies in everything from campaign creation, to media planning, to media buying.

So where does search come into play? Paid search and paid keywords—at least for the time being—are the crux of online advertising and online ad platforms. As Google has proven, beyond a shadow of a doubt, paid search is profitable.

However, while Microsoft may have built up a solid pool of searchers since it jumped into the search market a couple of years ago, so far, those searchers

---

[15] Platforms & Services President, Kevin Johnson, walked Wall Streeters, step-by-step, through his view of how Microsoft can and plans to play in the paid-search marketplace during Microsoft's 2007 Financial Analyst Meeting. The transcript of his explanation: www.microsoft.com/msft/speech/FY07/JohnsonFAM2007.mspx.

haven't been doing much searching using the company's consumer search engine, Live Search (the product formerly known as Windows Live Search).

Throughout 2007, Microsoft's search-engine market share hovered around 11 to 13 percent (compared to Google's 50% and Yahoo's 25% shares).[16] According to Microsoft's internal estimates, by mid-2007, it had managed to get 30 percent of the total number of Web searchers to try Live Search. But these searchers were providing it with only a little more than 10 percent of all Web queries. Put another way: While Microsoft, with 230 million Web searchers, had nearly as many folks doing occasional searches with its Live Search engine as Yahoo (with 250 million Web searchers), it had nowhere the number of Web *searches* being done using its engine.[17]

> *"The Softies have experimented with 'gaming' the destination-search numbers via a couple of different programs, with mixed results."*

The vast majority of Web searches conducted to date have been *destination searches*, meaning that users go to a specific web page—like www.google.com, www.yahoo.com, or www.live.com—and type a query into the Search box to obtain results. Catching Google (or even Yahoo) in this arena—even if you could prove that your results were more thorough and accurate—is a tough task, as even Microsoft's own execs admit.

---

[16] Several research outlets track search-market share using an evolving set of metrics. ComScore, the most-often quoted of the search researchers, changed its computational engine in mid-2007. In spite of the new algorithm, Microsoft still hovered between third and fourth place (trailing Google, Yahoo, and, by some estimates, the Chinese Baidu search engine) throughout 2007. The introduction by Microsoft of the Live Search Club contests created a slight, temporary gain in the Softies' search share, but Microsoft still remained substantially behind Google and Yahoo in the search-share results.

[17] Microsoft officials admit they've lagged their competitors substantially in search share. But the Redmondians don't look quite so bad when the number of searchers (and not searches) is compared. Microsoft Search Business Unit General Manager, Brad Goldberg, said in mid-2007 that Microsoft had convinced a third of all searchers worldwide to try Windows Live. But because they didn't use Live Search consistently, Microsoft's search-query share hovered at 10 percent throughout last year. Read more on this dichotomy here: http://blogs.zdnet.com/microsoft/?p=579.

The Sofites have experimented with "gaming" the destination-search numbers via a couple of different programs, with mixed results. On the consumer side, Microsoft launched in mid-2007 the Live Search Club (with its pointed motto, "Changing the Game So Everybody Wins").[18] By playing one or more Live-Search-centric games (like Chicktionary, Dingbats, Clink), users earn rewards like T-shirts, copies of Microsoft products, Xboxes, and the like. They also can opt to use their points to donate to causes and charities of their choosing. While the Live Search Club helped goose Microsoft's search results one month last year, the promotion didn't seem to have a lasting effect.

On the Enterprise side, Microsoft instituted a "Microsoft Service Credits for Web Search" program last year, as well. Under that program, Microsoft paid a company a low, medium, or high fee (something between $2 and $10 per computer annually, plus a $25K "enrollment credit") for agreeing to get its users to try Microsoft's Live Search for their Web-querying needs for a year. By committing to additional incentives—such as making Internet Explorer the default browser; getting the CEO to send out e-mail encouragements to get users to switch, etc.—participating companies received increasingly greater payback. Microsoft planned to sign up 30 companies in North America, Europe, and Japan by the end of March 2007 to participate in the year-long trial program. Microsoft planned to target companies with a minimum of 5,000 PCs per organization for the Live Search and Windows Live Toolbar promotional trials.

Stepping Gingerly through the Minefield of Search Integration

Destination search is just one piece of the puzzle. Another is what Microsoft officials call *convenience search*. By embedding Live Search into its own sites and products—starting with two of the largest sites on the Web (www.MSN.com and www.Microsoft.com), Microsoft believed it might have more of a fighting chance to grow its search share.

During 2007, Microsoft officials noted repeatedly that convenience search would become more and more important to Microsoft's strategy—as well as to the growth of the search market as a whole. Somewhat confusingly, however, company officials have shown signs that Microsoft may be poised to change its claims—and its course—with Microsoft now banging the destination

---

[18] Microsoft's Live Search Club, which is focused on "Changing the Game So Everybody Wins," is here: http://club.live.com/. The site includes various Live-Search-based games and contests that encourage users to search more using Live Search in order to win prizes.

search drum again. I guess it all goes to show what a difference an acquisition like Yahoo can (potentially) make....

The importance of convenience search to growing overall search share was one of the biggest reasons Microsoft reversed course in regard to the future of MSN.com in 2007. While it looked at the start of last year as if Microsoft was moving away from investing any more money or resources into MSN, by the end of the year, it was apparent that Microsoft was looking to the 380-million-unique-users-per-month-strong MSN.com audience as a captive one for Live Searching.

On the product front, Microsoft is slowly but surely embedding Live Search and other Microsoft search technologies into its various wares.

> *"On the product front, Microsoft is slowly but surely embedding Live Search and other Microsoft search technologies into its various wares."*

Take "Tafiti," the Microsoft-developed showcase mash-up between Live Search and Silverlight that the company introduced in September 2007, for example. Tafiti allows users to store and share search results across multiple queries and sessions. While Microsoft has declined to discuss when, how, and if it plans to commercialize Tafiti, the Tafiti app/service is another way for Microsoft to increase visibility and use for Live Search.

Xbox Live is another arena where Microsoft has been actively looking to turn its six-million-plus-strong online gaming users into Live Searchers. The search engine on the Xbox Live site is "powered by Live Search."

Even in cases where the consumer-oriented Live Search isn't the optimal search solution, Microsoft is still looking to integrate other Microsoft-developed search technologies directly into its own products. Office SharePoint Server, for instance, includes a Microsoft-developed Enterprise search module. SharePoint's search is not based on Live Search, however; instead, it is a separate technology that Microsoft made part of the first release of SharePoint Portal Server in 2001, allowing users to search across text files, HTML files, TIFF files, computer-aided design files, PDFs, faxes, Office documents, and more. At one point, Microsoft was using this search technology to power a number of its other search-related sites and products, including MSN Search, the search facility built into Office, and so on.

Another example: Windows Vista integrates Microsoft's desktop search technology—a derivate of MSN Desktop Search known as *Instant Search* that allows users to search for files and messages on their PCs. Microsoft officials have said the company is planning to continue to enhance the search facility embedded in future iterations of Windows, and moved the "Casino" desktop search team from the Windows Live unit directly into the Windows group in late 2006 to work on that project.

> *"Microsoft has been required to proceed with caution. That's one of the biggest reasons why Microsoft didn't end up integrating its Windows Live Services directly into Vista."*

If Microsoft had its way, it no doubt would have integrated Live Search and other home-grown search technologies into all of its current products and sites, buoying its search presence many times over by now. But given all the legal scrutiny that its bundling practices have attracted in the United States and abroad by the U.S. Department of Justice, state attorneys general, the European Union, the Japanese FTC (and, behind the scenes, its rivals), Microsoft has been required to proceed with caution. That's one of the biggest reasons why Microsoft didn't end up integrating its Windows Live Services directly into Vista; instead, it provided links to Live Services downloads via a startup screen.

In 2007, to head off a new potential antitrust suit, Microsoft agreed to change the search facility integrated in Vista to give third-party search engines equal access and compatibility. With Vista Service Pack (SP) 1, Microsoft introduced several changes to Vista to appease (primarily) Google and released search-protocol documentation to help third-party search providers implement the changes. The Redmondians changed preferred search results, delivered via the Vista Start Menu and Explorer, to display not just Microsoft's integrated Vista search, but other options, as well.

A New Business Model for Online Advertising?

While search makes the current paid advertising world go round, Microsoft is—not surprisingly—hoping a new metric might supplant search in the not-too-distant future. And, again, unsurprisingly, it's counting on technological advances to help develop new alternatives.

In the fall of 2007, Microsoft officials began planting the seed of its contention that search may not be the most accurate way to measure advertising effectiveness. Brian McAndrews, Senior Vice President of Microsoft's Advertiser and Publisher Solutions (APS) Group, told the *The New York Times* that Microsoft was trying to decouple online advertising from Web search. Instead of tying advertising to search results, Microsoft is proposing a new ad-measurement system called *conversion attribution*, which

> would track all of the online places where consumers see ads and give advertisers a fuller picture of the various ways that consumers reach them. Tracking is important, because the site that gets credit for prompting a user's visit is the one that gets paid for it.[19]

Microsoft's claim: Users don't necessarily click on an ad because they discovered it via Google's search engine. Consumers often check out a product after seeing information about it elsewhere. The Atlas division of Microsoft's aQuantive subsidiary has been working on technology that will allow advertisers to see "a log of all the places on the Internet where people see ads before going to the advertisers' Web sites," *The New York Times* said. The data Microsoft is looking to collect are "based on individual computers' electronic signatures, not individual people," officials said.

In February 2008, Microsoft announced that its proposed ad-measurement metric would be called "Engagement Mapping." And its "Engagement ROI" (return on investment) is a new integrated reporting capability for the Atlas Media Console, one of aQuantive's ad platforms that is now owned by Microsoft. The private beta kicked off in early March 2008.

> *"Microsoft's claim: Users don't necessarily click on an ad because they discovered it via Google's search engine."*

Another avenue for Microsoft to change the advertising metric game is in the authentication space, officials have hinted. What if advertisers were more interested in the number of authenticated users an advertising platform vendor offered, than in the total number of users—many of whom may use an online service sporadically or

---

[19] Former aQuantive CEO and current head of Microsoft's Advertiser and Publisher Solutions, Brian McAndrews, defined *conversion attribution* and explained why Microsoft believes it is a more accurate traffic measure in this fall 2007 interview with *The New York Times*: www.nytimes.com/2007/09/26/technology/26adco.html?_r=1&oref=slogin.

even once and then never again. Microsoft's newest incarnation of its Web-authentication system is known as Windows Live ID. By mid-2007, Microsoft claimed 380 million active Windows Live IDs, meaning that users needed to sign into one or more Microsoft services every 30 days to keep them active. (Microsoft claimed that Yahoo was at 245 million active registered users, and Google at 75 million signed-in users by mid-year last year.)

Platform & Services boss, Kevin Johnson, emphasized this importance of a registered, active user base to advertisers during Microsoft's Financial Analyst Meeting last year:

> Live IDs in these services are sticky. People sign on and they use these services because it's about contacts that are important to them, data that's important to them, information and their profile in services that they use that's important to individuals. So it's a very sticky service. … We can drive what I call direct revenue per live ID, the display ads or the in-screen videos or the searches done from these services as well as indirect revenue for Live ID. Indirect revenue per Live ID is as they come into the network, our ability to route traffic and flow them to other services, other parts of the network creates another revenue monetization opportunity.[20]

Further out, Microsoft is investigating other ways to make search more targeted and predictive. The company's adCenter Labs employ more than 100 researchers and developers to look at how technology can improve paid search, behavioral targeting, contextual advertising, social-network analysis, and image/video mining. The results of this work will be poured back into adCenter, Microsoft's online advertising platform, which as of mid-2007, supported 80,000-plus advertisers. Among some of the kinds of tools developed by adCenter Labs: ExplorerMSN, a tool for analyzing publisher web-site content and its audience to provide advertisers insights for ad placement and targeting; a keyword extraction tool that will allow advertisers to extract in an automated fashion representative keywords from web page content, and a tool to deliver ads on social networks.

---

[20] As you can probably tell, Microsoft Platforms & Services, Kevin Johnson, talked about almost nothing other than Microsoft's online advertising plans at the 2007 Financial Analyst Meeting. His comments on how to build stickiness in online services is part of those same remarks, which can be found here: www.microsoft.com/msft/speech/FY07/JohnsonFAM2007.mspx.

The Future of MicroHoo in Microsoft's Future

In early February 2008, Microsoft took an unprecedented—and controversial—step to shore up its online-advertising presence by making a hostile takeover bid for Yahoo. Even if Microsoft is successful in its bid for a company that has rebuffed the Redmond software maker's various buy-out and partnership attempts for the past couple of years, it's too soon to know whether Yahoo will provide all the search, datacenter, services, and advertising inventory from which Microsoft believed it would benefit when it initially made its take-over bid.

One thing's for sure: if the acquisition passes shareholder approval, as well as antitrust hurdles (which wasn't a done deal at the time I had to submit my manuscript for this book), Microsoft will be a very different company from what it is now.

If Microsoft manages to successfully add Yahoo to its mix, online services—and specifically online advertising—will become more than a struggling side business for Microsoft. Microsoft's pitch: A Yahoo acquisition will allow Microsoft to take advantage of scaled economies in search, online advertising, and the data-center infrastructure to run online advertising and other Web-based services.

Microsoft has been beefing up its online-advertising-focused investments for months now by buying a variety of smaller companies that own pieces of the online advertising pie. Until now, the biggest acquisition Microsoft had ever made was $6 billion for online-advertising powerhouse aQuantive, which Microsoft bought in 2007. While that buy had substantial impact on Microsoft's overall strategy and priorities, it still didn't result in Microsoft becoming more of an advertising vendor than a software vendor.

But a Yahoo seemingly would change Microsoft's business mix far more quickly than Ballmer and other Softies have been projecting. Will Microsoft end up spinning off its Yahoo unit as a separate, independent subsidiary? Will it kill off Yahoo offerings that are redundant with Windows Live, MSN,

> *"If Microsoft manages to successfully add Yahoo to its mix, online services—and specifically online advertising—will become more than a struggling side business for Microsoft."*

Microsoft adCenter, and other existing Microsoft properties? There are more questions than answers right now. I'll speculate on some potential scenarios in the Conclusion to this book, "Microsoft 3.0."

Adding Up Microsoft's Ad-Funded Wares

Whether or not Microsoft somehow breaks free of the search-result-centric/pay-per-click advertising model, the company is leaving no advertising stone unturned. Microsoft CEO Steve Ballmer has said that within a few years, Microsoft expects as much as a quarter of its revenues to come from advertising. (And he said that before Microsoft made its acquisition bid for Yahoo.)

> *"Microsoft also is testing whether users will tolerate ads in certain software products in exchange for them being free."*

The company has been experimenting with making a number of its fledgling services ad-funded. Officials have said they're considering making Microsoft's Popfly mash-up tool ad-funded. And Microsoft's patient-information service/software, HealthVault, also is likely to rely on ad-funding in order to keep the service free for consumers, officials said last year. (Currently, the beta of HealthVault doesn't target Web results or the ads based on data in a user's HealthVault record, but Microsoft hasn't ruled out these possibilities.)

Microsoft also is testing whether users will tolerate ads in certain software products in exchange for them being free. Microsoft is testing a pilot of an ad-funded version of its low-end desktop-productivity suite, Microsoft Works. The pilot version is being distributed by a select group of OEMs who are pre-loading it on new systems. The trial was set to end in mid-2008—at which time Microsoft will decide whether to make an ad-funded Works an option alongside the $40 ad-free version of the product.

Ad-funded software and services is just the tip of the Microsoft advertising iceberg, however. Other areas where Microsoft's been beefing up its advertising stable:

- **Mobile Advertising**—In May 2007, Microsoft acquired European-based mobile-phone advertising company ScreenTonic. It also purchased in mid-2007, MotionBridge, another mobile-search vendor.

- **In-Game Advertising**—In 2006, Microsoft bought Massive Inc. to help the company embed ads in games.
- **Widgets**—Microsoft is encouraging its partners to build Vista gadgets that are elaborate, interactive ads.
- **Community-Based Mash-ups**—Microsoft is seeking new ways to get members of its Live communities to build mash-ups around ads. They want to find a way to repeat the success of the Microsoft "Gears of War" trailer that took on a mash-up life of its own on YouTube.
- **Voice-Activated Search**—In March 2007, Microsoft bought TellMe, a mobile search service that responds to voice commands..
- **Vertical Search**—Microsoft bought health-search-vendor MedStory in February 2007, enabling it to add more integrated health results into Live Search, as well as launch a new, more health-search-focused service, HealthVault. It sounds like Microsoft plans to add more vertical search sites in the future.
- **Ad Exchanges**—In July 2007, Microsoft acquired AdECN, a company that provides an auction exchange for display ads.

Licensing (and Protecting) IP Is Big Business

While the Softies are looking to advertising as a future moneymaker, IP protection and licensing is already starting to line the company's coffers. IP licensing is so core to Microsoft now that it is called out specifically on its "About Microsoft" section of its Microsoft.com site under the "Business Model" section:

> The Microsoft business model also embodies respect for the rights of innovative companies and individuals worldwide. To survive and grow, local ICT (information and communications technology) industries must be able to protect their innovations and reap the benefits from widespread use of the technology they create. Protecting intellectual property rights and building local ICT industries and economies also enables governments to benefit from their ongoing support of education, research, and technology development. The tax revenue governments derive from a growing economy can then be reinvested to provide more community services.

> *At Microsoft, we have seen how the development opportunities for local ICT industries can be diminished by software licensing schemes that do not provide economic incentives for innovation, or that create disincentives by requiring innovators to give up all rights to their work. Conversely, commerce in intellectual property within a legal framework can stimulate innovation and local economic development. We work closely with governments and law enforcement agencies around the world to help them develop or strengthen laws that protect intellectual property and promote economic development.*
>
> *Microsoft has paid hundreds of millions of dollars in licensing fees to companies around the world for the right to incorporate some of their technologies into its own products. In fiscal year 2004, we also announced a program to license Microsoft's intellectual property more broadly, on fair and reasonable terms, as a way to assist innovators and companies around the world.*[21]

In 2003, Microsoft hired Marshall Phelps from IBM, where he helped Big Blue create a patent-generation revenue program in the mid-1980s. Phelps oversees Microsoft's intellectual property (IP) groups—which are responsible for trademarks, trade secrets, patents, licensing, standards, and copyrights.

Microsoft is working to protect its IP via the Genuine Advantage programs, as discussed in Chapter 6. In short, Microsoft is looking to grow Windows and Office revenues—despite the fact that Microsoft has cornered the market with these products—by making sure users pay for them. The Genuine Advantage program, which Microsoft officials have said they plan to expand to cover just about every Microsoft product in the not-so-distant future, is all about anti-piracy. Just as with Software Assurance (Microsoft's volume-licensing annuity program), Genuine Advantage provides users with some incremental "benefits." But Genuine Advantage's raison d'être is to enable Microsoft to collect in the United States and abroad on all those copies of its products on which the company is currently being short-changed.

---

[21] These IP protection goals come straight from Microsoft's "About Our Business Model" section of its Global Citizenship web site here: www.microsoft.com/about/corporatecitizenship/citizenship/knowledge/businessmodel.mspx.

At the same time as it cracks down on pirates, Microsoft also is looking to step up its revenue pace by licensing Microsoft-developed IP. Before Phelps joined the staff, Microsoft forged occasional patent-exchange and IP-licensing relationships with vendors on a variety of fronts. But once Phelps settled in, Microsoft's IP-licensing program became a lean, mean fighting machine. Microsoft employees are applying for patents to the tune of 3,000 per year. In 2006, Microsoft was granted its 5,000-th patent. Simultaneously, the Redmondians have forged far-reaching patent-exchange agreements with Novell, Sun Microsystems, Fuji-Xerox, Samsung, LG Electronics, Toshiba, and many other major tech vendors.

Microsoft began licensing more rigorously some of its own technologies that it had previously given away for free. The FAT (file allocation table) file system—for which, Microsoft claimed, it was denied and later awarded a patent—is a prime example. FAT is used to keep track of the location and sequencing of files stored on a hard drive. Several Windows and Linux programs make use of FAT, as do many devices, including cameras, Flash memory cards, and others.

> *"While the Softies are looking to advertising as a future moneymaker, IP protection and licensing is already starting to line the company's coffers."*

In 2005, under Phelps's tutelage, Microsoft also launched a new business unit called IP Ventures. IP Ventures' charter is to find companies potentially interested in a couple dozen technologies that Microsoft developed in its R&D unit but hadn't brought to market itself and help them secure outside venture funding to take these technologies to market. Among the initial IP venture licensees are the government of Ireland, Inrix, Skinkers, and Wallop Inc. (In a couple of cases recently, Microsoft either invested in and/or licensed for its own use technologies developed by these IP venture licensees. For example, Microsoft has a minority stake in Skinkers, which is developing LiveStation, a product for getting live TV on a PC.)

Patent-Lawsuit Threats as Revenue Generator

Licensing a patent war chest can generate some respectable revenues, as IBM has shown. But using the threat of patent lawsuits can generate them, too, as Microsoft has proven during the past year-plus.

In May 2007, Microsoft announced, via an interview with *Fortune* Magazine, that free and open-source software violated 235 of its patents, by the company's count. Microsoft wouldn't say which patents were in violation or how, "lest FOSS (free and open source software) advocates start filing challenges to them," Microsoft licensing chief, Horacio Gutierrez, said. All that company officials would reveal was that they believed the Linux operating system violated 42 Microsoft patents; Linux GUIs (graphical user interfaces), 65; Open Office violated 45; various free/open e-mail programs, another 15; and other free/open-source software programs violated an additional 68 Microsoft patents.[22]

> *"Licensing a patent war chest can generate some respectable revenues, as IBM has shown. But using the threat of patent lawsuits can generate them, too."*

While Microsoft execs claimed they weren't interested in suing customers who might find themselves on the wrong side of the patent tracks, they also suggested that users who worried about patent violations might want to make sure they were working with particular open-source vendors to minimize their risks—specifically, those who signed patent-protection licensing agreements with Microsoft.

Novell was the first vendor to sign such a deal. It did so in the fall of 2006, before Microsoft went public with its patent saber-rattling. Even though Novell—and to a lesser extent, Microsoft—attempted to position their joint agreement as a technology partnership (heavy on the interoperability synergies), Ballmer repeated in numerous interviews that Microsoft did the deal with Novell to provide users worried about potential patent infringements by open-source software on Microsoft products with indemnification by

[22] Questions remain about why Microsoft decided to throw gasoline on the then-just-smoldering open-source fires by using *Fortune* Magazine to go public with tallies of how many of its patents company officials believed open-source software violated. In spite of public claims to the contrary, many Microsoft officials (especially those involved in building bridges with the open-source community and customer bases) seemed caught completely off-guard by the move. *Fortune*'s article detailing Microsoft's claims is here: http://money.cnn.com/magazines/fortune/fortune_archive/2007/05/28/100033867/.

Microsoft. (That guarantee got a lot squishier in mid-2007, when Microsoft disavowed itself from promising to cover customers using Novell software licensed under the GNU General Public License v3—but so be it.)

After it shook the patent-threat cages, Microsoft signed up several more Linux distributors under the auspices of "technology partnerships," including Xandros, TurboLinux, and Linspire. These vendors inked patent-protection partnerships similar to the one Novell did.

Microsoft has trotted out, in several press releases, customers extolling the benefits of the technology partnership/patent-protection agreements it signed with these vendors. Among the fans of the deal Microsoft has rounded up for quote over the past year: AIG Technologies, Deutsche Bank, Credit Suisse, HSBC, and Wal-Mart. Novell reported in the fall of 2007 that it had garnered $100 million in revenue from Linux—a 243 percent gain—the first three quarters of that year, thanks primarily to its deal with Microsoft. (As part of the arrangement, Microsoft offers its customers SuSE Linux coupons and support.)

Microsoft's Open-Source Strategy: from LAMP to WAMP

Does Microsoft have an open-source strategy, beyond attempting to crush Linux and other open-source software (OSS)? Sam Ramji, Microsoft's Director of Platform Technology Strategy and the company's Open Source Software Lab, says it does.

> *"Microsoft wants to encourage the coexistence of two software stacks."*

"Our focus is getting OSS on top of Windows," Ramji told me in early 2008.[23] "And I'm focused on (providing) interoperability between the LAMP (Linux, Apache, MySQL, PHP) and Windows stacks."

Microsoft wants to encourage the coexistence of two software stacks: a Microsoft Windows stack comprised of Windows, Internet Information Services, SQL Server, and .NET, and a Linux-free/Windows-centric LAMP (Linux, Apache, MySQL, PHP) stack–something like a "WAMP."

---

[23] I explain in greater detail—with an illustrative PowerPoint from Ramji—exactly how Microsoft is looking at open-source software (OSS) in a January 31, 2008, blog post, entitled, "Microsoft's Open-Source Strategy: A Picture Is Worth a Thousand Words": http://blogs.zdnet.com/microsoft/?p=1142.

Microsoft is looking at OSS as just another flavor of independent software vendors (ISV) software. Microsoft's goal is to convince OSS vendors to port their software to Windows. But Microsoft doesn't want OSS software to just sit on top of Windows; the company wants this software to be tied into the Windows ecosystem by integrating with Active Directory, Microsoft Office, Expression designer tools, System Center systems-management wares, and SQL Server database. And in cases where customers and software vendors want or need Linux to still be part of the picture for some reason, Microsoft will suggest that they use Hyper-V, its forthcoming virtualization hypervisor, to run Linux and Linux-dependent applications.

For Microsoft, this OSS strategy makes a lot of sense. It's another way for Microsoft to try to make Linux obsolete, and not look as obviously ruthless doing so. And for OSS vendors who are selling a lot of their software on Windows—Ramji repeated a couple of times that more than 50 percent of JBoss's business these days is from software running on Windows—Microsoft's OSS push seemingly isn't a bad deal, either.

So, Has the "Open Source = Evil" Wall Really Fallen?

It would seem, from the apparent fiscal success of at least the Novell tech partnership, that the era of "open source is communism" at Microsoft is officially over. Has Microsoft really come to the realization that free (as in beer) can be the basis for a legitimate—and maybe even lucrative—business model? That seeding a market with open-sourced software still leaves plenty of room for profits from complementary, value-added software, hardware, and services?

In a word, no. Microsoft officials have admitted that more of its customers are interested in complementing their Microsoft closed-source products with open-source ones, and that its open-source partners are interested in teaming on open-source (not Shared Source) projects with the Redmondians. Microsoft went so far as to submit in the summer of 2007 a couple of its Shared Source licenses for consideration as bona fide "open-source" status under the guidelines created by the Open Source Initiative (OSI). In October, following some renaming and reworking of those two licenses, Microsoft got the nod from the OSI for a new Microsoft Public and a Microsoft Reciprocal License.

In spite of these developments, however, Microsoft continues to give open source more lip service than to actually put its money where its mouth is.

With the hiring of open-source expert, Bill Hilf, from IBM in 2003, Microsoft got itself a visible and credible Linux champion. Hilf started out running Microsoft's on-campus Linux lab. In the fall of 2007, he was promoted to a wider-scoped, higher-visibility position: General Manager of Windows Server Marketing and Platform Strategy.

In 2005, Hilf described his job as one dominated by repairing years of damage and distrust—inside and outside Microsoft. From an interview I conducted with Hilf once he first went public about his new job at Microsoft:

> *Hilf said he spends a lot of time "making Linux more transparent to Microsoft managers," doing a lot of educating around the open-source development, testing, deployment and licensing models. Hilf's job sometimes involves telling the Microsoft product managers "where we suck" vis-à-vis open source. And sometimes it involves showing the Microsoft teams "where the big holes are in open-source environments."*

"The bulk of my job is spent with the [Microsoft] product teams on where open-source software is going," he said.[24] Hilf made considerable headway in getting many inside Microsoft to think differently about open source and in convincing several vendors and users in the open-source community to see Microsoft as less of an out-and-out adversary. Microsoft tried fielding a few third-tier technologies, like its Windows Installer XML (WiX) toolkit under bona fide open-source licenses. Some Softies admitted they actually found a lot of open-source procedures and processes things that Microsoft would do well to emulate. The "wisdom of the crowds" philosophy, more rapid release schedules, and tighter sense of community that worked for

> *"Has Microsoft really come to the realization that free (as in beer) can be the basis for a legitimate—and maybe even lucrative—business model?"*

---

[24] About a year after Bill Hilf joined Microsoft, I had a chance to interview the then-head of the Microsoft Linux Lab. Hilf already knew he had his work cut out for him—needing to change the perceptions of many Microsoft insiders about open source's strengths and weaknesses, as well as to win over open-source stalwarts who saw Microsoft as nothing more than The Evil Empire. My 2005 interview with Hilf is here: www.microsoft-watch.com/content/operating_systems/meet_the_head_of_microsofts_linux_lab.html.

open-source vendors looked appealing to Microsoft. And, as noted in Chapter 2, being associated with the word *open*—especially when bidding on government contracts specifying "open standards"—had its pluses, as well.

But Microsoft's détente with the open-source community was only skin-deep. The aforementioned patent-violation saber-rattling by Microsoft's licensing/legal departments undid quite a bit of the goodwill that Microsoft had managed to build with the open-source community. At the same time, Microsoft's previously mentioned move to submit two of its Shared Source licenses to the OSI met with a lot of hostility and questions. Microsoft's announcement in October 2007 that it was releasing the .NET source code under its Shared Source (but not open-source) license met with just as much anger and hostility from many in the open-source community who didn't feel that Microsoft was going far enough. Microsoft's decision to dismantle its maligned "Get the Facts" anti-Linux propaganda site (full of market research studies paid for by Microsoft that highlighted Windows' superiority to Linux) was dulled by the replacement of that site with yet-another anti-Linux marketing hub, the Microsoft /Compare site.[25]

Last fall, Ballmer reopened old wounds again, by spouting off about Red Hat violating Microsoft's patents and its need "to compensate us." Ballmer rubbed salt in the wounds[26] by adding that he expected other vendors—such as Eolas, the company that sued Microsoft for browser-related patent infringement and

---

[25] Get the Facts vs. Compare: Over the past few years, Microsoft has fielded two marketing sites designed to provide users with data to help evaluate Microsoft products vs. open-source equivalents. The first of those sites ("Get the Facts") was definitely an anti-Linux propaganda site, stocked with research papers (most of which were commissioned by Microsoft) emphasizing Windows Server's superiority over its open-source alternatives. In 2007, Microsoft softened and rechristened the site as "/Compare." The goal remains the same, however: Provide users with (primarily Microsoft-funded) data that show Windows as superior in terms of ROI, security, and several other metrics, vis-à-vis Linux. Since the Get the Facts site was replaced by the /Compare site, side-by-side comparisons of the two are impossible. The /Compare site is here: www.microsoft.com/windowsserver/compare/.

[26] Just when it looked like the patent-violation flare-up had ebbed a bit, Microsoft CEO, Steve Ballmer, reopened old wounds by claiming during a speech in September that Red Hat was in violation of a number of Microsoft's (and possibly other vendors') patents and needed to be brought to justice. See here: www.vnunet.com/vnunet/news/2200717/microsoft-sharpens-aims-patent. Red Hat is one of the few Linux distributors that has declined to sign a patent-protection agreement with Microsoft, like the ones inked by Novell, Linspire, Xandros, and TurboLinux.

ended up settling with the Softies in August 2007—to sue open-source vendors for patent infringement. Not the best rhetoric if you're supposedly courting open-source vendors and their customers and want them to believe that you are in favor of working *with* them, not *against* them. ...

But back to business models. ... Ballmer said back in late September 2007 that he didn't have a problem with open-source business models. From a Q&A session between Ballmer and press/vendors in London:

> *I'd also tell you the following is true. ... I would love to see all Open Source innovation happen on top of Windows. So we've done a lot to encourage, for example, the team building PHP, the team building many of the other Open Source components. I'd love to see those sorts of innovations proceed very successfully on top of Windows. Because our battle is not sort of business model to business model. Our battle is product to product, Windows versus Linux, Office versus OpenOffice.*[27]

Bottom line: While Microsoft outwardly seems to have decided to try to join 'em rather than beat 'em when it comes to open source, the company's current brass hasn't changed its views on open source. Microsoft wants to cash in on open source's popularity,

> *"Microsoft's détente with the open-source community was only skin-deep."*

especially among government users. But, in spite of rhetoric and definitions to the contrary, the company isn't planning on turning away from a completely proprietary/closed-source business model any time soon—if at all.

Amateur Coders and Hobbyists Are Back in Style Again

When Bill Gates founded Microsoft more than 30 years ago, amateur coders and hobbyist programmers were the first and foremost target audience for its

---

[27] More Ballmerisms from the aforementioned speech in September that got several open-source backers' knickers in a twist. More coverage of Ballmer's comments that he wants to see open-source innovation happen "on top of" Windows is here: www.groklaw.net/article.php?story=20071008205138925.

products. Until fairly recently, however, Microsoft seemed to have abandoned that demographic, in favor of professional Enterprise coders.

Recently, however, Microsoft began a concerted effort to return to its hobbyist roots on the developer division side of the house. The thinking behind the move seemed similar to the motivations driving the Windows client group: If you've saturated a market, you need to grow it in order to grow yourself. And it doesn't hurt to cultivate an entry-level audience (tinkers and students) who might someday morph into bigger-item buyers.

> *"Microsoft wants to cash in on open source's popularity, especially among government users."*

Microsoft's primary "hobbyist" brands are its Express products. There's Visual Studio Express, SQL Server Express, Search Server Express, and XNA Game Studio Express. Microsoft's Robotics Studio development environment fits here, too. One could argue that Windows Home Server does, as well.

Dan Fernandez, the former lead product manager for Visual Studio Express, explained the "hobbyist renaissance" at Microsoft this way:

> *Programming is still too hard today and, in a lot of cases, Express is still too high end for where we want to go. You should not need a four-year degree to create or modify applications, period. The future is always murky, but I can only promise you that there are lots of very cool projects going on inside Microsoft that will redefine the experience for the next generation of developers.*[28]

One of those "very cool projects" ended up being Popfly, Microsoft's mashup editing tool. Popfly was designed to allow everyday users (whether or not they considered themselves "hobbyists" or "programmers") to build mashups, gadgets, web sites, and applications using pre-built "blocks." When the alpha of Popfly launched in mid-2007, there were 40 Web-programming blocks from which users could choose, including Flickr, Windows Live Spaces, Virtual Earth, and news service blocks. Popfly creations were all

---

[28] Read the full 2006 blog post on the "hobbyist renaissance" from Visual Studio Express Product Manager, Dan Fernandez, here: http://blogs.msdn.com/danielfe/archive/2006/08/10/the-hobbyist-renaissance-at-microsoft.aspx.

stored in the Windows Live Storage cloud. Popfly is currently free; Microsoft officials have gone on record saying they are contemplating making the Popfly tool ad-funded.

Going forward, Microsoft is likely to add more hobbyist-focused products to its line-up. Fernandez presciently outlined in 2006 Microsoft's thinking about how it planned to attack this market. My synopsis of his summary:

- **Different Design Goals**—Simplicity is key. If a feature wasn't key, remove or hide it.
- **Different Pricing**—From $99 to free is the target zone.
- **Different Product Size**—Don't think multi-CD, multi-gigabyte install. More realistic is a 50-MB download.
- **Different Distribution**—Use the Web—not retail or reseller—as the primary channel.

Will any of Microsoft's Express and/or future hobbyist products themselves evolve to be major moneymakers for the company in the next few years? Doubtful. But the hobbyist market is back on the Redmondians' radar (as it needs to be) in order to attract a new audience for its products now and going forward.

> *"Going forward, Microsoft is likely to add more hobbyist-focused products to its line-up."*

Microsoft as Hardware Maker

For years, Microsoft has been building and selling peripherals, like keyboards, mice, and joysticks. At the start of this decade, it broadened its hardware business and started building Xbox gaming consoles, then Zune multimedia players. In early 2008, there were rumors circulating that Microsoft might go so far as to buy hardware-peripheral maker Logitech. Shortly thereafter, Microsoft ended up buying Danger Inc., a company best known for inventing the Sidekick mobile phone (though Redmond claimed to buy the company for its consumer-mobile-services, not its hardware, prowess.) And, with the company's official unveiling of Surface, aka *Milan/PlayTable*, Microsoft is also now in the business of manufacturing large-screen, multi-touch, gesture-recognizing computing devices.

(Microsoft is building, at least as part of its first-generation Surface wave, not just the software, but also the "coffee-table"-type devices running the software. Ultimately, Microsoft has said it will likely encourage hardware makers to build some Surface systems. But so far, there's no firm timetable or commitment by Microsoft for this.)

> *"Has Microsoft decided that it needs to be in the hardware business in order to sell more software?"*

Has Microsoft decided that it needs to be in the hardware business in order to sell more software? Matt Rosoff, an analyst with the independent Directions on Microsoft market-research firm, was doubtful when I asked him last year. Rosoff said he believed that Microsoft originally got into the hardware business with keyboards and mice in order to help the graphical user interface (GUI) take off. He said he viewed the Surface as primarily a manifestation of a new UI, rather than a new hardware form factor.

Rosoff also noted that the Redmondians haven't stuck with hardware when its forays met with tepid user acceptance.

"Recall their quick exit from the 802.11 wireless router market, for instance. With Xbox, they had to make the hardware because it's so heavily subsidized. With Zune, they had to make the hardware because they saw that customers preferred convenience and experience over choice [of stores and devices]," Rosoff said.[29]

Me? I'm not quite as sure as Rosoff that we won't see more Microsoft-developed hardware in the near- and longer-term future. To be clear, I am not basing this impression on anything that OEMs or other sources inside or outside Microsoft have told me.

But think this through: Given Microsoft's increasing interest in playing in consumer markets, it wouldn't be surprising to see the Redmondians build more hardware. I think we'll see Microsoft use the "it's just a prototype" defense (as it did with the Surface tabletop) to explain why it might develop a mobile phone, an ultra-mobile PC (UMPC), a Microsoft-software-powered

---

[29] My brief Q&A with Directions on Microsoft analyst, Matt Rosoff, on Microsoft's designs (or lack thereof) on becoming more of a hardware vendor is here: http://blogs.zdnet.com/microsoft/?p=484.

PBX/phone system, and/or other devices. I'm also not 100 percent convinced that Microsoft is going to exit the hardware business once it has managed to get a market seeded, given its seeming disappointment with some of the form factors and price points that its partners have rolled out with their hardware for new Microsoft software platforms.

Microsoft's Apple-envy plays in here, too, no doubt. Hardware obviously isn't a business that Microsoft knows as intimately as software. And its risks are quite high. Remember the $1 billion charge Microsoft took to make good on the "Three Rings of Death" hardware failures experienced by a number of Xbox users? Yet Microsoft has planted a stake it doesn't seem interested in removing in the gaming console and digital-media-player markets. And even though margins on tech hardware are nothing approximating those of software, I'm not counting Microsoft out of the hardware space.

How big a contributor to Microsoft's bottom line hardware will be in the next 3, 5, or 10 years is not something about which I'd attempt to speculate. But I am watching for the Microsoft software juggernaut to get a growing percentage of its revenues from hardware sales in the next few years.

The Big V: Virtualization

Out of all the "untried but unavoidable" business models explored in this chapter, the biggest potential game changer for not just Microsoft, but all companies in the software market, is virtualization.

Virtualization technology, as it exists today, provides users with several interesting options. By running a user's environment in a virtual state, virtualization enables companies to consolidate their data centers; better prep for disaster recovery; and run older/customized applications on new hardware without incompatibility glitches.

> *"Virtualization also makes a user's operating system choice less of a barrier to entry."*

Virtualization also makes a user's operating system choice less of a barrier to entry. While several Windows users haven't switched to a Mac or Linux box because they need to make use of applications that only run on Windows, that justification is disappearing rapidly. Apple users running Apple's Bootcamp can run their old Windows software on shiny new Apple boxes using these virtualization products.

Microsoft already offers several different wares that fall under the virtualization heading. The company has said it wants to cover the gamut, meaning hardware-, operating-system-, and application-level virtualization. On the current and near-term Microsoft virtualization product docket:[30]

- **Virtual PC**—Microsoft's desktop virtualization offering for hosting legacy apps on top of Windows and/or applications not designed to be compatible with Windows.
- **Hyper-V**—Also known as the "Windows Server Virtualization" hypervisor (formerly codenamed *Viridian*) that Microsoft is baking into Windows Server 2008 to allow users to run multiple machines as "guests."
- **System Center Virtual Machine Manager**—A product for managing host configuration, virtual machine creation, library management, Intelligent VM placement, monitoring, rapid recovery, self-provisioning, and automation.
- **Virtual Server**—Microsoft's current server-based offering that allows users to run guests on top of Windows Server as a host.
- **SoftGrid**—Microsoft's application virtualization technology.
- **Terminal Services**—Microsoft's Terminal Services facility is being fleshed out so that Microsoft can sell it as its "presentation virtualization" solution.

There are a few different reasons—and ways—that virtualization could have a major impact on Microsoft's product line-up in the next two+ years. Some approaches to virtualization are more "dangerous" (in terms of cannibalizing Microsoft's existing revenue streams) because they enable users looking to switch from one environment to another a relatively easy way to do so. A hosted virtual-machine monitor runs on top of a host operating system, but a hypervisor runs guests on hardware directly and doesn't require a "host" operating system.

---

[30] Microsoft published in October 2007 a comprehensive white paper outlining its many virtualization products and their positioning. The paper is downloadable here: http://download.microsoft.com/download/4/3/1/431c0627-02ae-418f-9af2-89c0866d226d/Whitepaper-Virtualization-CoreIO-FY08.pdf.

Predictably, Microsoft is attempting to keep a tight leash on exactly how, when, and under what kinds of licensing mechanisms its customers can use virtualization today and tomorrow in order to prevent virtualization offerings from eroding the company's hard-won Windows and Office market share. Restricting which of its products are sanctioned to work on its competitors' virtual products is one way Microsoft can "control" how much of an impact virtualization will have on its user base.

Microsoft is expected by many to make its *Viridian* hypervisor an integrated part of Windows 7, due out in 2010. It also is expected to make SoftGrid more of a tightly integrated Windows component and possibly a deliverable available only to Software Assurance licensees.

But virtualization as a service is where things really get interesting. This is the modern version of utility computing, or going back further, Sun Microsystems' idea that "the network is the computer." Via virtualization, Microsoft can stream a "presentation layer" or entire applications to users, installing only minimal bits on their desktops and allowing most of the processing power to reside in the cloud. Microsoft officials have made vague references to making Windows Server a cloud-hosted service. What would that look like, beyond providing users with all their Active Directory contacts available anytime/anyplace/on any device?

> *"Restricting which of its products are sanctioned to work on its competitors' virtual products is one way Microsoft can 'control' how much of an impact virtualization will have on its user base."*

As in several other new markets where it's pushing to build a presence, Microsoft is a latecomer and has a long way to go to become a leader in the virtualization space. But that doesn't mean Microsoft won't be a player. As it is doing in the hosted-office space, Microsoft will likely latch onto a virtualization strategy that will provide its users with some of the benefits of virtualization without offering all its products to be used, willy-nilly, in virtualized environments.

Conclusion:
On to Microsoft 3.0

Any technology that is going to have significant impact over the next 10 years is already at least 10 years old. That doesn't imply that the 10-year-old technologies we might draw from are mature or that we understand their implications; rather, just the basic concept is known, or knowable to those who care to look.

—Microsoft Research Principal Scientist Bill Buxton,
"The Long Nose of Innovation," guest editorial,
BusinessWeek, *January 2, 2008*

E ven though technologists have barely begun to scratch the surface of what people call "Web 2.0," its successor, "Web 3.0," already is being bandied about. There's even a Wikipedia Web 3.0 page that attempts a definition:

> *Web 3.0 is a term used to describe the future of the World Wide Web. ... Views on the next stage of the World Wide Web's evolution vary greatly. Some believe that emerging technologies such as the Semantic Web will transform the way the Web is used, and lead to new possibilities in artificial intelligence. Other visionaries suggest that increases in Internet connection speeds, modular web applications, or advances in computer graphics will play the key role in the evolution of the World Wide Web.*[1]

It's apparent that no one really knows exactly what Web 3.0 will look like and when it will "arrive." The same can be said about "Microsoft 3.0"—the

---

[1] The full—and constantly evolving—Web 3.0 page on Wikipedia can be found here: http://en.wikipedia.org/wiki/Web_3.0.

Microsoft that will come into being as of the next major milestone in the company's history.

When will Microsoft 3.0 kick off? Some might say when the other half of the Bill Gates–Steve Ballmer odd couple finally decides it's time to move on—something Ballmer has gone on record saying is unlikely for another decade or so. Or perhaps it will be when (and if) Microsoft morphs from software vendor to services vendor, or from software vendor to more of a consumer-electronics vendor. Or maybe it's the day (if and when it comes) that Yahoo becomes fully integrated with Microsoft.

In Chapter 5—on Microsoft's "big-bet" products that are in the pipeline—I covered some of the products and services that the Redmondians seem likely to field in the few years. But there are clues out there about the kinds of arenas upon which Microsoft is likely to focus even beyond that. This chapter will attempt to touch on some of these longer-range strategies and initiatives.

Factoring for the Yahoo Wildcard

February 1, 2008, will be etched in my memory for years to come. I had finished my draft of this book just days before. Then Microsoft did something I thought they'd never do—in spite of a couple of years of rumors to the contrary: The software giant made a bid to acquire Yahoo.

> *"Microsoft did something I thought they'd never do—in spite of a couple of years of rumors to the contrary: The software giant made a bid to acquire Yahoo."*

As of the time this book went to press, it was still uncertain whether Microsoft would be successful in its Yahoo purchase quest; while some Yahoo shareholders were pressuring the Yahoo board to sell to Microsoft, neither the actual sale, nor any potential antitrust investigations had yet come to pass. Even if the Microsoft-Yahoo deal gets the official nod from all parties, the near-term plans outlined in this book will likely remain unchanged, as it will take Microsoft months to even begin assimilating Yahoo's various assets. The Microsoft entities that will be affected first will be the various online services and products, especially Windows Live and MSN.

However, a Microsoft acquisition of Yahoo will change dramatically Microsoft's longer-term plans. How will Microsoft combine its own Live Search with Yahoo Search? Will Microsoft trash some of its Windows Live properties that overlap with Yahoo's offerings (or vice versa)? Will Microsoft keep Flickr around? What about Zimbra? De.lici.ous? Will Microsoft kill off Yahoo's Panama ad platform or morph it into its own adCenter? How will Microsoft's back-end data-center infrastructure be combined with Yahoo's, so as to allow Redmond to gain the network effects it keeps touting as one of the main reasons for the deal?

Rather than make a bunch of wild predictions, as crystal-ball-gazers are wont to do, I figured I'd take a more measured approach and turn this into a "living book." As more details and specifics on the Microsoft–Yahoo deal come to light, I'll provide ongoing updates on the web site that accompanies this book (www.microsoft2.net).

Microsoft Goes to Pieces

Even without a "forcing function" (to invoke some Microspeak for a disruptive event) like a multi-billion acquisition, Microsoft reorganizes itself—a lot. Traditionally, at least twice a year, Microsoft management has moved the employee chess pieces around, in the hopes of discovering the optimal organizational structure. But to date, Microsoft has focused its reshufflings internally and has not done much in terms of moving divisions or groups outside of the mothership. In the future, that situation may change.

What if Microsoft is thinking even bigger and is looking to sell off multiple businesses and/or divvy itself up to become a federation of Microsofts, all in the name of agility?

Many Microsoft observers base their belief that Microsoft will never sell off any of its business units on the past. In the late 1990s, some of Microsoft's adversaries (and even some of its advocates) were pushing for Microsoft to split itself into multiple businesses. The critics—and many Microsoft employees and managers—believed that a chopped-up Microsoft would be a weakened Microsoft that would be less likely to be able to leverage its monopoly power. But others, including some Softies, believed that cleaving Microsoft into two or more parts (along Windows-vs.-everything-else lines) would make the software giant more agile. Microsoft management would have none of either argument and insisted that a united Microsoft was a strong and healthy Microsoft.

These days, I'm not sure the Microsoft brass is as adamant about the need to keep Microsoft whole. Microsoft was "forced" (by Bungie employees threatening to quit) to spin off its Bungie gaming acquisition in late 2007. But Microsoft managed to keep an undisclosed financial stake in the Halo development shop.

Microsoft's not the sheriff in town, its own officials are gradually coming to realize. And in some cases, even if Microsoft allegedly is the highest bidder for a company (think DoubleClick, FaceBook, etc.), Microsoft's money is no good. Web 2.0 darlings want to be acquired by Google, not Microsoft. As a result, Microsoft's management is being pushed to be more open-minded about differently structured business arrangements than it once might have been.

> "These days, I'm not sure the Microsoft brass is as adamant about the need to keep Microsoft whole."

It's not just on the online-services side of the house that this new willingness to think differently may be taking hold. Sure, Microsoft did make an attempt to buy business-software rival SAP back in 2003. But would Microsoft consider selling its Dynamics ERP/CRM product lines to SAP (as one of my ZDNet blogging colleagues recently suggested might happen)? Interesting question. I could see Microsoft making a case for focusing its business on infrastructure software and getting out of the Dynamics applications business all together. ... Whether antitrust regulators would OK such a plan is, of course, an entirely different matter.

Another example that might not be outside the realm of possibility: Microsoft structuring Yahoo as an independent subsidiary, rather than munging bits and pieces of Yahoo into different, disparate Microsoft business units. In January 2008 (before Microsoft made its official Yahoo bid), Wall-Street-analyst-turned-industry-pundit Henry Blodget blogged:

> As we've argued, the Internet industry will not support four major generalists—Google, Yahoo, AOL, and MSN—and two of them need to combine. We like the Microsoft–Yahoo combination a lot, but we think a simple Microsoft swallowing of Yahoo would be a disaster. We think Microsoft should sell its Internet business to Yahoo in exchange for a significant chunk of equity. The resulting public entity would be able to recruit top talent, more effectively

compete with Google, and operate independently of the Windows/Office machine.[2]

Blodget's sequitur: "Of course, that would only happen over Steve Ballmer's dead body." There, I disagree.

Microsoft isn't going to sell off its entire Online Services Business to Yahoo or anyone else. That would only happen over Ballmer's ice-cold corpse, given that Microsoft needs search and other consumer/business services if it plans to become, as execs have said, a leading player in the online-advertising realm. But what if Microsoft, instead, kept Yahoo intact, thereby creating fewer disruptions to its busi-

> *"But what if Microsoft, instead, kept Yahoo intact, thereby creating fewer disruptions to its business—not to mention fewer angry, likely-to-defect employees?"*

ness—not to mention fewer angry, likely-to-defect employees?

Another way that Microsoft is moving toward dividing itself is along the consumer/business fault line. Microsoft's brass is convinced that real innovation is coming more from the consumer-tech world than the business-tech one. And, at least on the platforms (Windows and services) side of its operating structure, Microsoft increasingly is organizing its marketing/business troops along the consumer/enterprise split. Platforms & Services Division (PSD) Kevin Johnson acknowledged this split in his February 2008 post-corporate-reorg e-mail to Microsoft's employees. Johnson explained:

> We have revamped our engineering approach and the team is making progress on key user scenarios across the PC, phone, and Web. As we look to the future, we must reinvent our approach to consumer marketing, the pre-sales experience, the way we work collaboratively with our PC partners, and how we communicate our brand and what it stands for. To do this, we will make changes to bring all consumer audience marketing across PSD

---

[2] In a January 2008 blog posting, Web pundit Henry Blodget made his case for why Microsoft will sell parts of its business to Yahoo long before Microsoft ever buys Yahoo. Read it here: www.alleyinsider.com/2008/01/microsoft-to-buy-yahoo-again.html.

into a single organization. This will enable us to align marketing resources, eliminate silos, communicate the end-to-end experiences, and better connect with consumers.

Johnson added:

Today, looking globally, our sales and marketing organizations are not as well aligned by customer segment as needed, particularly as we compete in the consumer segment with companies such as Apple and Google.[3]

Tiptoeing along the Bundling Tightrope

Speaking of the good old/bad old Department of Justice days, Microsoft has come to the realization and acknowledgement that any and every business decision it makes will result in legal scrutiny. This is especially true in Europe, where Microsoft adversaries have found antitrust regulators willing to take on the Redmond software maker on a moment's notice.

> *"Microsoft isn't likely to go so far as to bundle its Windows Live services with new versions of Windows. That would be too brazen."*

Yet there are increasing signs that, in spite of the possible wrath of Google, Adobe, Opera Software, and others, Microsoft is going to push the envelope in the 2010-and-beyond time frame by more closely syncing up its Windows and Windows Live technologies and strategies.

Microsoft isn't likely to go so far as to bundle its Windows Live services with new versions of Windows. That would be too brazen—and too easy a target for its lawsuit-ready competitors. But Microsoft is moving actively to increase the synergies between Windows

---

[3] The full text of Johnson's internal February 14, 2008, e-mail is available here: http://gigaom.com/microsoft-memos/kevin-johnson-memo. Johnson and the rest of the Microsoft brass are trying to recreate the "halo effect" that Apple and Google have demonstrated in the market. In Apple's case, that halo effect has taken the form of iPod and iPhone sales translating into greater MacBook sales. In Google's, consumers' appreciation for the Google search experience has made them more receptive to trying Gmail, Google Docs and other new Google services.

and Windows Live. As a summer 2007 planning memo for Windows Live Wave 3 (excerpts of which are included in Appendix A) spells out:

> *While we will target a seamless experience on Windows Vista, we will make a bet on the Windows 7 platform and experience, and create the best experience when connected with Windows 7. We will work with the Windows 7 team and be a first and best developer of solutions on the Windows 7 platform. Our experiences will be designed so when they are connected to Windows 7 they seamlessly extend the Windows experience, and we will work to follow the Windows 7 style guidelines for applications.*

The memo continues:

> *Windows Live Wave 3 will be designed so it feels like a natural extension of the Windows experience. … We will "light up" the Windows experience with Windows Live. … What's the relationship between a Windows account and a Windows Live ID (Microsoft's Web-authentication technology)? Should we have a LiveID connected to account settings?*

The bottom line, according to the planning memo:

> *Windows Live will have value for every Windows customer. If you have an email account and use the Internet, Windows Live will make your experience better.*[4]

In early 2008, the European Commission announced it was launching new "probes" into Microsoft's business practices, which might morph into full-fledged antitrust suits. One of these, spurred by a complaint by Microsoft browser rival Opera Software, is reopening the can of worms involving Microsoft's decision to bundle its Internet Explorer browser with Windows. (Microsoft's IE-Windows bundling was analyzed extensively in the late 1990s by the U.S. antitrust courts and ultimately left legally unchallenged.) Another complaint, brought by a handful of Microsoft rivals known as the European

---

[4] The Windows Live Wave 3 planning memo—authored by Windows Live execs, Chris Jones and David Treadwell, and Mobile Services Corporate VP, Brian Arbogast—dates back to the summer of 2007. I've included excerpts in this chapter, as well as in Appendix A, which highlight some of the priorities for the Live team with its next services release.

Committee for Interoperable Systems, cited Windows Live as one of several technologies blocking companies from being able to interoperate with Microsoft.

Even though the constant threat of antitrust scrutiny has made Microsoft more cautious than it otherwise might be about tying/bundling its software and services, the company is continuing to look for ways to "embrace and extend" that won't run afoul of the antitrust busters. If Microsoft's new integration attempts aren't thwarted, it will be interesting to see how far the company will try to go, as time goes on—in the name of integration on behalf of consumers.

Spelunking inside Microsoft Research for Future Clues

Planning memos can only take you so far, however. If you're really looking for clues about more-distant Microsoft futures, there are a couple of other options.

> *"There are a few problems with predicting future directions based on patents, including the vagueness of many of them."*

One way would be to examine patents for which the company has applied and been granted in recent years. Microsoft was granted more than 1,600 patents in calendar 2007.[5] Microsoft Chairman Bill Gates's name is on dozens of patent applications, as is Chief Software Architect Ray Ozzie's. But there are a few problems with predicting future directions based on patents, including the vagueness of many of them; the likelihood that they'll be challenged in court and overturned; and the fact that many patented ideas are never even meant to become products—they're simply designed to preempt a company's competitors from being able to do so.

Another, better way to make guestimates about Microsoft's future is to explore some of the hundreds of research projects on which Microsoft is working.

---

[5] Microsoft was No. 6 in terms of companies granted patents in 2007, according to a January 2008 report by IFI Patent Intelligence. IBM still remained No. 1, securing 3,148 patents, compared to Microsoft's 1,637, however. For more on IFI's tabulations, go here: www .networkworld.com/news/2008/011408-patent-list.html?fsrc=netflash-rss.

Microsoft spent more than $7.5 billion in fiscal 2007 on research and development. In 2007, the company employed 700 full-time researchers at Microsoft Research facilities in Redmond; Mountain View; Cambridge, U.K.; Beijing; and Bangalore, India. (In 2008, Microsoft also announced plans to add a new Microsoft Research outpost in Cambridge, Massachusetts, which is set to open this summer.) Microsoft also has launched a couple of joint ventures involving Microsoft researchers and employees of its adCenter online-advertising unit (adCenter Labs) and its Windows Live group (Live Labs).

> *"Microsoft Research's charter is to look '10–15 years beyond current product-development cycles to identify and invent key technologies that will shape users' experiences in the future.' "*

Microsoft Research's charter is to look "10–15 years beyond current product-development cycles to identify and invent key technologies that will shape users' experiences in the future."[6] As such, the group has been dabbling with various new ways to enable users to interact with their PCs and devices. Like the Chairman who has dominated the company since its founding, Microsoft Research has put a lot of time and energy into voice, handwriting recognition, and touch. Elements of their inventions have found their way into various Microsoft products. In some cases—such as the Surface multi-touch tabletop system—years of Microsoft Research work yielded an actual commercial product. But as the Softies repeat often, there are no guarantees that any Microsoft Research products will find their way to the commercial market. In spite of that caveat, Microsoft Research has proven a good place to look when thinking about Microsoft's future directions.

What does all this mean for what's on Microsoft's longer-term roadmaps? Here are some predictions.

---

[6] The Microsoft Research web site includes all kinds of information on the people, the projects, the history, and more behind Microsoft's hundreds of research projects scattered around the globe. An overview of Microsoft Research and its charter is available here: http://research.microsoft.com/aboutmsr/overview/default.aspx.

How Far on the "Horizon" Is Windows Live Core?

How quickly are customers and vendors going to make the move to cloud computing? That's the $64,000 question. Some vendors like Google already are betting 100 percent on it today. Author Nick Carr's 2008 business bestseller, *The Big Switch*, makes the case that the services model is well on its way to becoming as ubiquitous among consumers as a utility like electricity.[7]

But Microsoft—and this author—are a lot more cautious in our expectations of how quickly cloud computing will take the world (beyond students and tech-minded early adopters working primarily in small businesses) by storm.

> *"Will Horizon be available for free or for a fee? Will it be expandable? And when will it be available?"*

So far, Microsoft has been hedging its bets with Software + Services. But Microsoft's long-term cloud-computing vision revolves around Windows Live Core and another subproject code-named *Horizon*.

Horizon, from the little I've been able to learn about it, is a Web-storage service meant to give users the feeling that wherever they are—on their own PC, a mobile device, or some remote system/device—they are logged into their own machine. Horizon will include a combination of a Web interface and storage service, some kind of file synchronization mechanism, and a client.

Horizon will allow users to sync files from PC to PC (with a client install); open, edit, and save files to the cloud from a browser; share documents from/inside the cloud; and/or connect remotely to any PC. The way I've heard it described, Horizon will be an evolution of the back-end storage service that is currently used by existing Live services, including SkyDrive and Windows Live FolderShare.

Will Horizon be available for free or for a fee? Will it be expandable? And when will it be available? There's no word on any of these pesky details yet, but

---

[7] Author Nick Carr, in his book *The Big Switch: Rewiring the World, from Edison to Google* (W.W. Norton, 2008), makes the argument that utility computing soon will be as pervasive and ubiquitous as electricity (another utility). Carr's web page for the book is here: www.nicholasgcarr.com/bigswitch/. Microsoft is mentioned a few times in Carr's book—there's an entire chapter entitled "Goodbye Mr. Gates"—but there's little information on Microsoft's services and data-center strategies.

it sounds like Microsoft is planning to begin testing Horizon, the backbone for its forthcoming "meshes" of devices and social networks in 2008, so stay tuned.

Horizon somehow seems connected with a Microsoft project codenamed *Cosmos*. Cosmos is a "high-scale distributed-computing-service platform." From source reports I've received, it sounds as if Cosmos is a type of distributed file system—maybe the realization of the WinFS (Windows File System) that was slated in the early part of this decade to be part of Windows Longhorn.[8] Cosmos also is the storage layer that underlies Microsoft's Windows Live Search infrastructure.

Horizon and Cosmos, like objects in your rear-view mirror, may be closer than they appear—and really should be if Microsoft intends to stay ahead of its Web competitors.

Mobile Devices as Next-Gen Mobile PCs

The United States is a laggard in terms of how we use our mobile phones. For us, they are not replacements for PCs; they are adjuncts to them (and many times, completely disconnected adjuncts).

More than a few market researchers have bullishly predicted that cell phones will supplant laptops, tablets, and the less-than-successful ultra-mobile PC form factors in the not-too-distant future. If this happens quickly, however, Microsoft is going to be in a lot of trouble. While the company's share of the mobile operating-system market is growing, even Softies admit that Windows Mobile as it exists today leaves a lot to be desired.

> *"Microsoft is cognizant that the first place where cell phones become users' default mobile-computing platforms will be in developing nations."*

---

[8] There's next-to-no information available publicly about Microsoft's distributed file system/ storage system code-named *Cosmos*. There is, however, lots of historical background material on WinFS, the Windows file system that Gates portrayed years ago as one of the major selling points of Windows Longhorn. (A good starting point is this backgrounder: http://msdn .microsoft.com/msdnmag/issues/04/01/WinFS/.) After several years of undelivered promises, Microsoft finally pulled the plug on WinFS in June 2006, promising to deliver much of the file-system functionality in future releases of SQL Server and other products.

Microsoft is cognizant that the first place where cell phones become users' default mobile-computing platforms will be in developing nations. Sailesh Chutani, director of External Research & Programs with Microsoft Research, explained Microsoft's thinking here:

> This [the cell phone] is the only computing platform that most people in the world will have for the near future, but there are lots of roadblocks. It's difficult to program. Relatively few APIs (application programming interfaces) have been built with the view that somebody will want to use them to extend that platform. The power of the platform is manifest when you have services in the cloud to leverage. Currently, that's not easy, either. And depending on which part of the world you live, the carriers control this tightly, so it's not easy for people to experiment with the functionality.
>
> But those things will get sorted out, because the value proposition is too strong. We have seen evidence of this in the work we have done in digital inclusion: Yes, this can be leveraged and used effectively as a platform.[9]

In the United States and other first/second world countries, the dynamic is different, but Microsoft's need to step up its mobile efforts is the same. Whether smartphones end up complementing or supplementing PCs in the coming years, Microsoft's mission with the next few releases of Windows Mobile seems to be to take a product that the company built to satisfy business/Enterprise users and make it more palatable to consumers.

At a late 2007 Microsoft-hosted event known as *Mobius*, company officials admitted to participants that Microsoft won't be resting on its laurels as Apple's iPhone and Google Android phones eat away at the company's roughly 10 percent mobile-operating-system market share.

Microsoft knows that Windows Mobile needs a lot of work. Microsoft has some ambitious plans for adding new features and functionality—including touch- and gesture-recognition support—to its mobile operating system. But these improvements are not really on the fast track. Windows Mobile 7, which

---

[9] A Microsoft Q&A with Director of External Research and Programs Sailesh Chutani from the 2007 Faculty Summit can be found here: http://research.microsoft.com/displayArticle .aspx?rc=n&id=1758. The future of cell phones is just one of several topics he addressed.

will provide touch but only for certain carriers' headsets, isn't expected to hit until 2009.[10] Currently, it takes carriers at least six months, and oftentimes a year, to release phones built on a new Microsoft operating system, which would put consumer availability of Windows Mobile 7 around 2010.

Some time after Windows Mobile 7 (probably two to three years later, if Microsoft sticks to the way it has been staggering its mobile operating-system updates), the company will deliver Windows Mobile 8. While it's very early to be talking feature lists for an update not likely to go live until 2011 or 2012, on the supposed Windows Mobile 8 short list are a completely redesigned user interface, "revolutionary" features like global search, and new concepts such as automation and connections within the phone, ideas borrowed from other smartphone operating systems. As bloggers at Gizmodo explained:

> This means that you'll be able to go from viewing a person's
> address info in his contact card to seeing where he lives in map
> view in one click. There will be much more of this intuitive flow,
> and far less digging through menus.[11]

In February 2008, as previously noted, Microsoft acquired Danger Inc., the inventor of the Sidekick mobile device. Microsoft officials emphasized that Microsoft wanted Danger not so much for its hardware design past, but for its expertise in consumer-focused mobile services. To date, with Windows Mobile, Microsoft has focused almost exclusively on business customers. But under Roz Ho—one time head of Microsoft Mac Business who is now corporate vice president, Premium Mobile Offerings, the Danger team will work on consumer-focused premium mobile offerings.

---

[10] Inside Microsoft blogger Nathan Weinberg broke the news on some of the touch- and gesture-recognition technologies that Microsoft is planning to deliver as part of Windows Mobile 7. Weinberg's synopsis of an internal Microsoft document on Windows Mobile 7 user interface enhancements is here: http://microsoft.blognewschannel.com/archives/2008/01/06/exclusive-windows-mobile-7-to-focus-on-touch-and-motion-gestures/.

[11] Gizmodo and several other bloggers and press focusing on the mobile market were invited by Microsoft to participate in its annual Mobius look-ahead. Other attendees said Microsoft required them to sign non-disclosure agreements that stipulated they could not share much of the content at the event. Yet Gizmodo went ahead and published at the end of 2007 a synopsis of Microsoft's remarks in a blog post on what's in store for Windows Mobile 7 and 8. The full post is here: http://gizmodo.com/gadgets/what.s-wrong-with-windows-mobile/whats-wrong-with-windows-mobile-and-how-.

Microsoft's new mobile charter, going forward, is to take aim at an expanded set of mobile-market arenas, specifically:

- **Business productivity**: Microsoft's—and its handset partners' primary target market to date for Windows Mobile.
- **Personal productivity**: Phones that offer Hotmail, Windows Live Messenger and other consumer services.
- **Mobile Internet**: Devices that are first and foremost gateways to the Internet, rather than voice-centric models.
- **Entertainment**: A platform for delivering music, gaming and other entertainment services. The Danger platform will be the focal point here. (And interestingly, Microsoft officials have said they have no plans to drop the Danger OS/platform—which is based on Java—any time soon, in favor of Windows Mobile.)

It's the End of Windows as We Know It

Windows Mobile is just one of the many "Windows" platforms Microsoft is rushing to advance.

Some day, maybe not so far out there, Windows is going to become more of a liability than an asset to Microsoft. Even with Windows Vista, the ball and chain of guaranteed backward compatibility hurt Microsoft, in terms of how well or poorly the operating system worked with existing drivers and applications. Many Microsoft watchers figure it's only a matter of time until Microsoft cuts the cord and launches a new post-Windows product that won't be so bogged down by legacy baggage.

> *"Some day, maybe not so far out there, Windows is going to become more of a liability than an asset to Microsoft."*

It's worth noting that not everyone believes Microsoft is going to have to take this radical course. I've also heard that Microsoft has been working on some kind of architectural solution to this problem, which would allow older apps and drivers to be virtualized and run in that mode alongside more modern, native applications. Or maybe Microsoft will end up taking the route that Apple did with Carbon, by introducing a programming interface/environment that provides backward compatibility for older software. Or maybe

Microsoft can circumvent many of its backward-compatibility issues by simply decoupling elements from Windows like mail, photo storage, and audio/video players and delivering them as optional Windows Live services. That way, Microsoft could lessen complexity, while simultaneously pulling the rug out from under antitrust investigators (at least on the bundling front).

On the research side of the house, Microsoft has developed a non-Windows-based microkernel operating system, known by the codename *Singularity*. Singularity also encompasses a new programming language (Sing#) and new software verification tools. As the Microsoft researchers behind Singularity explained:

> *The Singularity project started in 2003 to re-examine the design decisions and increasingly obvious shortcomings of existing systems and software stacks. These shortcomings include: widespread security vulnerabilities; unexpected interactions among applications; failures caused by errant extensions, plug-ins, and drivers, and a perceived lack of robustness.*
>
> *We believe that many of these problems are attributable to systems that have not evolved far beyond the computer architectures and programming languages of the 1960's and 1970's. The computing environment of that period was very different from today. ...*
>
> *From the beginning, Singularity has been driven by the following question: What would a software platform look like if it was designed from scratch, with the primary goal of improved dependability and trustworthiness?*[12]

Microsoft researchers have written Singularity in 100 percent managed code, which means, in a layperson's terms, that the code is managed by Microsoft's Common Language Runtime, the heart of its .NET Framework. Managed code is supposedly more secure by design. Singularity is being

---

[12] A considerable amount of information is available on Microsoft Research's Singularity Project web page: http://research.microsoft.com/os/singularity/. The quotes on Singularity's purpose come from an April 2007 white paper entitled "Rethinking the Software Stack," which is available in PDF form: http://research.microsoft.com/os/singularity/publications/OSR2007_RethinkingSoftwareStack.pdf. Interestingly, there is no mention of "Midori" in the Singularity pages.

designed, from the outset, to minimize internal subsystem dependencies—a problem that has been the plague of Windows. There's been talk that Microsoft also has been investigating what a Singularity-plus-Viridian-hypervisor combo might bring to the table.

Microsoft researchers completed Version 1.0 of Singularity in 2007 and shipped a research-development kit for it to several universities, stipulating that it be used for research purposes only. The Microsoft Research team has moved on to working on Singularity 2.0.

> "There's a seemingly related project under development at Microsoft that has been hush-hush."

There's a seemingly related project under development at Microsoft that has been hush-hush. That project, code-named *Midori*, is a new Microsoft distributed-operating-system platform. Midori is in incubation, which means that it is a little closer to market than most Microsoft Research projects, but not yet close enough to be available in any kind of early preview form.

What's also interesting about Midori is who is running the project. One-time Gates heir-apparent, Eric Rudder, is heading up the effort. Midori is being incubated under Chief Research and Strategy Officer Craig Mundie's wing. "Everyone under him [under Rudder on Midori] is a multi-year vet, has a super fancy title, and is going back to their roots and writing code like they probably did in the old days," one Microsoft tipster told me.

Midori sounds a lot like a secret Microsoft project known as *BigTop*. BigTop was an incubation project under then-Chief-Technology-Officer Mundie. BigTop was designed to allow developers to create a set of loosely coupled, distributed-operating-systems components in a relatively rapid way. Some described BigTop as a distributed, grid-computing operating system. Big Top was to be composed of three major components:

- **Highwire**—Highwire is a technology designed to automate the development of highly parallel applications that distribute work over distributed resources.
- **Bigparts**—Bigparts is code designed to turn inexpensive PC devices into special-purpose servers by enabling real-time, device-specific software to be moved off a PC, and instead be managed centrally.

- **BigWin**—BigWin sounded like the precursor to Microsoft's Software + Services (S+S) strategy. BigWin apps are just collections of OS services that adhered to preset "behavioral contracts."

Microsoft ended up axing the BigTop project in 2006. But it sounds like a lot of the thinking is living on with Midori.

When and how Microsoft will roll out Midori is still a mystery. But Microsoft seemingly believes the project is serious enough to dedicate a considerable amount of time/people/resources to it.

Deciphering Future Data-Center Deliverables

Rudder's mystery project isn't the only one involving Microsoft's systems and networking futures. Microsoft is expanding its focus on high-end computing technologies—clustering, fault-tolerance, parallel computing, and other related computing arenas. These technologies aren't being designed for Microsoft customers only; they're also likely to find homes in Microsoft's expanding network of data centers that are powering its various Live/Online services.

Microsoft Research labs in Redmond and other locations are engaging in several projects in the distributed-computing, parallel-computing, and fault-tolerant areas.

The Microsoft Research Dryad team, based in Mountain View, is developing software that is designed to provide operating-system-level abstractions for large clusters (thousands) of PCs in a data center. Dryad is considered Microsoft's answer to Google's MapReduce, its software framework to enable parallel computations across large clusters of computers.

> *Converting a sequential and/or single-machine program into a form in which it can be executed in a concurrent, potentially distributed environment is known to be hard. ... The Dryad project is an attempt to generalize this approach to provide a programming model which scales from future single-machine many-core PCs up to large-scale data-centers,*

explained Microsoft on the Dryad Web site.[13]

---

[13] Microsoft Research's Dryad web page is here: http://research.microsoft.com/research/ sv/dryad/. My ZDNet blog post that summarizes some of Microsoft's Dryad work is here: http://blogs.zdnet.com/microsoft/?p=18.

> *"These technologies aren't being designed for Microsoft customers only; they're also likely to find homes in Microsoft's expanding network of data centers that are powering its various Live/Online services."*

The Dryad team is focusing initially on a few key areas: composability (decomposing a program skeleton into a set of simple operating classes), fault tolerance, and applicability (discovering paradigms best suited for distributed programming, especially in computer vision, speech, and machine learning). The Dryad researchers are working hand-in-hand with the MSN/Windows Live product groups, as a result of those groups' need for ever-increasing scalability and bandwidth.

One aside: No matter how fault-tolerant and reliable systems are, downtime and outright system failure are unavoidable. Microsoft and other vendors seem to be talking less about 99.999 percent uptime guarantees these days. Instead, they're focusing more on "graceful degradation," "self-restoration," and other realities. The Microsoft Research Eclipse project[14] is all about designing distributed/fault-tolerant systems while taking performance realities into consideration. And Microsoft big-picture thinker Pat Helland has been talking about the future of the data center as being many, tiny, cheap, and flaky computers with less power and fewer transaction demands.[15]

The Many Pieces of Many-Core

Another future computing trend that is having an increasingly important impact on both Microsoft and its customers is the move to multi-core/many-core processors.

---

[14] Public information on Microsoft Research's *Eclipse* project—the successor to its discontinued *Boxwood* effort—is available on this page: http://research.microsoft.com/research/sv/eclipse/.

[15] Pat Helland's TechEd EMEA 2007 talk focused on the implications of using lots of cheap, unreliable servers harnessed together to power data centers. The slides of his talk are available from his blog: http://blogs.msdn.com/pathelland/archive/2007/11/25/the-irresistible-forces-meet-the-movable-objects-closing-general-session-at-teched-emea-in-barcelona.aspx.

Not just in servers, but in desktops/laptops as well, multi-core processors are becoming the norm. But operating systems (Windows and others), as well as programming tools, aren't currently able to accommodate applications that make full use of *many-core* systems.

Mundie has been leading the charge for far-reaching changes in software design and development to accommodate the shift to many-core systems. In 2007, he began to step up his campaign to make many-core development a top priority for Microsoft.

> *"Not just in servers, but in desktops/ laptops as well, multi-core processors are becoming the norm."*

"As the microprocessor has grown dramatically in capability, as has the whole system, the concept of the app hasn't fundamentally changed that much," Mundie told Wall Street analysts and members of the press who attended Microsoft's 2007 Financial Analyst Meeting. "And so the question that looms in my mind for Microsoft and ultimately for the industry is: What are those future applications and what might they look like?"[16]

The cloud-services development/deployment model meshes well with multi-core, Mundie said, given that multi-core apps will be more asynchronous, loosely coupled, concurrent, composable, decentralized, and resiliently designed.

There are several Microsoft initiatives focusing on various aspects of the many-core challenge.

Microsoft Research's MS-ManiC is one of these projects. According to a page on the Microsoft Research site, the MS-ManiC (Memory Systems for Many Cores) project

> is focused on designing scalable memory system architectures for future many-core processors. The memory system is not only one of the major performance bottlenecks in chip multiprocessors, but its design can lead to serious energy inefficiency, unpredictability, and security holes. Our goal is to design a scalable and balanced

---

[16] A transcript of Mundie's remarks from FAM 2007, which included his thinking on what kinds of new applications will be enabled by many-core/multi-core systems, is here: www.microsoft.com/msft/speech/FY07/MundieFAM2007.mspx.

memory system using a holistic hardware/software approach. We are interested in designing a high-performance, energy-efficient, and secure memory system that at the same time provides quality of service to applications utilizing it.[17]

On the commercial side of the Microsoft house, the company's Parallel Computing Platform team is working on solving a piece of the many-core puzzle by developing new compilers and tools that will support parallel-computing systems. These new tools are expected to be built on Phoenix, the Microsoft Research code-analysis/transformation framework[18] that's been in development for several years.

People, Products, and Strategies Subject to Change

> *"Chief Software Architect Ray Ozzie: Will he stay or will he go?"*

The same way that Microsoft itemizes as part of its own financial statements the various near- and longer-term risks to its future business, I, too, want to handicap my Microsoft 3.0 predictions with a list of risk factors that could influence the future. Any of these could end up changing substantially the pace/products that Microsoft will roll out in the next decade. In no particular order:

- **Yahoo**—Will Microsoft finally realize its goal of buying Yahoo and clear all the antitrust hurdles needed to acquire Yahoo? Will the company find some other way to structure the deal as more of a partnership/independent subsidiary that will make it more palatable to Yahoo management and employees?
- **Chief Software Architect Ray Ozzie**—Will he stay or will he go? And if he stays, will he become more of a behind-the-scenes developer, or emerge as the kind of tech leader Microsoft needs?

---

[17] I provided on my ZDNet blog in late 2007 a synopsis of what's happening inside Microsoft Research with the MS-Manic project: http://blogs.zdnet.com/microsoft/?p=668.

[18] Background on Microsoft Research's Phoenix code-analysis and transformation framework is available on the Microsoft Research site at http://research.microsoft.com/phoenix.

- **CEO Steve Ballmer**—Will Ballmer stick around another nine or 10 years, as he's said he plans to do? Will he remake Microsoft more in his own image by bringing in more sales guys (like Stephen Elop, the former Chief Operating Officer of Juniper Networks, who is replacing Microsoft Business Division President Jeff Raikes)? Will he alienate any more current/potential Microsoft partners—and investors—by mouthing off about open source, Microsoft's online investments, or other hot buttons? A number of Microsoft watchers have opined that if the Yahoo acquisition becomes a disaster—financially and/or management-wise—Ballmer could be ousted by the Microsoft board.

- **Google**—Will Microsoft's online rival manage to gain traction for anything other than its search engine? So far, in spite of all the headlines they garner, Google's other online services and products have not attracted the masses.

- **Apple**—Will Apple's growing consumer PC and mobile-phone operating-system share, as well as its domination of the digital-media player market, make Apple more of a threat to Microsoft? Up until this point, Microsoft has looked to Apple as a user-interface-design leader and a vendor of one of many platforms for Microsoft Office, but not spent many cycles worrying about Apple as a viable rival.

- **Adobe**—Will Adobe become a much bigger thorn in Microsoft's side? Adobe is on Microsoft's radar screen as a development-tool rival, as well as an emerging competitor to its office-productivity business. Adobe also has dropped the L word (lawsuit) at least once to get Microsoft off its turf. Wide-ranging alliances between Adobe and Apple and/or Adobe and Google would likely give Microsoft pause.

- **Silverlight**—What's the future for Silverlight? Up until now, Silverlight has carved out a niche for itself as a minor Flash competitor. But Microsoft has bigger dreams and plans for Silverlight, which will come to light over the coming years. Microsoft's goal is to get Silverlight on all of its users' systems (without getting sued for antitrust violations in the process). Silverlight will be a key piece of several Microsoft services and products, ranging from Astoria to various Live Labs online-advertising tools.

- **DRM**—What if DRM dies? Microsoft has been banking on its Windows Genuine Advantage (WGA) and Office Genuine Advantage (OGA) anti-piracy mechanisms—and DRM technologies in sheep's clothing—to help line the coffers of Windows and Office by forcing pirates to pay up. Microsoft underestimated how much legitimate customers would end up loathing WGA/OGA. In 2007, Microsoft released a version of Internet Explorer 7 without WGA and softened the WGA "punishment" metered out to customers whose copies of Windows were deemed to be "non-genuine." With DRM falling out of favor in the music world, too, DRM may end up far less useful to Microsoft as a revenue generator than the company had been expecting.

- **IPTV**—What if IPTV never turns into the barn-burner market that Gates has been promising for the past decade? Microsoft continues to try and try again to capture a chunk of the soft and squishy IPTV market. Microsoft has been pouring money/resources into IPTV for years and, as of early 2008, still had only 1 million users.

- **Generation X/Y/Z**—Will Microsoft win over the next generation? It's not a given. Apple has found a way into younger users' hearts and pocketbooks in a way that Microsoft would love to emulate. Microsoft has stepped up its student-focused marketing campaigns, building new web sites (like Channel 8) and offering substantially cheaper—or even free—versions of some of its products to attract younger users. Xbox and Zune are giving the Redmondians more of a toehold among the younger demographic. This next generation is the next generation of information workers and IT managers, as Microsoft knows all too well.

- **The OLPC Generation**—Will Windows (and other Microsoft products) take hold in the developing world? Microsoft has been building up its Unlimited Potential team and its family of offerings steadily. But Linux and its biggest booster in developing nations, Nicholas Negroponte's One Laptop per Child (OLPC) project, are giving the Softies a run for their money. Microsoft has worked with the One Laptop Per Child (OLPC) team and various PC partners to test if and how Windows XP can run on Linux-based XO laptops. One of the favored solutions is to enable XP and other Microsoft software to run on an SD card that will be inside the XO. Microsoft may end up boosting its efforts here to stave off Linux's growing appeal, if nothing else.

Can Innovation Be Learned?

What better way to end a book on Microsoft's future than to ask a question that Microsoft (quietly) has been puzzling over itself: Can innovation be bottled, documented, and turned into a repeatable, understandable process?

> "What if IPTV never turns into the barn-burner market that Gates has been promising for the past decade?"

As covered in Chapter 2, Microsoft officials from Gates on down have been publicly adamant that Microsoft is an innovator and will continue to be one. Late last year, at a Microsoft-hosted event for Web enthusiasts, Gates bristled when a questioner brought up the "myth" that Microsoft doesn't innovate:

> Did we do personal computing? Who did that damn personal computing thing? When I bought that 8008 for $360 down at Hamilton (Avenue), what was that?
>
> Anyway, tablet computers, is there somebody else out there doing tablet computers? IPTV, is there somebody else out there doing—by definition what we do is the baseline. Everything Microsoft does is the baseline, and what we don't do, that's what's innovative I guess. And by that definition the other guys do all the innovative things.[19]

As yours truly and others have pointed out, however, the bulk of Microsoft's true innovations have not gained traction. The company's top brass know this. And they're dabbling with several ways to improve Microsoft's batting average here.

The aforementioned Microsoft incubations[20] and cross-over labs (adCenter Labs, Live Labs, etc.) are aimed at getting more Microsoft-Research-developed

---

[19] Gates's full rant on why Microsoft gets no respect when it comes to innovation can be found in the transcript of his Q&A during the December 2007 Mix-and-Match event that was posted by LiveSide.Net: www.liveside.net/files/folders/6910/download.aspx.

[20] How "incubation" works at Microsoft: The ResponsePoint example—a case study from Microsoft Research—is available here: http://research.microsoft.com/news/featurestories/publish/Incubation.aspx?0hp=n1.

technologies into consumers' hands more quickly. The Microsoft Surface touch-centric tabletop, PhotoSynth photo-stitching technology, Deepfish Mobile browser—all of these forward-looking technologies—are the products of Microsoft research ventures. And Microsoft's 70 or so "quests" that are maintained on an internal SharePoint wiki-style site are another way the Microsoft management is hoping to get a better handle on what should be at the top of Microsoft's priority list.

> *"The bulk of Microsoft's true innovations have not gained traction. The company's top brass know this."*

There's another internal mechanism Microsoft is using to foster innovation that has been under the dominion of Randy Granovetter, Microsoft's General Manager of Innovation. An internal community platform, known as *IdeAgency*,[21] is designed to define an idea, seed, try, and prototype it before delivering an early version to customers. IdeAgency is designed to lead employees toward incubation and not perpetually looking outside for the next new thing or next big thing. There was a big internal kickoff for IdeAgency, but lately it's been awfully quiet, my Softie sources say.

Here are a couple of final points to ponder, regarding where Microsoft should be (and is) setting its future priorities.

Microsoft Program Manager J.D. Meier had a thought-provoking blog post at the very end of 2007, entitled "Love Your Dogs." The post, inspired by an article on behavioral economics in *strategy+business* magazine, argued that conventional wisdom is wrong in terms of how companies should treat their worst-performing businesses. Instead of abandoning the "dogs," a company would be better served by investing in them. Meier quotes the article by Harry Quarls, Thomas Pernsteiner, and Kasturi Rangan:

> *There is, in fact, reason to believe that the conventional wisdom is wrong. Corporate managers often rely on accounting metrics to*

---

[21] A write-up on IdeAgency and Microsoft's evolving thinking on innovation appeared in the *Triz* Journal in September 2007: www.triz-journal.com/commentary/archive/microsoft_national_innovation_forum_part_iii_innovation_practices.html—Microsoft tries to figure out innovation.

make business decisions. However, these metrics are based on past performance; the market is interested only in the future. And past performance is generally a poor predictor of the future. Thus, when performance is assessed over time, greater shareholder value can be created by improving the operations of the company's worst-performing business. The way to thrive is to love your dogs.

Just as some fund managers earn superior returns by identifying and buying undervalued "market dogs"—better known as value stocks—corporate leadership can learn to identify "value assets," hold and nurture them, and produce superior performance. This in turn will ultimately lead to an increase in shareholder value.[22]

Insert "IPTV," "Zune," "Windows Mobile," or any other struggling/new Microsoft business for "dog" and the message is loud and clear.

Another related bit of food for thought comes from Microsoft Research Principal Scientist (and former Xerox PARC researcher) Bill Buxton. Buxton also argued against

> *"Instead of abandoning the 'dogs,' a company would be better served by investing in them."*

hasty retreats when it comes to future innovations. In January 2008 in a guest editorial in *BusinessWeek*,[23] Buxton wrote

> *My belief is there is a mirror-image of the long tail that is equally important to those wanting to understand the process of innovation. It states that the bulk of innovation behind the latest "wow" moment (multi-touch on the iPhone, for example) is also low-amplitude and takes place over a long period—but well before the "new" idea has become generally known, much less reached the tipping point. It is what I call The Long Nose of Innovation. ...*

---

[22] J.D. Meier's full "Love Your Dogs" blog post from December 31, 2007, is available here: http://blogs.msdn.com/jmeier/archive/2007/12/31/love-your-dogs.aspx.

[23] Microsoft researcher Bill Buxton's Long Nose editorial, which ran in the January 2, 2008, edition of *BusinessWeek*, is here: www.businessweek.com/innovate/content/jan2008/id2008012_297369.htm.

Innovation is not about alchemy. In fact, innovation is not about invention. An idea may well start with an invention, but the bulk of the work and creativity is in that idea's augmentation and refinement.

> *"If Microsoft were still the company it was 10 or 20 years ago, with the simultaneously ruthless and cautious Gates at the helm, I'd have no qualms predicting that the Redmond vendor will be successful in its next decade-plus transition."*

Whether you buy these "innovation for the long-haul" arguments or not, one thing's for certain: Microsoft is starting its next corporate chapter, 2.0, with lots of seemingly risky long-term investments on the books. One could argue, as CEO Ballmer has repeatedly, that because software doesn't really ever wear out, Microsoft needs to be thinking—and taking risks—in order to keep its revenue stream healthy as customers and the industry move to new paradigms.

If Microsoft were still the company it was 10 or 20 years ago, with the simultaneously ruthless and cautious Gates at the helm, I'd have no qualms predicting that the Redmond vendor will be successful in its next decade-plus transition. But can a company that is becoming more and more MBA-heavy (not to mention employee-heavy, with a workforce approaching 100,000 if/when the Yahoos are added) be guaranteed of continued success in an ever-more technology-driven, nimble and Web-centric world? In a word, no.

As Microsoft Turns

I'll be providing regular updates on the people, products and strategies that the new, post-Gatesian Microsoft will be promoting this year and beyond. For ongoing post-print-publication updates on Microsoft's products and strategies) make sure to check out the web site: www.microsoft2.net.

Memos, Letters, and E-mails (Just in Case Someone Hits That Delete Button)

I've been a student of all things Microsoft for more than 20 years. One of the hard lessons I've learned over that time: Don't count on e-mails, blog posts, and other forms of historical documentation sticking around forever. Sometimes interesting information disappears within minutes of it (accidentally or intentionally) going public. Other times, it takes years, but it still ends up falling off the edge of the Internet.

Some of this information deserves to be preserved for posterity, in my opinion, since it provides important context for what's coming next from the Softies. I've selected a few key documents that I want to make sure don't go by the wayside because of their relevance to Microsoft's future.

I'm including synopses of these documents here. I will include the full text of several of them on the web site that will accompany this book (www.microsoft2.net).

Chief Software Architect Ray Ozzie's Internet Services Disruption Memo (October 2005)

First up is Chief Software Architect Ray Ozzie's first big-time memo as a Microsoft employee. Ozzie joined Microsoft in March 2005, following Microsoft's purchase of Groove Networks. Just days before Microsoft was set to outline publicly its "Live" services vision, Ozzie distributed this memo to the Microsoft Executive Staff and his direct reports. This memo, although three years old now, has proven to be an amazingly accurate blueprint for what Microsoft did and intends to do in the Internet services space.

Although I don't know this for a fact, I strongly believe that Microsoft leaked this memo to select members of the press, with the stipulation that they not run it in full. Luckily, for the rest of us, RSS Pioneer Dave Winer got a copy and did run it in full on his Scripting.com web site at `www.scripting.com/disruption/ozzie/TheInternetServicesDisruptio.htm`.

I am including a few of what I consider the most telling excerpts from that memo, which Ozzie sent to the Microsoft executive staff, and his direct reports on October 28, 2005.

Ozzie set the stage, mentioning online advertising, online distribution, and the growing importance of consumer-friendly user experiences as forces with which Microsoft needed (and still needs) to reckon. He noted that three key tenets are driving key shifts in the tech landscape, and that all three are related in some way to services. The three:

- The power of the advertising-support economic model
- The Internet as a key enabler for technology delivery and adoption (via limited trial use, ad-monetized, free reduced-function use, subscription-based use, online activation, digital-license management, etc.)
- Compelling, integrated "user experiences" that "just work" on all kinds of form factors (PCs, TVs, cell phones, gaming consoles, etc.)

Ozzie then went on to explain how Microsoft could take its existing software products and platforms and Web-ify them. In his memo, he went methodically through each of Microsoft's main three divisions (Platforms & Services, Business Division, and Entertainment and Devices) and itemized some of the ways that they could make better use of the Internet.

Microsoft has said repeatedly that its mission is to introduce a service element to all of its products, going forward. Ozzie outlined the game plan for doing this. In the Platforms & Services (which is the business unit that encompasses Windows Client, Windows Live, and other Microsoft services) unit, Ozzie outlined four broad areas in which Microsoft could make better use of the Internet and Internet-specific technologies.

Ozzie talked about the need for Microsoft to become more agile in delivering both software and services. Instead of betting on a slow trickle of big-bang releases, Microsoft needed to find its groove (pun intended) by rolling out substantial "base" experiences, as well as "additive" smaller updates. Ozzie wrote:

> We should consider many options as to how we might bring user experience, innovations, and enhancements to users worldwide.

Specifically, we should consider the achievability, desirability, and methods of increasing the tempo for both "base" OS experiences as well as "additive" experiences that might be delivered on a more rapid tempo. In doing so, we would better serve a broad range of highly-influential early adopters.

Ozzie emphasized the "service/server" synergy of which Microsoft needed to find a way to take advantage. He explained:

A tension has emerged between our products designed for the enterprise and those for the internet. Exchange/Hotmail, AD (Active Directory)/Passport, and Messenger/Communicator are but three examples. All our enterprise clients and servers must interoperate with and complement our internet services. Our functional aspirations are generally "server/service symmetry," but architectural considerations dictate that different implementations may be required to economically reach internet scale. We must quickly find the best path to achieve seamless user, developer, and administration experiences involving servers and services.

Microsoft also needed to start thinking about making software development and development tools more "lightweight" and agile, Ozzie said. Microsoft had some history turning out lightweight tools for Access and SharePoint power users, but perhaps there was more to be done. Ozzie said:

The rapid growth of application assembly using things such as REST, JavaScript, and PHP suggests that many developers gravitate toward very rapid, lightweight ways to create and compose solutions. … We should revisit whether we're adequately serving the lightweight model of development and solution composition for all classes of development.

Ozzie emphasized that Microsoft would need to stay within its legal bounds as it moves toward a software-plus-services vision. While "tight integration" would be OK, bundling would not. Ozzie noted:

We will design and license Windows and our internet-based services as separate products, so customers can choose Windows with or without Microsoft's services. We'll design and license Windows and our services on terms that provide third parties with the same ability to benefit from the Windows platform that Microsoft's services enjoy. Our services innovations will include tight integration with the Windows client via documented interfaces, so that competing services can plug into Windows in the same manner as Microsoft's services.

Windows/Windows Live Dev Chief Steven Sinofsky's 'Translucency vs. Transparency' Blog Post (July 2007)

When long-time Windows chief Jim Allchin passed the Windows-development torch to Microsoft veteran Steven Sinofsky in late 2006, many things changed. One of the biggest was Microsoft's policy on "transparency."

Under Allchin, Microsoft's Windows division was uncharacteristically open with its own thought processes around the development of Windows. Blogging was encouraged. Many roadmaps were matters of public record. When Microsoft came to the realization in 2004 that its Longhorn (Vista) course was off-course, the company went public about its decision to "reset" its Windows client direction. In March 2006, when the Windows team realized it wasn't going to hit its internal ship targets and would miss the holiday 2006 selling season, that information, too, was shared.

Sinofsky, who came to the Windows team from the Office one, had some radically different thoughts about the best way to run a development shop. Sinofsky was known inside Microsoft for keeping Office on schedule, preferring secrecy to information sharing, and for keeping code close to the vest.

Following a couple of service pack code and information leaks in July 2007, Sinofsky wrote a post on his internal blog explaining why he believed "translucency," instead of "transparency," is the best approach for his team and for customers. Because Sinofsky's philosophy is so integral to how Microsoft 2.0 is attempting to operate, I feel it is important to discuss it.

Sinofsky's internal Microsoft blog post from July 9, 2007, entitled "Transparency and Disclosure," was provided to me by a source who asked not to be named.

Sinofsky started out his post by making a distinction between *transparent*, meaning "easily seen through or detected; obvious," and *translucent*, or "easily understandable; lucid."

Sinosky emphasized to his readers that the highest goals to which Microsoft should aspire, when it comes to its shareholders and customers, is to communicate accurately and truthfully. He went on:

> This does not mean free from ability to change down the road. It does not mean silence until the very last minute. What it does mean is that we should recognize the potential impact our communications can have on customers, partners, and our industry, and we should treat folks with great respect because, when we do disclose what we're working on, people pay attention—and they do more than listen as they make plans, spend money, or otherwise want to count on what we have to say.

However, in the same breath, Sinofsky made it clear that admitting a change in plans wasn't something to be undertaken lightly.

> When we have to change our plans, modify what has been said, or retract/restate things we not only look like we don't have our act together, but we cause real (tangible) pain to customers and partners.

Sinofsky cited Microsoft's experience with Longhorn Vista and "us being out there talking broadly before we really were able to speak with the accuracy our customers and partners assumed," as one of the key reasons for the new translucency policy. Even though "premature disclosure might make us feel like we were helping," it's best to be avoided. Sinofsky claimed Microsoft still would be able to be "just as open and just as transparent about roadmaps and plans as we ever were" in the new world order.

> Just as we plan the software we will plan to disclose our work. It means that we will develop the messages (so expectations are correctly set), the supporting information (so all the details are there), and the overall communication plan (so we don't leave anyone out).

Sinofsky emphasized that Microsoft will take very seriously who discloses and how. Leaks are a no-no. Only product management is charged with disclosure and communication with the outside world, he said.

> I know many folks think that this type of corporate "clamp down" on disclosure is "old school" and that in the age of corporate

transparency we should be open all the time. Corporations are not really transparent. Corporations are translucent. All organizations have things that are visible and things that are not. Saying we want to be transparent overstates what we should or can do practically—we will share our plans in a thoughtful and constructive manner.

Microsoft Chairman Bill Gates ThinkWeek Paper: 'An Edge Computing Network for MSN and Windows Live Services' (December 2006)

Twice a year, Microsoft Chairman Bill Gates was known for going off on sequestered "ThinkWeeks" to read papers submitted by Microsoft employees with ideas for new products and technologies that they believed Microsoft should be considering, going forward.

In the early Microsoft days, these papers were secret. But in the middle of this decade, Microsoft began sharing these ThinkWeek papers publicly inside the company, allowing employees to comment on them and to see Gates's and other key Microsoft executives' comments on them.

One of these papers, provided by a source who requested anonymity, provided a good sense of some of the "cloud-computing" infrastructural issues with which Microsoft has been—and needs to be—grappling.

Because Microsoft is spending so much on building out its data centers and people in the online business space in order to gird for the Web 2.0 and 3.0 battles, the issues described in this paper are especially interesting. And with recent rumors that Microsoft might be interested in buying Limelight or some other content-delivery-network (CDN) provider, many of the points raised in this paper are still applicable, although they were first raised in late 2006. Additionally, there are some hints about the still-under-wraps Microsoft CloudDB and Blue technologies that are also rather intriguing.

The December 15, 2006, ThinkWeek paper, entitled, "An Edge Computing Network for MSN and Windows Live Services," by Jason Zions, outlined some of Microsoft's back-end infrastructure challenges. Zions discussed at length the concept of an "edge computing network," or ECN, that "extends Microsoft's existing core network and data center infrastructure with intelligent computing nodes at the 'edge' of the network cloud."

This distributed computing network provides a set of network, computing, storage, and management resources and services closer to end-users. It would go beyond traditional content distribution networks (CDNs) "to enable a wider range of application architectures that offer improvements to performance and robustness and reduction or elimination of some operational challenges," according to Zions.

The rest of the ThinkWeek paper outlines Microsoft's online-business challenges as a result of the company's infrastructure implementations, describes the ECN vision, and provides a couple of examples of how an ECN could be used to advantage by Microsoft's 150 online properties.

The paper notes that CDN services are costly. Microsoft spent about $40 million on CDN services in fiscal 2006 and expected to spend as much as $130 on them by fiscal 2011, Zions said. An ECN could cut some of these costs and more efficiently address Microsoft's data-center needs, Zions argued:

> *The Edge Computing Network comprises roughly 24 nodes distributed worldwide. Most Internet users will be no more than 20 msec roundtrip time away from at least one node. Each node provides traditional CDN services and also provides distributed computation and storage services capable of hosting elements of Microsoft's own on-line properties. Each node would have egress capacity to the Internet end-users in the region. The nodes would be connected to each other and to existing Microsoft datacenters by a network overlaid on the Internet and on private links leased or owned by Microsoft.*

Zions explained that each ECN node serving that region would be provisioned so as to provide an appropriate subset (and capacity) of these services:

- *Small object caching*

- *Large file downloads*

- *Media streaming*

- *Peer-to-peer file transfer*

- *Smart (business-rule and load aware) traffic management and load balancing*

- *Traffic and user analytic data*

- *Logging to support billing, regulatory compliance, and forensic demands*

- *Monitoring and management of services*

By providing these services in-house, Microsoft could extend and enhance these services beyond what is possible through external CDNs, Zions said. Many of these services could be delivered in partnership with a third-party CDN; however, that CDN would be free to sell those same enhanced services to others, including Microsoft's competitors. "Our intellectual property would be used to the benefit of the very companies over which we seek to build competitive advantage," Zions lamented. Buying CDN technology looked like a more viable option, he argued:

> Microsoft already has considerable intellectual property in this space; we hold a substantial portfolio of patents across these technologies. While we could implement all of these services from scratch, the most cost-effective way to get these capabilities deployed and working to our advantage is to acquire existing, functioning technology from one or more CDN providers.

Zions's paper goes on to discuss the distributed computation and storage needs for ECN. Each ECN node for a region would provide the appropriate capacity of services like application containers; replicated and local BLOB storage; replicated and local transaction-oriented database storage; distributed file systems; billing; diagnostics; and monitoring and management of services. These services would interact in the following way:

> Applications need to store chunks of data for a variety of uses; some are purely local to an instance, others are intended to be shared amongst all instances of the application running anywhere in the Edge Computing Network. An application would tell the BLOB (binary large object) storage infrastructure about the replication needs for each category of BLOB data: local to this instance, local to the node or a set of nodes, and/or replicated to a backing store in one of Microsoft's large-scale datacenters. The BLOB store would be built on top of the Cheap File Store (used by Windows Live Spaces), Blue (used by Windows Live Mail), or some variation on those which accommodates the extended replication needs of ECN.

Some applications need transactional storage; again, replication needs would vary by application. For properties needing distributed database semantics, a service like CloudDB would be provided. Properties needing a database purely local to a node would use SQL Server on top of local non-replicated storage; a property which needed off-node replication of data for business-continuity and backup could build such a mechanism using existing and forthcoming services provided by the major datacenters (e.g. Blue).

Zions mentions that Microsoft attempted to buy an unnamed CDN vendor but wasn't willing to pay the asking price. Consequently, the company decided to license technology from "one or more" CDN vendors in order to jump-start the ECN implementation. Microsoft made a list of 24 locations for ECN nodes and selected the sites to accommodate specific Windows Live Infrastructure teams managing Microsoft's major data centers, he said. The rollout plan, as of late 2006, was to build the first three sites by the end of fiscal 2007 (i.e., June 2006), the second three by mid-fiscal 2008 (December 2007), and the remaining sites by the end of fiscal 2009 (June 2008).

CEO Steve Ballmer's Microsoft Priority List (February 2007 Financial Analyst Briefing)

There are some Microsoft watchers who have experienced, first-hand, Microsoft's tendency to say one thing and do quite the opposite. (Does anyone else remember Microsoft making intentionally misleading statements around OS/2, while the company secretly developed Windows NT?) There've been plenty of other more recent examples of the Redmondians' proclivity toward bending the truth, as well.

That said, when Microsoft officials talk to Wall Street, there seems to be a tad more truth serum running through their veins. So when CEO Steve Ballmer in early 2007 itemized for the financial community Microsoft's biggest growth areas for the next three-plus years, that list has some weight and credibility, in my book.

Here are some of the meatier excerpts from Ballmer's February 15, 2007, Strategic Update presentation to analysts on Wall Street. For the time being at least, the full transcript of Ballmer's remarks can be found on Microsoft's investor web site at www.microsoft.com/msft/download/transcripts/fy07/Financial%20Analyst%20Brief.doc.

Note: Ballmer provided a more recent Strategic Update to Wall Street in early February 2008. His priority list was nearly identical, albeit somewhat less detailed—hence my decision to analyze the 2007 preview speech Ballmer gave, rather than the 2008 version.

Ballmer kicked off his 2007 remarks with a few reminders:

> We have elected certainly to invest in a broader portfolio of business opportunities where that implies more R&D, more skill development than I think anybody has ever tried certainly in the technology business, and we think that is a fundamental part of the value that we bring, particularly since many of the technologies are well shared across all four of our cores, and perhaps additional cores in the future.
>
> The Live transformation, I'm going to talk more about this, but the evolution of the software business to being a business of software and service is fundamental. And we are investing in that as if it is fundamental. We will evolve our business models from transactions to in some cases subscription, in some cases hosting, in some cases advertising, in some cases we'll continue on the transaction model, but our business models will evolve with the evolution of our business to have much more of a service component.
>
> I view this as a huge opportunity for us. People can say, isn't it also a huge threat? Sure, all great transformations have both aspects to them. But in some senses the more we can have an ongoing, continuous relationship with our customers, be those large account customers or consumers or small businesses, the more we can have an ongoing relationship, the more opportunity we have to add value. So, I think of this as fundamentally a very, very good thing, but nonetheless it brings with it a world with new competitors and new challenges.

In his 2007 update, Ballmer outlined nine "opportunities" that Microsoft pegged as providing at least half a billion dollars of new gross-margin growth over the next three years (fiscal 2008, 2009, and 2010). He ordered them from largest to smallest.

In spite of all the hullabaloo over services, online advertising, gaming, and so forth, the No. 1 on Ballmer's projected revenue list was Windows. Forget about growing the business by eliminating piracy or by capturing a bigger share of the elusive "emerging markets" business. Plain old Windows, pre-loaded on new PCs, is where Microsoft's bread will continue to be buttered—first and foremost—for the next three years, Ballmer said.

The rest of Ballmer's list for top near-term growth spots for the company included Office, server revenues, online advertising, Xbox, and Windows Mobile on cell phones. Ballmer also itemized six additional up-and-coming technology growth areas that are poised to contribute more to the company's bottom line in the next three years, including savings from cutting piracy, Office Live, Office Online (the Microsoft-hosted versions of SharePoint, Exchange, etc.), Zune and "attached" hardware/software/services add-ons, TV, and healthcare.

In 2008, Ballmer's list looked almost identical, minus the focus on IPTV (that never-ending sinkhole into which Microsoft has been pouring money for years) and anti-piracy programs and mechanisms like Windows Genuine Advantage and DRM. Although he made his remarks just days after the company offered $44 billion to acquire Yahoo, Ballmer mentioned online advertising and Web portal revenues as just one of a number of priorities for the company in the next few years.

A transcript of Ballmer's February 4, 2008, Strategic Update remarks for the Wall Street community is here: www.microsoft.com/msft/download/transcripts/fy08/steveb020408.doc.

Windows Live Wave 3 Planning Memo (Summer 2007)

When it first began fielding Windows Live services, Microsoft allowed its employees to run amok. During 2006, new Windows-Live-branded services were tossed over the transom sometimes weekly, if not even more frequently. Every time Google or Yahoo launched a new web service, Microsoft rolled out something similar. (A few times, the Redmondians even beat Google and Yahoo to the services punch, though not often.)

Such agility made for a lot of excitement, as well as uncertainty. I remember several times calling Microsoft for comment on some new Windows Live service spotted in the wild that no one on the Microsoft marketing and/or public-relations team seemingly knew existed. The "let's just throw it out there and see what sticks" mentality also made for a lot of half-baked services that didn't work properly. A number of Windows Live services went to testers, only to disappear days or weeks afterwards, with no one willing to comment on their fate.

Enter Chris Jones, Corporate Vice President of Windows Live Experience. In 2007, Jones, along with colleagues David Treadwell, Corporate Vice President of Live Platform Services, and Brian Arbogast, Corporate Vice President of Mobile Services, began trying to bring some discipline and regimentation to the Windows Live development effort. In the summer of 2007, that gang of three issued a Windows Live Wave 3 planning document that demonstrated just how much they planned to change the modus operandi on the Windows Live team.

While theme planning, milestones, vision checkpoints, and other Windows-like conventions, if successfully implemented, will make Windows Live services more predictable and reliable, they also threaten to slow the pace of Windows Live development and deployment. The fastest Microsoft seems willing to say it can deliver a new version of Windows is every two to three years. Windows Live needs to be on a much quicker turnaround schedule—especially if Microsoft hopes to keep pace with Google, continuing to espouse the idea of rolling out new trial services without a lengthy planning/testing process.

The Windows Live Wave 3 Planning Memo—shared with me by a source of mine who asked not to be named—demonstrates some of the new planning, development, and testing conventions that the Live team is adopting. It will be interesting to see if Microsoft will be able to roll out, as officials have said they intend to do, a spring and fall update of its major Windows Live and Live Search properties while jumping through all the new, Windows-like hoops that the Live management team is establishing.

As the Planning Memo authors noted, the planning memo covered the state of the market and outlined their strategy for Windows Live Wave 3 (down to the level of feature detail) and Wave 4 (more general investment areas). And it included an internal timeline and schedule.

Much of the planning document focused on the new levels of management and checkpoints that the Windows Live team is instituting to bring more discipline into the Windows Live process. The unanswered question: Does this kind of rigor and planning negate the agility and spontaneity required to go head-to-head with Google and other Web 2.0 companies? Now, with "themes" and "pillars," the Windows Live team is starting to look more like the Windows team than a services provider.

An example from the memo:

> In Wave 2, themes were provided as guidance to feature teams. In
> Wave 3, themes will be the foundation of our planning

process. Each theme will have an owner (generally a GPM and/or PUM), a product planner, and, in most cases, a design lead. Each theme owner will produce a presentation and a high-fidelity click-through prototype for each theme. The role of the owner will be to coordinate the investigation of each theme, working with product planning, product management, design, development, testing, and other discipline leaders. They will work across dependent teams as they are writing their drafts and make sure that scenarios or features that span teams are covered end to end. They will outline the proposed scenarios and customer promise.

These theme checkpoints provide scoped and refined themes to the feature teams, who will then work on planning their work for Wave 3. Once we have scoped the themes, we will have a set of feature team checkpoints, where the teams will describe what they believe can be delivered for Wave 3 based on our themes. These feature teams are the experts on the scenarios and specifics for their area and are responsible for building best of breed solutions to meet customer demand. Any conflicts or disagreements between teams should be resolved as part of the checkpoint meetings.

But wait; there's still more checks and balances in the new Live processes:

Following these checkpoint meetings, we will decide on the pillars for Wave 3 and write the vision document. The GPMs and/or PUMs will work with Chris Jones and David Treadwell to create a single draft vision document that spans the work in Windows Live Wave 2. This will include the value proposition, tenets, top level schedule, shared bets, and feature commitments across our teams. We will load balance as required across teams to make sure that the themes and scenarios are delivered for the Wave.

The feature teams will use the vision document and resource plan to build the final feature list and schedule for their area. Following their detailed schedules, we will have a vision week with team members and partners where we walk through the vision, demonstrate the prototypes, and commit to the shared schedule. For Windows Live Experience teams, we will then move into M1 and coding for Windows Live Wave 3.

It's not only the Windows bureaucracy that increasingly will influence the Windows Live team. It also is Windows itself. Microsoft's goal is to integrate Windows Live Wave 3 with Windows 7 more tightly, according to the planning document.

> *We have a unique opportunity to provide a seamless experience for customers who choose to use our services with Windows and Internet Explorer. While we will target a seamless experience on Windows Vista, we will make a bet on the Windows 7 platform and experience, and create the best experience when connected with Windows 7. We will work with the Windows 7 team and be a first and best developer of solutions on the Windows 7 platform. Our experiences will be designed so when they are connected to Windows 7 they seamlessly extend the Windows experience, and we will work to follow the Windows 7 style guidelines for applications. We will work with the Internet Explorer 8 team to make sure we deliver an experience that seamlessly extends the browser with our toolbar and other offerings.*

Annotated Reading List

Here's my "Everything You Wanted to Know about Microsoft" reading list. I have read or skimmed most of the books listed here. A few I'm including even though I haven't because they are considered Microsoft classics. There are hundreds of books that are directly or indirectly about Microsoft on the market, written by everyone from former employees with axes to grind to Chairman Bill Gates himself. If you ask me for my personal favorite on this list, hands-down it is G. Pascal Zachary's (now out-of-print) *Show Stopper!*, a book about the making of Windows NT, which in its character treatment, plot, and conclusion, says so much about how Microsoft became the company that it is today.

In order of publication date, here are my picks (with brief annotations about each from the Amazon.com web site):

Hard Drive: Bill Gates and the Making of the Microsoft Empire
James Wallace and Jim Erickson
Collins (May 26, 1993)

In a biting biography and computer-industry expose, two *Seattle Post-Intelligencer* journalists here relate in dramatic detail how a moody, computer-dazzled prep-school whiz kid, a Harvard dropout at age 19, formed his own company, now Microsoft Inc., with a few friends.

Gates: How Microsoft's Mogul Reinvented an Industry—And Made Himself the Richest Man in America
Stephen Manes and Paul Andrews
Touchstone (January 21, 1994)

According to this "independent" biography, the computer whiz kid, Harvard dropout, youngest self-made billionaire ever, William Henry "Bill" Gates III (b. 1955), has dominated the immense, dramatic story of America's electronic revolution. Manes, a former columnist for *PC/Computing magazine*, and *Seattle Times* high-tech reporter

Andrews combine authoritative discussions of technology with a clear and entertaining prose style.

Show Stopper! The Breakneck Race to Create Windows NT and the Next Generation at Microsoft
G. Pascal Zachary
Free Press (June 1, 1994)

Show Stopper! is a vivid account of thecreation of Microsoft Windows NT, perhaps the most complex software project ever undertaken. It is also a portrait of David Cutler, NT's brilliant and, at times, brutally aggressive chief architect.

The Road Ahead: Completely Revised and Up-to-Date
Bill Gates, Nathan Myhrvold, and Peter Rinearson
Penguin Books, Revised edition (November 1, 1996)

Love him or loathe him, Mr. Microsoft is certainly an influential voice in the modern business world, and *The Road Ahead* is definitely an important addition to any business library. Gates's description of the beginnings of the information age, while somewhat overemphasizing his own contributions and downplaying those of his competitors, is nonetheless as clear and enlightening as any in print today.

Business @ the Speed of Thought: Succeeding in the Digital Economy
Bill H. Gates
Business Plus, 1st edition (May 15, 2000)

His vision changed our world. But in this monumental work, Bill Gates argues that the capabilities of computers, software, and networks are only beginning to be harnessed and that your company must start building a modern, digital nervous system now in order to compete quickly and intuitively in the new millennium. Here, one of the world's most successful, strategically thinking CEOs explains how to turn your hardware and software into a powerful, evolving network of information by looking at the digital systems in place at Microsoft and other leading corporations.

U.S. v. Microsoft: The Inside Story of the Landmark Case
Joel Brinkley and Steve Lohr
McGraw-Hill, 1st edition (August 10, 2000)

Six chapters take the controversy from 1995 (when Assistant
Attorney General Joel Klein joined the Justice Department and
started looking at Microsoft's behavior) to 1998 (when the lawsuit
was filed) and up to the present. While the bulk of each chapter consists of reprinted *Times* articles on the trial, each with the date on
which it ran, a new and detailed essay explaining part of the case,
often relying on new interviews, opens each chapter, and new sum-
maries and explanations are interspersed as well.

**Proudly Serving My Corporate Masters: What I Learned in Ten
Years As a Microsoft Programmer**
Adam Barr
Writers Club Press (December 2000)

First-time author Barr describes his 10 years of experience as a software developer for Microsoft. Beginning with a detailed account of
the hiring process, especially the interviewing methodology for new
hires, Barr goes on to trace not only his career but the history of software development over the past quarter-century.

**Breaking Windows: How Bill Gates Fumbled the Future of
Microsoft**
David Bank
Free Press, 1st edition (August 13, 2001)

Wall Street Journal reporter Bank charts the downward spiral of
Microsoft's public image: Over the past five years, the company went
from fearless New Economy pioneer to a predator vilified by its competitors and brought to trial in a landmark antitrust action. For those
hungry to know how golden boy Bill Gates could end up looking like
a defensive old-school monopolist, Bank has provided a hard-hitting
yet evenhanded account.

Pride Before the Fall: The Trials of Bill Gates and the End of the Microsoft Era
John Heilemann
Diane Pub Co. (October 2003)

Navigating the myriad twists and turns of the landmark antitrust suit against Microsoft, Heilemann forges a gripping, breakneck account of contemporary law applied to business conduct, peopled with rival visionaries, guardians of the public interest, and brilliant trial lawyers. A former staff writer for the *New Yorker* and the *Economist*, Heilemann covered the case as a special correspondent for *Wired* in November; this is an expanded version of that extensive article.

Beyond Books with Blogs and Web Sites

Books aren't the only way aspiring Microsoft followers can keep up with the Softies. There are thousands of blogs from Microsoft employees, resellers, customers, and competitors that make for great reading, too. Thanks to my trusty RSS reader, I subscribe to lots of Microsoft-related content, including the 5,000+ MSDN and TechNet blogs from Softies all over the company. There are lots of Microsoft blogs that are hosted in other places, too (including on the company's Windows Live Spaces platform), as well as on various private domains across the Web.

I tried to winnow my list down to 20 top picks for anyone interested in keeping up with Microsoft. Here are my must-reads (including my own blog, of course) in alphabetical order:

http://adcenterblog.spaces.live.com/Blog—The team blog for the Microsoft adCenter online-advertising unit.

www.activewin.com—A Microsoft aggregation site with some good original reviews and gaming coverage.

http://apcmag.com/—*APC* (*Australian PC*) Magazine's site, which focuses heavily on Windows and competing operating systems from a fairly geeky perspective.

http://bink.nu—Dutch blogger Steven Bink's Microsoft-tech-news aggregation site.

http://blog.seattlepi.nwsource.com/microsoft—*Seattle Post-Intelligencer* reporter Todd Bishop's Microsoft blog (from Microsoft's backyard).

`http://blogs.msdn.com`—Microsoft's aggregated site for all of its employees' blogs on the Microsoft Developer Network (MSDN).

`http://blogs.msdn.com/ie/`—The Internet Explorer team blog.

`http://blogs.msdn.com/somasegar/`—Microsoft Developer Division Chief Soma Somasegar's blog. Somasegar is one of the highest ranking (if not the highest ranking) Microsoft officials with an active blog.

`http://blogs.technet.com`—Microsoft's aggregated site for all of its employees' blogs on TechNet.

`http://blogs.technet.com/windowsserver/`—The Windows Server team blog.

`http://blogs.zdnet.com/microsoft`—"All About Microsoft" by Mary Jo Foley.

`www.edbott.com/weblog/`—Windows expert Ed Bott has tips and tricks for techies and regular Microsoft consumers.

`www.istartedsomething.com`—Australian blogger Long Zheng on Microsoft patents, products, and more (with a heavy emphasis on design/interface issues).

`www.liveside.net`—An independent blog covering all things Microsoft-Live-related.

`www.microsoft.com/presspass`—All Microsoft press releases, all the time.

`www.neowin.net`—Aggregated Microsoft news, tech scoops, and good forum discussions for techies.

`http://uxevangelist.blogspot.com/`—Stephen Chapman's blog with lots of goodies on Windows and Office futures, as well as user-experience topics, in general.

`www.winbeta.org`—One of the most complete (and up-to-date) of the Microsoft aggregation sites.

`http://windowsvistablog.com/`—Vista Team Blog (which mixes news in with lots of marketing speak).

`www.winsupersite.com/`—Paul Thurrott maintains an archive of all kinds of Microsoft product news and reviews, as well as an accompanying blog.

Index